CARIBBEAN LANDS

CXC Edition

John Macpherson

Longman Caribbean

Addison Wesley Longman Limited,
Edinburgh Gate, Harlow,
Essex CM20 2JE, England
and Associated Companies throughout the world

Carlong Publishers Ltd
PO Box 489
Kingston 10
33 Second Street
Newport West
Kingston 13
Jamaica

Longman Trinidad Ltd
Boundary Road
San Juan
Trinidad

First published 1963
This edition 1990
Seventh impression 1996

ISBN 0 582 03987 8

Produced by Longman Singapore Publishers (Pte) Ltd.
Printed in Singapore.

Acknowledgements

The Publishers are grateful to the following for their
permission to reproduce the following photographs:-

ACP-EEC Courier for pages 54, 62, 77, 121 and 129;
Barnaby's Picture Library for pages 190, 229, 239 and
240; Anne Bolt for pages 16, 17, 18, 28, 29 top and
bottom, 46, 51 top left, 67, 90, 99, 124, 133, 139, 145
bottom, 197, 198, 202, 209 top, 214, 215 and 218; Camera
Press for pages 180 bottom and 224; J. Allan Cash Photo
Library for pages 108 and 236; Crown Copyright.
Reproduced with the permission of the Controller of Her
Majesty's Stationery Office for pages 30, 61, 211, 212
and 216; Cuban Embassy for page 171; David G. Foster
for page 44; French West Indies Tourist Board for page
150; Adam Gadsby for page 112; The Gleaner Company
Ltd. for pages 25 and 48; Robert Harding Picture Library
for pages 113, 157, 225 and 233; Hutchison Library for
page 209 bottom; Infoplan Ltd. for pages 8 and 160;
Jamaica Industrial Development Corporation for page 68;
Jamaica Tourist Board for page 53; Ministry of
Education, Barbados for page 32; Norton Studios for
page 85; Photo Researchers Inc. for page 145 top;
Popperfoto for pages 1, 86 and 182; Prensa Latina
Servicio Fotografico for page 170; Rex Features for pages
40 and 180 top; Dave Saunders for pages 11, 47 and 162;
Science Photo Library for page 24; Vivienne Tomei (PR)
Ltd. for page 80; Tropix/Richard Lane for page 31; J.S.
Tyndale-Biscoe for pages 7 and 78; Philip Wolmuth for
pages 51 top right, 51 bottom left, 51 bottom right, 87,
97, 119 and 141.

The Publishers regret that they have been unable to
trace the copyright holder of the photographs on pages
109 and 168 and would welcome any information
enabling them to do so.

The cover photographs have been kindly supplied by
the St. Lucia Tourist Board (top) and N.A.S.A. (bottom).

Contents

Metric conversion tables

Metric units are used throughout this book. Where necessary, comparison with the traditional units may be made by using these tables. However, it should be remembered that they are only approximately correct. For the sake of simplicity some conversions have been rounded off.

Table 1: Temperature

°C	0	10	16	21	22	23	24	25	26	27	28	29	30	31	32	35	38
°F	32	50	60	70	72	73	75	77	79	81	82	84	86	88	90	95	100

Table 2: Rainfall (*1 millimetre = 0.0394 in.*)

Millimetres	10	20	30	40	50	75	100	150	200	250	500	750	1 000	1 250	1 500	1 750	2 000	2 500	3 000	4 000	5 000	6 000
Inches	0.4	0.8	1.2	1.6	2	3	4	6	8	10	20	30	40	50	60	70	80	100	120	160	200	240

Table 3: Height (*1 metre = 39.37 in. = 3.28 ft.*)

Metres	1	2	3	4	5	7.5	10	15	20	25	50	75	100	150	200	500	1 000	2 000	3 000	4 000	5 000	6 000
Feet	3.3	6.6	10	13	16	25	33	50	66	82	164	246	330	490	660	1 650	3 300	6 600	10 000	13 100	16 400	19 700

Table 4: Area (*1 sq. kilometre = 0.386 sq. mile*)

Sq. km.	1	2	3	4	5	7.5	10	25	50	100	150	200	500	1 000	2 000	3 000	4 000	5 000	10 000	20 000	50 000	100 000
Sq. miles	0.4	0.8	1.2	1.5	1.9	3	4	10	20	40	60	80	200	400	800	1 200	1 500	2 000	4 000	800	20 000	40 000

Table 5: Distance (*1 kilometre = 0.621 mile*)

Km.	1	2	3	4	5	10	20	30	40	50	100	250	500	1 000
Miles	0.6	1.2	1.8	2.4	3	6	12	18	24	30	60	155	310	620

Table 6: Weight (*1 kilogram = 2.205 pounds*)

Kg.	1	2	3	4	5	10	20	30	40	50	100	250	500	1 000
Lb.	2.2	4.4	6.6	8.8	11	22	44	66	88	110	220	550	1 100	2 200

Table 7: Weight (*1 tonne = 0.984 UK ton*)

Tonnes	1	10	50	100	1000	25 000
Tons	0.9	9.8	49.2	98.4	984.	24 550.

Introduction

This book deals with the way we live and make a living in the Caribbean, and explains some of the contributing factors. These factors are of two kinds. First there are the physical factors of topography, climate and mineral wealth which play a big part in controlling what can and cannot be done. Thus sugar cane, oranges, jute and tea can all be grown in the Caribbean climate, whereas wheat and apples cannot. Second, out of the possibilities provided by nature, people motivated by the desire for gain or the need to subsist – have selected some ways of making a living rather than others. Thus sugar cane and oranges have been grown on a large scale here, whereas jute and tea have not. So we see that the ways by which we make a living in the Caribbean are influenced both by physical and by historical factors. Both therefore play an important part in this book. The former are dealt with in general in chapters one, two and three and in detail in the regional chapters; the latter in chapter four and also in the regional chapters.

At any time in history, the ways in which people have made a living have been limited by their skills. New skills have led to new achievements and to the moulding of new landscapes. One example of this is the rise of the sugar industry in the seventeenth century. This created a landscape which, in some places, has remained with little change to the present day. Another example is the development of Jamaican bauxite which for centuries had been regarded only as a poor kind of soil. Up to the 1950s no one had any idea that it would be the basis of a large, new industry. Of course, the discovery of new skills does not mean that they will be put to use in the same way at the same time

everywhere. Throughout the region it is commonplace to see the same physical environment used in different ways – as, for instance, a highly mechanised sugar estate lying beside unmechanised smallholdings.

Differences in resources and the use of resources are easy to discern between one place and another, and between one territory and another. Similarities also exist. These may be more obvious to tourists and other visitors to the Caribbean, and to West Indians living abroad, than to those who live in the Caribbean lands themselves. But the very fact that we immediately recognise a fellow inhabitant of the Caribbean wherever we meet one is evidence of this regional similarity. Similarities and differences within the Caribbean are an endless source of topics for discussion. Opportunities for discussing them and for making geographical comparisons and contrasts abound throughout the book.

This edition of *Caribbean Lands* has been extensively revised so as to include new information, take account of recent developments in the Caribbean, and give added emphasis to matters of social, economic and political importance as a preparation for informed citizenship. It has also been expanded by the addition of a final chapter which extends the study of geographical topics beyond the Caribbean to other parts of the world so that meaningful comparisons can be made. Often different aspects of these topics are dealt with in different parts of the book, and to consider them in detail it will be necessary to follow up the references given in the index. Familiarity with the use of an index is a valuable preparation for advanced studies not only of geography but of other subjects as well.

1

The Formation of the West Indies

The oldest rocks of the Caribbean region are those of the Guiana Highlands which lie to the south of the West Indies. These rocks belong to the oldest group of rocks in the world. They were formed during the immense period of earth history (probably about four-fifths of the total) which drew towards a close when the first primitive forms of life came into being. Other very old rocks have been found in Central America, for example in the Maya Mountains of Belize. The rocks of the West Indies themselves, as can be seen from Diagram 1.1, are not nearly as old.

The mountain-building periods

The great series of earth movements that formed these rocks into mountain chains fall into two main episodes. In the first, which began over 70 million years ago and lasted for several million years, the volcano-studded backbone of Mexico and Central America appeared. Two branches of these mountains extended eastwards, one to what is now Jamaica, and the other by way of southern Cuba, Hispaniola and Puerto Rico to the Virgin Islands. In

Evidence of past vulcanicity – Grand Etang, a crater lake in Grenada. Other examples of volcanic scenery are shown on pages 129, 133 and 157.

Geological Periods		Approximate time scale (years)	Development of Life	Major Caribbean Events
Quaternary Period	Recent	— 20 000	First human beings	Coral reefs, coastal plains, active volcanoes, river terraces
	Pleistocene	— 2 m		Jamaica bauxite
Tertiary Period	Pliocene			
	Miocene	— 25 m	Higher mammals Warm-blooded animals first became common	Creation of volcanic Lesser Antilles Trinidad oil Great thicknesses of limestone deposited
	Oligocene			
	Eocene	— 50 m		Central American and Caribbean mountain chains first formed
Cretaceous		— 100 m	Extinction of most reptiles. First flowering plants Flying reptiles	
Jurassic				
Triassic			First primitive mammals Dinosaurs	
Permian		— 200 m	Primitive reptiles and insects common	Oldest known rocks in the West Indies
Carboniferous			Swamp forests (now coal)	
Devonian		— 300 m	First amphibians	
Silurian		— 400 m	First land plants Lung fishes (first air-breathers)	
Ordovician			First fish-like creatures with backbones	
Cambrian		— 500 m	Sea plants and marine animals with hard shells became common	
Pre-Cambrian		— 700 m	First forms of primitive life	Guiana Highlands

Diagram 1.1 The main events in the geological history of the West Indies.

the south the Caribbean Coastal Range was uplifted. It stretched from what today are Colombia and Venezuela to Trinidad and possibly Barbados.

Even more striking than these mountain chains was the huge trench created by the downfold. If you look at Map 1.3 you can trace its path. The part of it that begins near Central America and passes between Cuba and Jamaica – called the Cayman Trench – is in places over 7 000 metres below sea level. North of Puerto Rico and the Virgin Islands is the Puerto Rican Trench which goes down even further. It is the deepest part of the Atlantic Ocean. If Mount Everest were submerged in it, its summit would not appear above the surface of the sea. From there the downfold continues along the outer side of the arc of eastern Caribbean islands to Trinidad.

This activity was followed by a quieter period when much of this land was submerged beneath the sea and great thicknesses of limestone were deposited. Volcanic activity died down and one series of volcanic islands including Anguilla, St Martin, St Barthélemy, Antigua, Désirade, Marie Galante and the eastern part of Guadeloupe never again became active.

The second great mountain-building episode, like the first, was part of a tremendous world-wide upheaval. It produced such great folded mountain systems as the Alps, Himalayas, Rockies and Andes. In the West Indies some parts were uplifted, others thrown down, and there was another outburst of volcanic activity. It was at this time that the volcanic islands of the Lesser Antilles began to be built up on the inner side of a great curving ridge which had been formed during the first period of mountain building and which reached up to, and in places rose above, the surface of the sea. These islands of the inner arc, which stretch from Saba in the north to Grenada in the south, are much higher than those in the outer arc, lying on the crest of the ridge itself. Guadeloupe shows the contrast most clearly, the western volcanic half being nearly 1 500 metres high, whereas the eastern limestone portion is very low.

Volcanoes and Earthquakes

Two or three of the volcanoes in the Lesser Antilles are still intermittently active and in historic times have caused much damage and loss of life. La Soufrière in Guadeloupe destroyed cultivated land in

1797. The St Vincent Soufrière erupted in 1812, and again on 7 May 1902 when it devastated nearly a third of the island and caused some 2 000 deaths. The very next day Mt Pelée in Martinique also erupted, utterly destroying the town of St Pierre and killing about 30 000 people. Nothing serious has happened since, though in 1976 Guadeloupe was threatened, and in 1979 the St Vincent Soufrière erupted causing extensive damage to crops and forcing the people living nearby to take refuge for a time in other parts of the island. Thermometers and other instruments in the craters of Caribbean volcanoes record everything that happens there so that warning can be given of impending danger.

In several other islands, notably Montserrat, Nevis, Redonda, St Lucia and Dominica, dying vulcanicity is shown by the presence of boiling sulphur springs.

Caribbean earthquake zones

Central America and the West Indies together form one of the world's major zones of earthquake activity. Today, scientists record the location and strength of every earthquake in the region, no matter whether it occurs beneath the land or the sea. The results show that a broad belt of earthquake activity stretches from California along the Pacific edge of central America to Panama. It then swings eastwards below the Gulf of Maracaibo to the Gulf of Paria, curves northwards along the Atlantic side of the Lesser Antilles and Puerto Rico, passes through Hispaniola, and follows the line of the Cayman Trench to Central America south of Belize. The rest of the Caribbean Sea, and the whole of the Gulf of Mexico and the surrounding lowlands, are almost free from earthquakes.

Most of the Caribbean lands have suffered severely from earthquakes at one time or another. The capitals of Guatemala and El Salvador were destroyed in 1917 and 1918. Managua in Nicaragua was destroyed in 1972 with the loss of over 10 000 lives. Four years later an earthquake in Guatemala destroyed fourteen towns, killed 22 000 people and left a million people homeless. Jamaica had a shock of such intensity in 1692 that most of Port Royal disappeared beneath

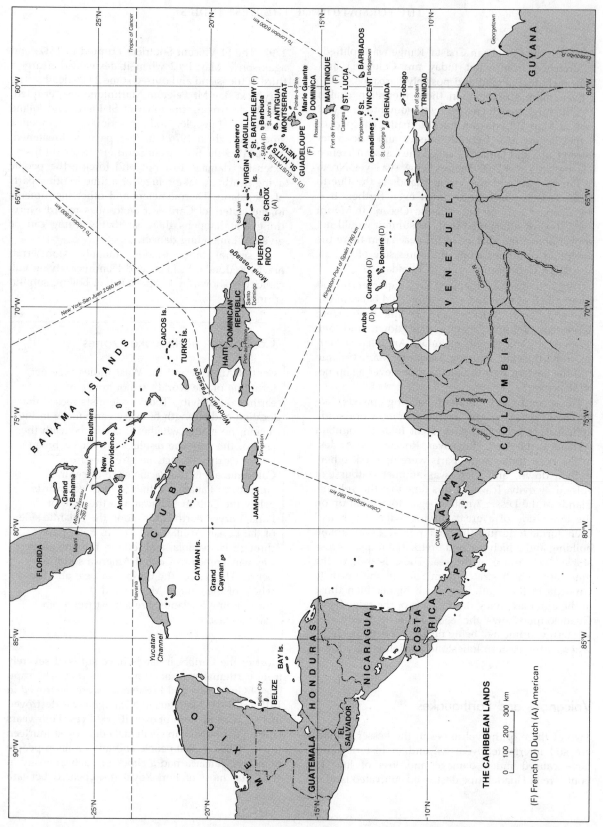

Map 1.2 The Caribbean Lands.

THE CARIBBEAN LANDS

0   100   200   300 km

(F) French (D) Dutch (A) American

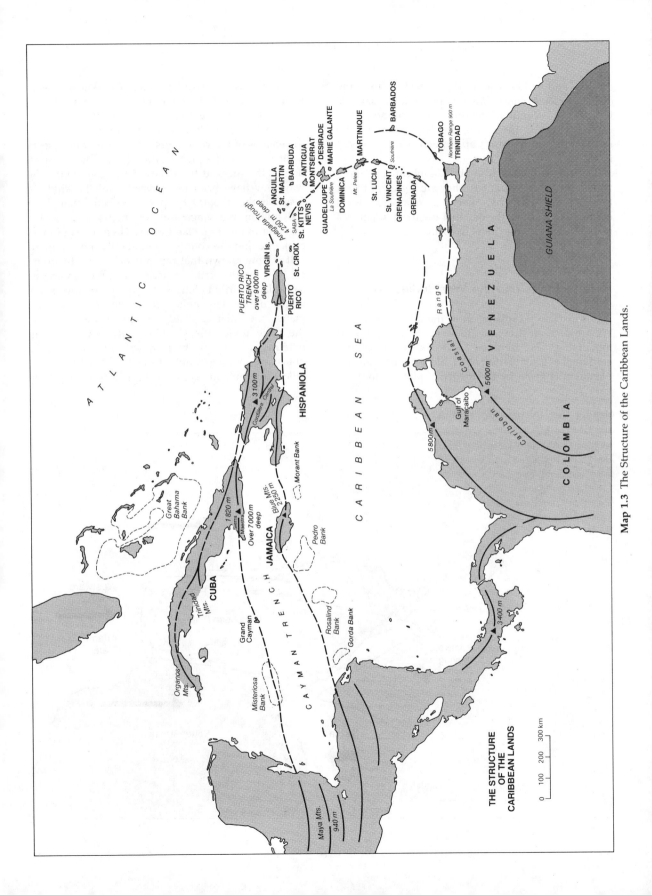

Map 1.3 The Structure of the Caribbean Lands.

the sea, and in 1907 Kingston was destroyed. Some of the Lesser Antilles suffered considerable damage in 1843, the Virgin Islands in 1867. Port-au-Prince was destroyed twice in twenty years in the eighteenth century and Cap Haitien was destroyed in 1842.

Because earthquakes in the Caribbean are more widespread than volcanoes, they are a greater threat, to life and property. Even a relatively small earthquake, such as the one that occurred in Jamaica in 1957, can prove extremely costly.

Plate tectonics and the West Indies

Any satisfactory explanation of the formation of the West Indies must be able to account for the folded mountains, the trenches, and the volcanic and earthquake activity described above. Such an explanation is given by the theory of plate tectonics.

The theory is based on two well-known facts. First, the lava that pours out of active volcanoes proves that temperatures below the continents are so high that rocks melt and are able to move. Second, the shapes of the continents are such that they seem to fit together like pieces of a jigsaw. Close inspection of the rocks at the edges of the continents, the way they have been magnetised, and the kinds of fossils within them, all support the belief that about 200 million years ago the continents were joined together in one huge land mass. Then the land mass broke up and the continents gradually moved apart.

It is now known that this movement is still going on. The earth's crust consists of a few enormous rock plates carried along very slowly by movements in the underlying molten rock. One of these rock plates, the Atlantic Plate, is moving west towards the plate under the Caribbean at about 3–4 centimetres a year. Such a movement may not be noticeable, but it amounts to 30–40 kilometres (20–25 miles) in a million years which, as can be seen from

Map 1.4 The earth movements which have created the West Indies.

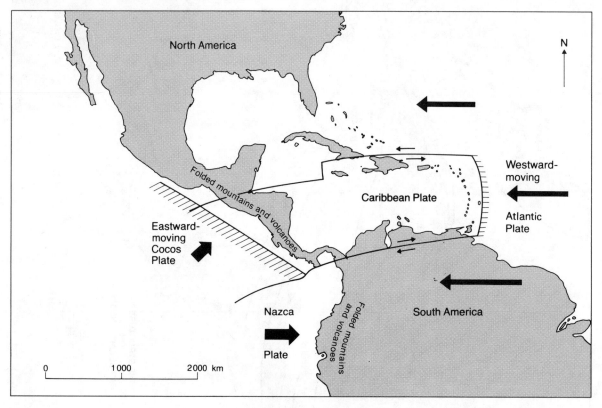

Evidence of past folding, and much subsequent erosion – the Jamaican Blue Mountains.

Diagram 1.1 is a very short period of geological time.

The approximate location and direction of movement of the plates which have created Central America, the northern part of South America, and the West Indies, are shown on Map 1.4. What happens where the Atlantic Plate meets the Caribbean Plate is shown in Diagram 1.5. The pressure between them is so enormous that the edge of the thinner Atlantic Plate is forced downwards – a process called subduction. As it descends its rocks become hotter and hotter until they melt and are destroyed. For this reason this kind of boundary is called a destructive boundary. Another name for it is a convergent boundary because it is the place where two plates meet head on.

Movement at the plate boundary is not continuous. Instead, there are many years of stability while the pressure mounts. Then a sudden movement at a point somewhere on the boundary releases some of the pressure. This is an earthquake. It may take place at or near the earth's surface, or at depths of as much as several hundred kilometres. Pressure may also be suddenly released when some of the molten underlying rock is forced up through cracks near the edge of the Caribbean Plate. This is volcanic activity.

Something similar must have happened some 60–90 million years ago to form the folded mountain chains of the Greater Antilles. However, for the last few million years, the Atlantic Plate and the Caribbean Plate in this part of the Caribbean region have no longer been moving towards each other but beside each other. As a result, the Cayman and Puerto Rican Trenches have been thrust downwards, and

A small low-lying island – Bimini in the Bahamas.

Diagram 1.5 A section (not to scale) through part of the earth's surface to show what happens at the boundary between the Atlantic Plate and the Caribbean Plate.

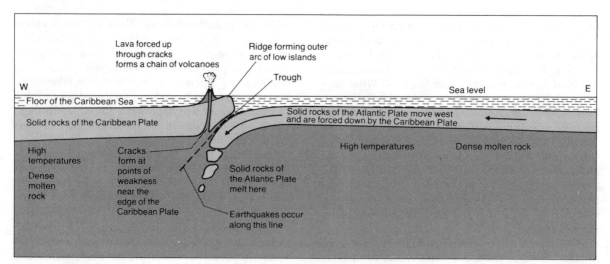

the Greater Antilles have been forced upwards. In parts of the islands the rocks have been split apart by great cracks. Some of these cracks, called faults, are hundreds of miles long. Where the land has been thrown upwards on one side of a major fault, and downwards on the other side, the line of the fault is easy to see. There is highland on one side, lowland on the other, and a steep slope in between. Small faults, of course, are less easily traced. So are faults where the rock movement has been horizontal rather than vertical.

Because the plates in this part of the Caribbean region are not converging, the boundary between them is not a convergent one. It is called, instead, a conservative boundary. Though there is no volcanic activity along it, movement between the plates causes frequent earthquakes.

A third kind of plate boundary also exists, though not in the Caribbean region. Known as a creative boundary, it is the line along which molten rock from deep inside the earth rises towards the surface where it cools to form the rigid rock plates. One of these creative boundaries runs along the floor of the Atlantic Ocean. Its path is marked by a number of mid-Atlantic volcanic islands, including Iceland, the Azores, Ascension Island, and Tristan da Cunha. It is at this boundary that the Atlantic Plate begins its movement westwards. On the other side of the boundary another plate, the African Plate, begins its movement eastwards.

Recent changes

Evidence in the landscape of uplift in recent geological time is provided by terraces, which are areas of flat ground lying between steep slopes. On parts of the coasts of Dominica, Tortuga and St Vincent, for instance, are found, just above the present shorelines, narrow platforms of rock which have been planed-off by the action of the waves and then uplifted. The raised coral terraces found in Jamaica, Barbados and elsewhere are somewhat similar.

More common than either of these are river terraces which are the remnants of river flood-plains left higher up the sides of a valley when the river itself is forced to cut down with renewed vigour, usually because the land has been raised. River terraces occur in Jamaica, Hispaniola, Trinidad and elsewhere.

In the few thousand years that have elapsed since the last Ice Age ended, new land has come into being in ways that are possible only in the tropics. First, new coastal lands have been added where mangrove roots have trapped mud and sand deposited by waves. Second, cays have grown up where sand has been blown and washed on top of coral reefs.

Coral is made by tiny animals that extract calcium carbonate from the surrounding sea water in order to build protective shells for themselves. These shells remain when the animals die. In time, as new corals grow on old ones, a reef is formed. There are three main types of reefs, all of which occur within the region.

1 *Fringing reefs*, the most common type, either touch the coast or are separated from it by only a narrow stretch of shallow water.
2 The *barrier reef* which lies several kilometres off the coast of Belize is separated from the land by water thirty and more metres deep.
3 *Bank reefs* are those which have been built on a broad, shallow submarine platform and are un-attached to any mainland. Bermuda and many of the Bahamas are of this type.

The erosion of West Indian landscapes

Every shower of rain that falls over land moistens the rocks beneath. When the rocks dry off again, small particles are loosened and flake off. Rainwater also affects rocks in a second way. The acids it picks up from dying and rotting vegetation attacks rock surfaces and loosens more particles. Still other fragments are broken off by the roots of plants. Gradually, over the ages, the land becomes covered with a layer of rock particles and soil. In some places the layer is very thin. In others it may be several metres deep.

Under the action of gravity, the surface layer of rock particles and soil tends to move downhill, a process called mass wastage. On gentle slopes the movement is too slow to be noticeable, but it can cause cracks to open in buildings made of brick, concrete or cement blocks. Very occasionally on some steep slopes a sudden movement may take place causing a landslide.

In limestone areas, rainwater acts in a special way. Wherever it enters cracks in the limestone, the acids in the water dissolve away some of the surrounding rock. The cracks are widened into sink holes which drain off all the water from the land surface. Where limestone areas begin, as they often do, as high plateaux, the landscape today takes several different forms. In some places it remains fairly flat. In others it has become gently hollowed. In still others the rock has been worn into steep-sided, cone-shaped hills and intervening pits. Everywhere, however, there is a shortage of surface water. Valleys contain no rivers; hollows contain no lakes; even ponds are uncommon. All the water is under the ground. There, in places, it has dissolved away so much limestone that huge caves have been formed.

Conditions are very different in mountains and highlands made of rocks other than limestone. Instead of disappearing underground, rainwater forms streams which join together and grow in volume as they flow downhill towards the sea. Fragments of rock carried along by the streams erode the rocks beneath. For most of the time this erosion is a very slow process. But after heavy rainstorms the rush of floodwater is so powerful that it carries along large boulders and vast quantities of smaller material. Erosion is then much more rapid. Gradually, deep, steep-sided valleys are carved into the hillsides (see photograph on page 7).

When the streams slacken pace, as they do on leaving the hills, they can no longer carry much material. They deposit it on their floors and along their banks. Each flood brings down more material and adds to the deposits which grow in thickness and are extended further and further away from the hills until they form wide alluvial plains.

As erosion proceeds over great lengths of time, landscapes gradually change their shape. This is particularly easy to see in volcanic areas such as those of the Lesser Antilles where there is a great contrast between the regular cones of active volcanoes, the ridges and ravines of recently extinct volcanoes and the rounded, low hills and wide alluvial plains of older areas.

Along the coasts of the West Indies another agent of erosion is constantly at work. This is the sea. When waves approach a coastline they pick up pebbles, sand and other beach material from the sea floor. Even in calm weather the power of breaking waves is sufficient to grind the beach material into smaller and smaller fragments. During storms the waves become enormously powerful. They fling the beach material against the base of cliffs with such force that a notch is cut between high and low tide marks. Gradually the notch undercuts the rocks above until the time comes when they can no longer support their own weight. They break off and fall into the sea.

In this way cliffs are eroded and made to retreat. The speed of their retreat depends on the type of rock they are made of. If the rock is resistant it is eroded slowly and remains as a headland. If it is not resistant it retreats more quickly and forms a bay.

As we have seen, breaking waves carry beach material with them. Depending on the force of the waves and the shape of the coastline, this material can be flung inshore or carried out to sea or transported along the coast. Beaches are built up wherever waves throw on to the shore more pebbles and sand than they are able to carry away. This happens in bays where waves lose much of their power. There is a beach at the head of most bays. It also happens at sheltered river mouths where the material brought down by the river is more than the waves can carry out to sea. In some places a ridge of sand, called a bar, is built up across the mouth of the river. In other places the material is swept along the coastline until, on reaching a headland, it is deposited on the far side to form what is called a spit. The best known example of a spit in the West Indies is Palisadoes in Jamaica. Several miles in length, it protects Kingston harbour and is the site of an international airport (see Maps 5.16 and 5.17).

With erosion taking place in some places and deposition in others, coastlines are constantly changing their shape. Sometimes the change can be dramatic. A single storm may be sufficient to make a beach noticeably wider if sand is added to it or narrower if it is swept away.

Where coral reefs grow, they affect coastal erosion in two ways. First they protect the shore behind them from wave attack. Second they provide a plentiful supply of beach sand. Many Caribbean beaches owe their existence to the presence of a living offshore reef. If through pollution or some other reason the coral dies, the beaches nearby may lose much of their sand. This has happened in some parts of Barbados. In some countries where beaches are under threat, measures are being taken to prevent further erosion. One of them is to construct groynes to trap the sand. Another is to plant types of seaweed which anchor the sand with their roots.

Part of the Palisadoes sand spit. Also shown are part of Kingston Harbour, Long Mountain where limestone is extracted for the cement factory; and the cloud-capped summits of the Jamaican Blue Mountains. By looking at the maps on page 77 say in which direction the camera was pointing.

Sea pollution

Pollution is harming the natural environment making it less healthy and less pleasant than it was before. Wherever people live in large numbers, the household and industrial waste they produce can cause pollution. Household waste contains germs that can cause outbreaks of typhoid and other diseases if they get into drinking water. It can also act as a breeding ground for flies which spread other kinds of disease. Industrial waste is dangerous in another way. It may contain poisonous chemicals. So may the water running off farmland on which pesticides have been used without proper care. The safe disposal of household, agricultural and industrial waste is therefore essential, no matter how much it may cost. This is true not only in highly populated industrial countries where the problem of waste disposal is becoming very serious but in the West Indies as well.

In many parts of the West Indies, household sewage is disposed of by letting it soak away underground. Care has to be taken to prevent pollutants from getting into this water. In other places drainage into the ground is not possible. This is commonly the case in coastal lowlands. When the sea is used instead pollution is possible here, too. Caribbean tides are small and are not always capable of carrying waste away from the shore. Coral reefs can be affected, even killed, thus allowing waves to attack the coastline and remove sand from the beaches. Landlocked harbours, such as Kingston, can become so polluted that fish and shellfish absorb so much poison that they are unsafe to eat. They may even be killed.

When tourists visit West Indian beaches, they expect to find the sea clear and the sand clean. Household and industrial waste must therefore be prevented from polluting the best beaches and harming the tourist industry. This sort of pollution is not difficult to control, by law if necessary. But on their own the West Indies can do nothing about another source of pollution – the Atlantic Ocean. More ships use the Atlantic than any other sea route in the world, and they throw an enormous amount of waste into the sea. Much of it sinks or rots away, but this does not happen to plastic cups, wrappers, and other plastic products. Nor does it happen to the oil sludge and tar that are pumped overboard when oil tankers wash out their tanks at sea. Because the Atlantic currents in latitudes 5°N to 25°N flow from east to west, anything floating in the water tends to be carried towards the Caribbean. Some of it is washed up on West Indian beaches where the oil, in particular, is difficult to remove. The worst affected islands are the Lesser Antilles, Puerto Rico, the Dominican Republic and the Bahamas, but none escape entirely. So far, pollution from the Atlantic is not serious. It cannot be compared, for example, with the Mediterranean, where people dare not bathe on certain beaches at certain times. But only international action can prevent Atlantic pollution from getting worse.

Questions and assignments

1 Where are the oldest rocks in the Caribbean region to be found? Roughly how old are they believed to be?
2 Name two types of rock which are being formed in the West Indies today. Name a place where each type is to be found.
3 What reasons suggest that the world's continents were once a single land mass?

4 What is the name of the theory that accounts for the submarine trenches, folded mountains, volcanoes and earthquakes in the West Indies? Name the two plates that have done most to create them. What happens at:
a) a convergent (destructive) boundary;
b) a conservative boundary;
c) a creative boundary?
Give an example of each.
5 What is mass wastage? How does it resemble and differ from landslides?
6 Name two limestone areas in the West Indies. What are the main characteristics of their landscapes? What problems are there in obtaining drinking water in these areas? (Check the index on pages 245 to 249 when answering this question.)
7 Draw and label simple diagrams to show:
a) How rivers carve valleys like those shown in the photograph on page 7.
b) How waves attack a cliff.
c) How the sea creates bays, beaches and bars.
8 In the district where you live find out what relationships there are between:
a) gradient and agriculture;
b) soils and agriculture.

2

Caribbean Climate

Temperature

Seasonal changes

The most outstanding feature of the climate of the Caribbean is the uniformity of its high temperature. This uniformity extends from one end of the region to the other. Consider a traveller arriving at a West Indian airport. He could land in the Bahamas or 2 500 kilometres to the south in Guyana. He could land in Barbados or 3 000 kilometres to the west in Belize. In all cases the airport temperatures could well be exactly the same, and on no occasion would they differ by more than a few degrees. There are few other parts of the world where the same would be true over such long distances.

The uniformity of temperature also extends from one month to another. The hottest months, with average temperatures about 27° to 28°C, are those

Diagram 2.1 The monthly progress of the overhead midday sun. It travels through 94° of latitude in 52 weeks. Work out on what dates it is directly above the place where you live.

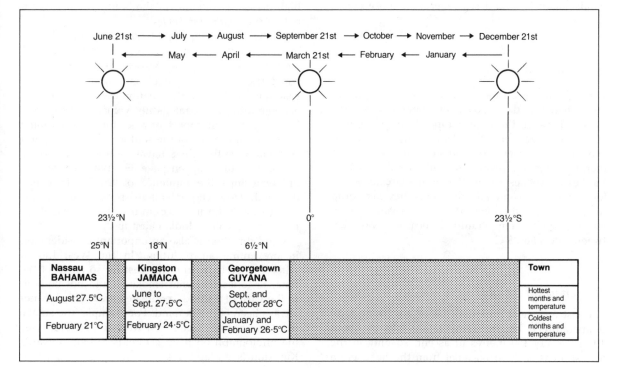

immediately following the passage of the overhead midday sun. The coolest months are those when the sun is south of the Equator, but even then average temperatures seldom fall below 24°C. Diagram 2.1 shows the relationship between the overhead mid-day sun and the average temperatures of three places in different latitudes.

Caribbean temperatures are so reliable that tourists in the Virgin Islands hotels are given their money back if the average daily temperature falls below 20°C or rises above 31°C. So far this has never happened and you will probably find that the scheme could apply just as safely to the territory in which you live.

This small annual temperature range is one of the distinguishing features of the tropical marine climate. It is partly due to the constantly high angle of the sun's midday rays. Another and stronger influence is the Atlantic Ocean. Like all oceans, the Atlantic has such a slow response to heating and cooling that its temperature varies little from one season to another. The steady temperature of the sea is imparted to the Trade winds, which blow over the islands and prevent day temperatures from rising to very high levels. Many houses are specially designed to make the most of the cooling effect of the Trade winds, or of land and sea breezes in those places where they occur.

Day and night changes

Throughout the Caribbean lands there is a greater range between day and night temperatures than there is between the mean temperatures of the hottest and coldest months. Day temperatures can exceed 32°C, even, occasionally, in the cooler months. Night temperatures regularly fall to 21°C in the Lesser Antilles and to 18°C in the Greater Antilles, where in exceptional conditions they may drop to 13°C even in the lowlands. The sea varies much less: its surface temperature is nearly always between 26°C and 28°C.

The effect of height

The last and most important factor governing local temperature is height. Temperature falls by about 1°C for every 160 metres of ascent, so only in the lowest areas is there no relief from the heat. From this point of view it is unfortunate that the largest towns in Caribbean lands are all ports and therefore lie at, or close to, sea level. However, in some islands, notably Jamaica, suburbs have been built in the foothills where people can live in comparatively cool surroundings.

In the Greater Antilles some of the highest peaks are subject to occasional frosts and there are large areas of highland where conditions are more suitable for the cultivation of citrus, coffee and temperate fruits and vegetables than for sugar cane, bananas, cocoa and coconuts.

Pressure, winds and rainfall

The most important pressure system affecting the West Indies is the North Atlantic high which extends from the Azores to Bermuda. Owing to the earth's rotation the winds blowing out of this system are deflected in a clockwise direction so that near Africa they blow as northerly winds and near the Equator they are almost due east. However, as they blow from the north-east for most of their journey, they are known as the *North-East Trade winds*. A similar high-pressure system over the South Atlantic gives rise to the *South-East Trades*.

In the old sailing-ship days the Trades had a marked influence on sea routes and on naval strategy in the Caribbean. Voyages from west to east could take five to ten times as long as those from east to west. An easterly situation was therefore both economically and strategically valuable. Thus Barbados became an important place for trans-shipping goods to other parts of the southern Caribbean, and Antigua was the chief naval base for the whole region (see the map on page 39). With the coming of steamships the influence of the Trade winds declined. However, it still exists to some extent, being shown, for instance, in the east to west alignment of most West Indian airstrips.

Wind direction is also an important consideration in preventing air pollution. In the West Indies, where winds blow from the east for so much of the time, factories that emit smoke should not be built to the west of a thickly populated area. This has not always been borne in mind. For example, the smoke from the cement factory on Kingston harbour (see the photograph on page 11) tends to blow towards Kingston (see Map 5.17).

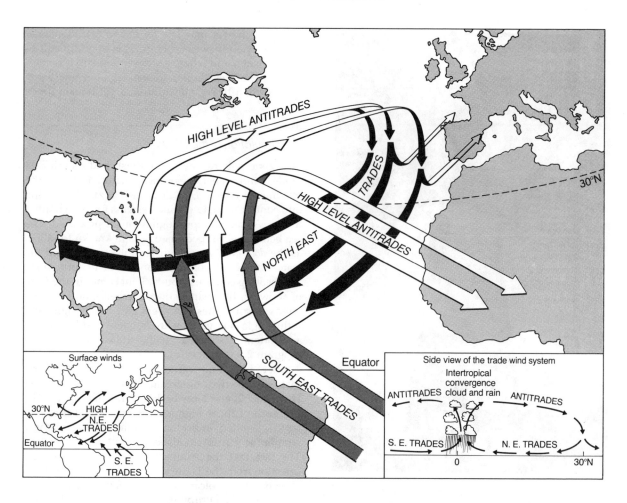

Diagrams 2.2 and 2.3(a), (b) Trade winds and the Intertropical Convergence Zone.

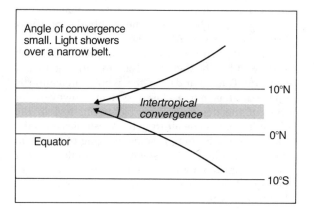

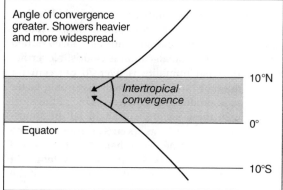

A light shower may last for only a few moments, a heavy one for over an hour. It is very difficult to predict when and where a shower will fall. It is common in the West Indies to stand only a few yards away from a heavy rainstorm and yet remain dry.

The circulation of the winds

The zone where the North-East and South-East Trade winds meet, near the Equator, is called the *Intertropical Convergence Zone* (the TCZ). On coming into contact these two wind systems force each other to rise. A colossal updraught of air is produced. The sea beneath is left becalmed; a calm known to sailors as the *doldrums*. As the air rises it is cooled and the water vapour it contains condenses to form huge rain-bearing cumulus clouds. Rain comes in the form of showers. If the angle of convergence of the Trade winds is small these showers are usually light, but if the angle is large they are frequent and heavy and are often associated with thunderstorms (see Diagram 2.3 on page 15).

After ascending vertically for several thousand metres the two airstreams turn, as shown in Diagram 2.2, and blow back towards the tropics. The presence of these high-level winds, called the *Antitrades*, is often indicated by thin, white, feathery strands of cirrus clouds composed of ice-crystals. The fact that the Antitrades blow in the opposite direction from the Trade winds has occasionally been shown when volcanic ash has fallen many miles north-east of an erupting volcano. Barbados has had several falls of ash following the eruptions of the St Vincent Soufrière. In 1835 Jamaica received some from Cosiguina in Guatemala. As the Trade winds blow constantly from the north-east, the only possible explanation of these incidents is that the ash rose high enough to enter the Antitrades and was carried north-eastwards by them.

When the Antitrades reach approximately 30° North and South, they sink back to earth again and form the Trade winds, so the whole circulation is repeated. It is not a closed system, however, for some of the descending air blows out to join the Westerlies and some air from the Westerlies joins the Trades. Similarly there is some merging of the air in the two Trade-wind systems. In addition, other winds at times blow into the region from the neighbouring land masses, particularly from North America in winter.

The fact that the Trade winds are strongest and most regular during the dry season was used to advantage in former times when windmills were built on many sugar estates to operate cane-crushing machinery – cane being reaped and crushed during the dry months.

Though the Trade winds are moisture-laden they are not normally rain-bearing and the most typical Caribbean weather conditions are blue skies dotted with white puffs of small cumulus clouds. Nevertheless, Trade wind humidity is over 70 per cent for most of the time, and only a small disturbing factor is required to produce rain showers. One of the most important of these factors is a slight fall of atmospheric pressure (such as occurs throughout the region in the summer months). Another is the passage of even a weak low-pressure system. Yet another is the interruption of the smooth flow of the wind by land.

Convectional rainfall

As we have seen, the Trade winds, though humid, are not necessarily rainy unless some rain-producing factor is present. Such factors are diverse, unreliable and often only of local significance. It therefore follows that rainfall varies from one place to another and that the rainfall of one year may bear no resemblance to that of the year before or the year after. There are, nevertheless, certain characteristics shared by all Caribbean countries. First, most of the rain falls in heavy showers. This is typical of hot as opposed to cool lands (eg Britain) where the rain usually falls more gently for longer periods of time. Second, the Caribbean has one season – summer – which is rainy and another season which is fairly dry. This is a distinguishing feature of the tropical marine climate. Monsoon countries, though similar, have a much more pronounced contrast between the wet and the dry seasons.

In spite of the fact that rain may come at any time of the year, drought is a serious problem in the West Indies. A long drought lasting for several successive months is a risk everywhere, not only in the low-lying dry islands. It can wither food crops and cause great distress in rural areas. It can reduce the sugar output of such islands as Barbados and St Kitts by more than a quarter, and can encourage the conditions under which soil erosion flourishes.

As the rain-producing factors vary in importance in different parts of the Caribbean, the region has been subdivided into three zones; the southern Caribbean, the Greater Antilles, and the eastern Caribbean.

The rainfall of the southern Caribbean

The two main factors affecting the rainfall of the southern Caribbean are the character and the position of the Intertropical Convergence Zone. The character of the ITCZ depends, as we have already noted, on the angle of convergence of the North-East and South-East Trade winds. When the angle is small, activity is light, the sky is blue, and the

Fine weather; blue skies dotted with white puffs of small cumulus clouds off the coast of Nevis.

weather is fine. But when the angle is large, activity is considerable. A zone of dense cloud may stretch from north to south for a hundred and fifty kilometres, and rainfall may be heavy and prolonged.

The position of the ITCZ is not constant throughout the year. Instead, it moves northwards and southwards a month or two behind the movement of the overhead sun. Thus in December, when the sun is furthest south (23½°S), the ITCZ is moving southwards across Guyana, and as Diagram 17.3 shows, December is a particularly rainy month there.

The ITCZ reaches its most southerly position (1°N to 3°N) in February. Then it moves northwards again, bringing a second rainfall maximum to Guyana in May and June. For the next three months the ITCZ lies between 10°N and 12°N, and this is therefore the rainy season in Trinidad. During this period it occasionally moves a few degrees further north. When this happens, Trinidad gets dry weather, and rain falls over Barbados and the most southerly islands in the eastern Caribbean chain.

The rainfall of the Greater Antilles

The size of the Greater Antilles and the height of their mountains are both factors sufficient to produce rainfall.

Rainfall and relief

In order to cross the mountains of the Greater Antilles, the Trade winds are forced to rise. In doing so they are cooled, and this tends to produce rain. Clouds not only commonly blanket the mountains themselves, but, as shown at the top of Diagram 2.5, extend a considerable distance to windward and a short distance to leeward of them. One of the best examples of this is found in Jamaica, where the Blue Mountains stand across the passage of the North-East Trades. Port Antonio, a town on the north-east coast, has 3 200 millimetres and the mountains themselves have over 5 000 millimetres of rain a year.

Showery weather; rain-bearing cumulus clouds building up off Port Antonio on the north coast of Jamaica.

Kingston, on the southern side, has only 760 millimetres a year and is said to be in rain shadow.

Some of the Lesser Antilles are high enough to produce occasional relief rain but not high enough to cause rain-clouds to form very far to the windward of the mountains. Their windward and leeward coasts therefore display less of a contrast than do those of the Greater Antilles.

Convectional rainfall

Convectional rainfall occurs in the Greater Antilles because of the size of each of the islands. Land has a quick response to heating and cooling influences, and soon after sunrise the temperature of these large islands rises rapidly. By mid-morning the air above the land is sufficiently hot for it to rise, and powerful convection currents are set up. As the air rises it gets cooler and the moisture it contains condenses to form cumulus clouds. If the air is very moist, these clouds grow and spread across the sky so that by afternoon they may cast large shadows over the land. In consequence the upward currents of air lose strength and heavy showers may fall from the clouds. Convectional showers of this kind are heaviest and most frequent in the months when the air is most humid. They are sometimes accompanied by thunder. Usually by evening the clouds disperse and the nights are clear and cool except over the sea, where it is often cloudy and occasionally rainy, especially just before dawn (see Diagram 2.6).

During the days a powerful sea breeze blows inland to replace the rising air. At night when the land is at a lower temperature than the sea the process is reversed. The cool air over the land sinks and blows offshore as a land breeze. Thus, over the coastal plains of the Greater Antilles the normal Trade wind system is interrupted and replaced by this day and night alternation of sea and land breezes.

Relief and convectional rain are not the only types of rain in the Greater Antilles. Rain is also brought to them by *northers* in winter and by *easterly waves* and *hurricanes* in summer.

The rainfall of the eastern Caribbean

The islands of the Lesser Antilles are small and therefore receive little convectional rain. Some rise high enough to have relief rain and there is a great contrast between those islands which are mountainous and wet and those which are low and dry.

When describing climate it should be noted that in the West Indies a month is said to be wet if its rainfall is over 100 millimetres, and moist if it is between 65 millimetres and 100 millimetres. Evaporation is so rapid, and the Trade winds have such a drying effect, that a month with under 65 millimetres is said to be dry unless it follows a wet month (in which case it can be called moist). Table 2.4 shows how this works in practice.

Easterly waves

Among the most important rain-producing factors in this region are easterly waves. These troughs of low atmospheric pressure are believed to form over West Africa. They move across the Atlantic Ocean along the northern edge of the ITCZ.

Table 2.4 Average monthly rainfall of a dry island and a wet island (*figures in millimetres*)

Grand Turk, Turks Islands

J	F	M	A	M	J	J	A	S	O	N	D	
66	46	30	33	56	48	48	43	79	112	127	61	mm
M	D	D	D	D	D	D	D	M	W	W	M	

(total 749 millimetres)

Castries, St Lucia

J	F	M	A	M	J	J	A	S	O	N	D	
137	102	91	89	145	234	236	260	236	244	227	188	mm
W	W	M	M	W	W	W	W	W	W	W	W	

(total 2 189 millimetres)

W = Wet M = Moist D = Dry

The axis of a typical easterly wave points roughly in a north to south direction, as shown in Diagram 2.7. Ahead of the axis, that is on its western side, the wind blows from the north-east or north, the weather is fine, and the sky is unusually clear. Along the axis the wind is light, and there is more cloud. Behind the axis the wind is at its strongest. It tends to blow slightly south of east and to rise upwards from the earth's surface. In doing so it creates towering cumulus clouds. Rain showers are common by day and by night, often accompanied by strong gusts of wind.

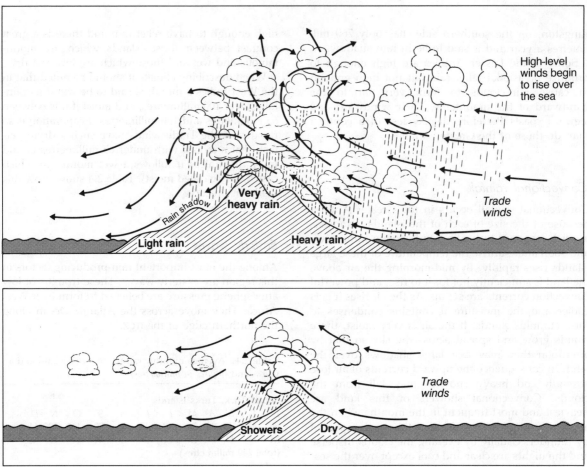

Diagram 2.5 Rainfall and relief.
(a) Showers falling over an island large enough and mountainous enough to force high-level winds to rise long before they reach it, so that showers fall over the sea and the windward coast as well as on the mountains themselves.
(b) Sometimes the showers which fall over a smaller, lower island drift downwind and fall mainly on the leeward slopes. Often lines of cumulus clouds extend for many miles to the leeward of the hill summits where they form.

The extent of the bad weather depends on the speed of the easterly wave. If the wave moves more quickly than the Trade winds it may bring little or no rain. But if, as happens more often, it moves slowly, showers may fall over a period of a day or two.

Easterly waves are most common between May and November. During this period they appear on an average every five days. From June to September there is seldom a day on which one is not present somewhere over the Caribbean.

Some easterly waves extend as far north as the Tropic of Cancer and pass over the Greater Antilles and the Bahamas. In doing so they add to the rainfall there.

Hurricanes and northers

Hurricanes

Sometimes an easterly wave over the North Atlantic Ocean or the Gulf of Mexico travels at the same speed as the Trade winds. When that happens it tends to become unstable, and it may develop into a hurricane. As a result of factors which are not fully explained, a powerful upward air current is set up, creating an almost circular low-pressure system. If this is far enough from the Equator (that is, north of 10°N) the winds drawn in to replace the rising air are deflected by the force of the Earth's rotation so that they spiral inwards in an anticlockwise direction, (see Diagram 2.8). Once the hurricane is born,

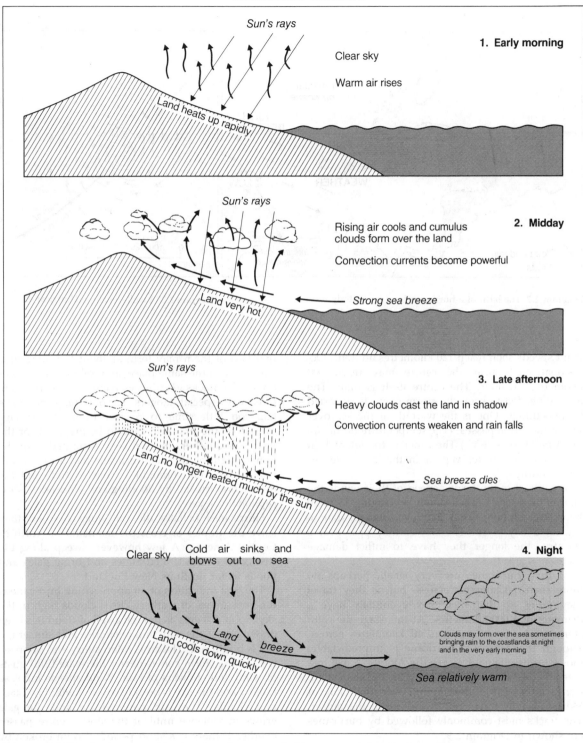

Diagram 2.6 The development of land and sea breezes and of convectional showers throughout the day on one of the larger islands.

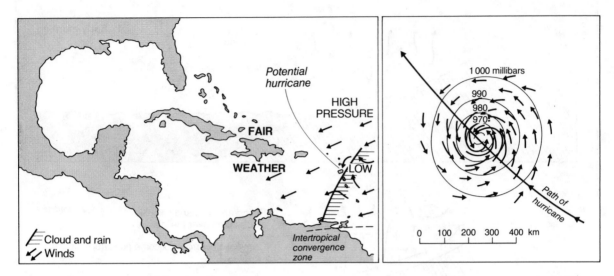

Diagram 2.7 The birth of a hurricane from an easterly wave.

Diagram 2.8 A well-developed hurricane.

wind speeds soon reach 120 kilometres an hour. Occasional gusts near the centre may reach 300 kilometres an hour. The centre itself is calm. The energy needed to keep the storm going is provided by two things. One is the warmth of the sea over which the storm passes. (The temperature of the sea must be at least 26°C.) The other is the latent heat released as the water vapour in the air condenses into raindrops.

In contrast to the terrific speed of their winds the storms themselves move slowly, averaging 15 to 20 kilometres an hour. They may even remain stationary for a day or so. The slower they pass over a country, the longer they have to inflict damage there.

At first, hurricanes are very small, perhaps no more than 8 kilometres across, but as they travel they grow, so that they may eventually have a diameter of 1 000 kilometres. At this stage the calm storm centre is as much as 40 kilometres across. Though the path of a hurricane is unpredictable, most storms originating over the Atlantic travel in a westerly direction into the Caribbean and then curve northwards. Those developing over the Gulf of Mexico usually travel northwards from the outset. The tracks most commonly followed by hurricanes are shown in Diagram 2.9.

An as yet unexplained feature of the hurricanes which originate over the Atlantic Ocean is the way that two of them may form at about the same time and in much the same place, and follow one another on similar tracks. Territories lying in their path are faced with special dangers. For one thing they have had too little time to recover from the damage caused by the first hurricane to be prepared for the next. For another, the soil is so saturated with the rain brought by the first hurricane that it can absorb none of the rain brought by the second, and the destruction caused by flooding and landslides is exceptionally severe.

Hurricanes usually die out quickly when they leave the tropics or cross the mainland of North or Central America. A few however, sweep along the east coast of the United States and bring gales and floods as far north as New England.

The first indication of an approaching hurricane is the appearance of feathery cirrus clouds high in the sky. Soon it seems as though a veil of cloud has been drawn across the sun, and at sunrise and sunset the sky is bright red. The air is calm, sultry and oppressive. As the storm comes nearer there are fitful gusts of wind and showers of rain. Wind speeds increase rapidly and the sky is quickly covered with low black rain clouds. The rain pours down and the gale grows in violence until, if the storm centre passes overhead, there is a short period of calm broken by a few sharp gusts of wind. Suddenly, with little or no warning, the winds reappear, blowing from the opposite direction. As the storm passes on its way the winds gradually drop, but the rain can continue for several more days.

The destructiveness of hurricanes has been recorded from the earliest days of West Indian history. Columbus weathered at least three. One of the worst years of all was 1780 when hurricanes destroyed a Spanish, a French and an English fleet in the Caribbean and took a toll on sea and land of 20 000 lives. Today such tragedies are rare because satellites and special aircraft report the movement of each hurricane, and ships are warned to keep well away from them. On land, although these warnings are valuable in saving lives, they cannot prevent the force of the wind, the torrential rain and sometimes an accompanying 'tidal' wave from destroying crops and buildings worth millions of dollars each year.

For example, in August 1980 Hurricane Allen moved in from the Atlantic. Passing close to Barbados and Grenada, it damaged property in both islands and destroyed over a third of Grenada's bananas, cocoa and nutmegs. Gathering force it crossed St Vincent and St Lucia, killing 16 people, rendering thousands homeless, and destroying over 90 per cent of the bananas there. Martinique and Dominica were the next islands to suffer. Dominica was still recovering from an even worse hurricane (David) the year before. Worse was to come. Hurricane Allen next struck Haiti where 200 people died and 150 000 were left without food or shelter. Curving north-westwards it destroyed the banana crop along the eastern coastlands of Jamaica. Finally it swept across Cuba, adding to the death toll there and doing extensive damage to the island's citrus trees.

Two years later, St Vincent and St Lucia suffered further setbacks from Hurricane Danielle. Then, in 1988, the Greater Antilles experienced one of the

Map 2.9 Common hurricane tracks.

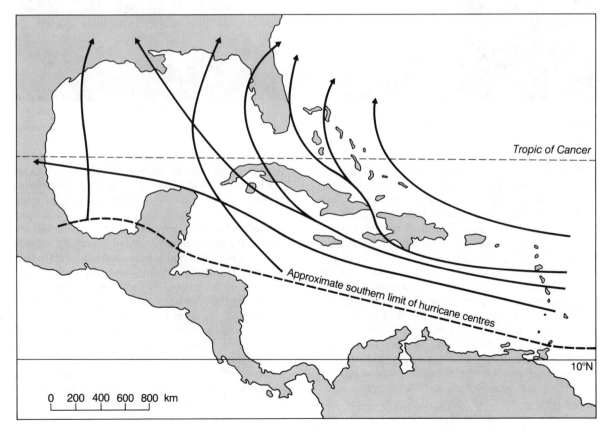

Tropic of Cancer

Approximate southern limit of hurricane centres

10°N

0 200 400 600 800 km

A satellite photograph of Hurricane Allen a day or two after it crossed Cuba in August 1980. By this time it was 1 000 kilometres across. Note the eye of the storm and the spiral of clouds.

fiercest storms in recent years. This was Hurricane Gilbert. Entering the Caribbean near St Lucia it soon developed wind speeds of 280 kilometres per hour over a wide area. It brought death and destruction to the Dominican Republic and Haiti. Next it crossed Jamaica from end to end. It caused further deaths, wiped out several hospitals, rendered 500 000 people homeless, destroyed or damaged 60 per cent of the coffee crop and most of the bananas, and cut off electricity supplies which in some places took several weeks to restore. It then went on to cause similar destruction in Central America. In September 1989 an equally powerful hurricane, Hugo, took a more northerly course than most storms. It crossed Guadeloupe, the Virgin Islands and Puerto Rico, and caused enormous damage not only in those islands but also in Antigua, St Kitts and Montserrat.

Fortunately in these days of international co-operation, governments of countries outside the Caribbean are ready to send relief to stricken areas. So are a number of religious bodies and other organisations which have been set up specially to provide assistance to developing countries in times of need.

No island in the Caribbean can be considered entirely free from danger. Trinidad, normally outside the hurricane belt, had a freak storm in 1933 which destroyed coconut plantations and oil installations in the south of the island. Barbados, storm free for the first half of the century, suffered in 1955 from a hurricane which went on to wreck Grenada.

The official hurricane season in the Caribbean lasts from June to November, during which time about eight hurricanes can be expected to develop. Not all of these will be severe, nor will they necessarily touch land. August and September are the months of the most numerous and violent storms.

A Jamaican hospital damaged by Hurricane Gilbert in 1988.

Northers

Northers are winds which occasionally blow out from the cold interior plains of North America in winter. They bring squalls, low temperatures, dull skies and rain to Mexico, the northern part of Central America, Cuba and Jamaica. These winds, which can last for several days at a time, are strong enough to damage and destroy such crops as bananas and cocoa, especially on exposed northward-facing slopes. Here too, the rainfall can be very heavy; indeed, northers cause as many floods in Jamaica as do hurricanes. In contrast, the southern side of the island is usually dry, and in Kingston the only sign of a norther may be a bank of white cloud looking like a huge roll of cotton wool lying over the mountain tops (see page 11).

In some winters northers extend no further south than 15°N. In others they reach as far as Trinidad and Venezuela. In travelling over the sea the winds warm up and lose their strength so that by the time they reach the southern Caribbean they are neither cold nor destructive. Instead, they produce a wide belt of cloudy skies and sometimes rain which may last for several days.

Climate and agriculture in the West Indies

Temperatures throughout the West Indies are very favourable for agriculture. There are no elevations where it is too cold for crops to be grown, though many mountains are too misty, too rainy and too steep to make cultivation worthwhile. There is no winter to slow up plant growth, and some crops – like bananas – bear throughout the year and are of particular value to the small farmer as they provide him with a steady income. Quick-growing crops, such as rice and vegetables, may be planted and reaped more than once a year.

The amount of rainfall has a great deal to do with the type of crop grown. Thus in the Lesser Antilles exports of such tree crops as cocoa, coconuts, nutmegs and citrus are limited to the rainy, mountainous islands. None of them are grown commercially in the lower, drier islands. The onset of the rainy season determines the date on which small farmers plant their food crops.

The chief climatic hazards are drought and hurricanes. Sugar cane stands up relatively well to both (in any case most has been harvested before the beginning of the hurricane season). This is one reason for the success of sugar cane in the West Indies. Bananas suffer very badly in hurricanes, but recovery is swift because new plants come into bearing within a year. Tree crops are worst affected and their output may be reduced for years afterwards.

Climate and health in the West Indies

Until it was known that disease was caused by germs, the climate was commonly blamed for ill health in the tropics. Evidence of this can be seen in the word 'malaria' which means 'bad air'. But in fact climate affects health only in an indirect way. For instance, the absence of severe frost in the West Indies encourages the growth and multiplication of disease-bearing organisms in man, animals and plants. On the other hand the plentiful sunshine destroys many of these organisms and now that we are able to control such diseases as yellow fever, cholera, typhoid, yaws and malaria, the West Indies are rightly regarded as health resorts for visitors from other countries.

There are varying beliefs about the psychological effect of the West Indian climate but it does seem that on some days the temperature and humidity are high enough to affect people's work. In order to make conditions more comfortable and to increase productivity, some businesses and offices are air-conditioned.

A more complex chain of events arising from the tropical climate affects the food supply and in turn the health of many people in the West Indies. Heavy rains remove most of the minerals from the soils and both grass and crops are thereby impoverished. Where grass does grow, its quality is usually poor and it cannot support as many animals as the grass of temperate countries. As a result the West Indies can produce only a fraction of their requirements of animal products. Imports are expensive and beyond the means of many people who therefore exist largely on a diet of vegetables and sugar. Unfortunately, again because of the climate, these foods are generally deficient in minerals and proteins. Indeed it has been stated that throughout the West Indies the poorer people live on diets that are inadequate, providing neither sufficient energy for long periods of manual work nor proper protection against disease.

Questions and assignments

1 Name the two months when the sun is directly above the equator, five months when the sun is south of it, and five months when the sun is north of it.

2 What is meant by the term 'annual temperature range'? Name one West Indian town with a small annual range and give two reasons why it is small. Name a West Indian town where the range is larger and say why it is larger.

3 What do the initials ITCZ stand for? Draw and label:
  a) a simple diagram to show how the North-East and South-East Trade winds meet at the ITCZ;
  b) a sketch map to show the position of the ITCZ in February and in June.
  What happens when the angle between the two Trade wind systems at the ITCZ is
  c) large, and
  d) small?

4 Draw and label bar graphs to show the annual monthly rainfall of the two places shown in Table 2.4. (You can use Diagrams 17.3 and 17.4 as models for this exercise.) Name one similarity and one difference between the rainfall of the two places.

5 What is
  a) relief rain, and
  b) convectional rain?
  Draw and label diagrams to show why they occur. What is meant by the term 'rain shadow'? Name three parts of the West Indies where rain shadow occurs.

6 Describe what is likely to happen when moisture-laden winds cross
  a) one of the low-lying, and
  b) one of the mountainous islands in the Lesser Antilles.

7 Draw and label a diagram to show the pressure, wind direction, and wind strength in a typical hurricane. (The book *Introducing Caribbean Weather Maps* has additional information on hurricanes.) From the information given on pages 23 and 24 show on a map of the Caribbean the tracks of Hurricanes Allen (1980), Gilbert (1988) and Hugo (1989).

8 What is the difference between weather and climate? With the aid of diagrams describe the climate of the place where you live.

9 By keeping daily weather records find out:
a) the highest and lowest temperatures that occur for each month;
b) the longest period over which there is no rain;
c) the time of day and the duration of the showers that fall in different months.

10 From whatever information is available and from your general knowledge make your own forecast of tomorrow's weather. Try to predict maximum and minimum temperatures, wind speed and direction, and the sky condition (cloudiness) at various times of the day.

Later, look back at your forecast. Which of your predictions were reasonably accurate? Which were not? Why can you always expect some to be better than others?

11 Draw a chart to show the relationship between the rainy and dry seasons and the planting and harvesting of the crops grown where you live.

3

Vegetation and soils

Vegetation

Forest formerly covered the greater part of the West Indies. Because of the variety of soils and climatic conditions, in its natural state it varied considerably in character from place to place. The cutting of forests by man and the introduction of many foreign species (eg logwood in Jamaica, marabú in Cuba and fruit trees everywhere) have greatly changed the make up of West Indian forest vegetation.

Along rocky or sandy coasts it is common to see sea grapes and other bushes bent low and permanently gnarled or flattened on top by the strong, salty breeze. In other places there are swamps – mangrove swamps wherever the water is salt or brackish, but filled with other plants where it is fresh. Mangrove trees, of which there are several kinds, are able to grow in or near salt water. Their tenacious root systems help to protect low-lying coastal areas from erosion by the sea, and may even

Coastal vegetation adapted to the wind and salt spray on an exposed coast.

Mangroves growing in mud on a sheltered coast.

Caribbean forests and woodlands

In the wettest lowland areas where conditions are most favourable for plant growth, *tropical rain-forest* occurs. This forest has been cleared from most of the inhabited areas but fine examples still exist in Guyana and parts of Central America, and some small stands remain in Trinidad and the Lesser Antilles. The rain-forest contains a great variety of tall, evergreen, broad-leaved trees, some of which rise to a height of 35 metres and more.

Lianas and epiphytes are common. Lianas are long woody vines which climb up the trunks of trees and along their branches. Epiphytes are plants that anchor themselves to the trunks, branches and even the leaves of trees and obtain their water and nutrients from roots which hang in the air and have no direct connection with the ground.

Wherever the land rises high enough the tropical rain-forest gradually gives way to *montane forest*. Here the trees are somewhat smaller than those on

Cactus thorn scrub (Antigua).

promote the extension of land by accumulating soil about their roots. Coconut palms grow well in the sand along the shore, as they are not harmed by the sea air. They are a useful source of food and other materials. These palms, however, are almost always planted; they do not form natural forests. Unfortunately, in some places (eg Grand Cayman), they have been nearly wiped out by disease in recent years, and other areas (eg Jamaica) are also suffering.

In the plains behind the coasts of Caribbean islands the type of vegetation depends mainly on the amount of rainfall, which as we saw in chapter two, varies greatly from one place to another.

In areas where there is a prolonged seasonal drought each year – that is, usually on the leeward side of an island – there is *semi-deciduous woodland*. Some of the trees, which are mostly short and often thorny, shed their leaves in the dry months. Burning, and shifting cultivation, have turned large areas of this woodland into scrub and thicket.

In a very few dry areas, notably the Cul de Sac plain of southern Hispaniola, the eastern tip of Cuba and part of the southern coastlands of Puerto Rico and Jamaica there is *cactus thorn scrub*. Cacti have long roots and tiny, spiny leaves especially adapted to withstand aridity.

Tropical rain forest (Guyana). What conditions support this type of vegetation? How do the conditions differ from those which give rise to cactus thorn scrub?

the lowlands and are more thickly covered with epiphytes such as orchids, bromeliads (wild pines), ferns and mosses. Tree ferns are common, particularly in areas which have been cleared at one time or another. Some kinds of trees occur that are absent or rare in the lowlands, for example the nearly pure stands of pitch pine which cover large parts of the interior mountain ranges of Hispaniola. Elsewhere the undisturbed montane forest consists of a complex mixture of trees and shrubs. It contains even more species than the lowland rain-forest, sometimes over one hundred to the acre. Thus the total woody flora of the West Indies is very rich, containing in all thousands of species. Many of these, however, are restricted to particular localities or islands, for example the pine barrens which exist on some of the low-lying islands of the Bahamas (see chapter twelve).

On exposed ridges and high peaks amidst the drifting clouds, where temperatures are rather low and the air is always saturated with moisture, *elfin woodland* grows. This vegetation is so called because the densely growing trees are stunted and twisted into strange contorted shapes that appear ghost-like in the mist. Their gnarled and dripping limbs are swathed with lichens and draped with tangled masses of sodden moss. Embedded in the moss grow many tiny epiphytic orchids and ferns belonging to species found only under such conditions.

All forests are affected by soil conditions as well as by moisture and temperature. For example, the Lesser Antillean lowland rain forest grows further up the slopes of young volcanoes (where the soils are new and rich in minerals) than of old, eroded volcanic areas where the soil is poorer. Again, the vegetation in limestone regions differs markedly from that in shaley or igneous areas. Thus in dry places where the porous nature of limestone increases the effect of aridity, dry *evergreen woodland* commonly occurs. It also exists on the porous white sand of Guyana.

Some species of trees and shrubs are limited to soils derived from limestone and seldom, if ever, occur elsewhere. Others cannot grow in limey soils. Many plants, on the other hand, are much more widely tolerant. The effect of salt in the soil can be seen in coastal areas throughout the West Indies. Relatively few species of plants can grow in salty soils, and these species usually cannot grow elsewhere. A special case of a different kind occurs in some of the Lesser Antilles where the sulphurous vapour given off from volcanic vents or fissures kills many plants, allowing to grow only those that can withstand the fumes. Examples occur in the Valley of Desolation, Dominica, and on the slopes of the Soufrière mountains in St Vincent and St Lucia.

In order to collect fuel, obtain building material, and clear the land for cultivation, man has removed most of the original forest cover from the accessible parts of the West Indies. Some islands, such as Antigua were cleared right up to the hill-tops by the sugar planters of the eighteenth century. If cleared land is later abandoned, the forest may never grow back in the same way as it was before. In some areas *secondary forest* takes its place. Secondary forest is characterised by fewer species, smaller trees and poor quality timber. Elsewhere the original forest is replaced by fern brake or by savanna followed later by poor scrub. In short, the present vegetation cover of most of the West Indies is secondary in nature; that is, it has succeeded, usually in some degenerate form or other, the original natural vegetation.

Tropical montane forest (Belize).

Caribbean Savannas

Savanna is tropical grassland which may or may not contain scattered scrub trees. Many savannas in the West Indies have been made by man and are maintained by annual fires; indeed the name 'Burnt Savanna' occurs in places. In a few other parts of the region savannas are the result of natural conditions. In the interior of Guyana the long dry season is too severe for forest growth and savanna occurs instead, except along the banks of rivers. Soils are the determining factor in Barbuda – the only island in the Lesser Antilles to possess a natural savanna. Here, a few inches below the surface, lies a layer of dense clay which tree-roots cannot penetrate. Moreover, this clay bed is impervious to water. As a result the thin overlying soil becomes waterlogged during the rains but dries out completely afterwards. Such conditions effectively prevent trees from growing, so the vegetation consists chiefly of drought-resistant grasses and water-tolerant sedges. In Trinidad and the Greater Antilles savannas are more common, and the word appears in several place-names, for example, Savanna-la-Mar in Jamaica, and Sabana Grande in Puerto Rico. In these islands savannas are usually the result of a combination of climatic, soil and human factors. They occur both in lowland areas and at higher elevations.

Soil formation

All over the world weathering agents are at work breaking rocks into smaller and smaller fragments. Different weathering agents act in different ways. For example, where days are hot and nights are cold, bare rock surfaces can expand and contract sufficiently for them to crack and for bits of rock to break off. This is one kind of 'mechanical weathering'. Another kind occurs where water collects in the cracks by day and splits the rock when it freezes at night.

In most places the most important weathering agent is acid rainwater. The acids in rainwater come

Badly eroded land in the Scotland District of Barbados. What measures do you know of for preventing soil erosion in the territory in which you live?

from two sources. One is the atmosphere. The other is the decaying vegetable and animal matter on the ground. The acids obtained from these sources are able to attack minerals in rocks and alter them chemically. This is called 'chemical weathering'. It can occur not only at the surface of the land but also deep underground.

One of the most common rock minerals in the world is feldspar. Acid water changes feldspar into clay, a rock composed of tiny particles so closely packed together that, as we have already seen, it is easily waterlogged. Another very common mineral is quartz, made of the chemical silica. When quartz grains are loosened from rocks by weathering they form particles of sand. Because these particles are larger than those of clay, they readily allow water to soak between them. Vast quantities of sand and clay are to be found in the lowlands of Guyana (see page 207). Both were formed by the ancient weathering of granite, a rock which is largely composed of feldspar and quartz.

The fragments of broken rock which form a surface layer on the land are not themselves soil. They are only the parent material. For soil to be formed, another component, humus, is required. Humus is the decaying vegetable and animal material on or near the surface of the ground together with all the living organisms that causes the material to decay. It gives life to the soil and enables it to support living plants. Its colour is dark brown or black.

Four factors that produce different soils

Four factors account for the many different kinds of soil in the world.

1 Parent material: the soils that form above granite, limestone, sandstone, shale, and volcanic rocks differ from one another in their mineral composition. There are even differences between one volcanic soil and another. Each of the volcanic outbursts in the Lesser Antilles produced somewhat different kinds of volcanic rock, and hence somewhat different soils.

2 The second factor affecting the nature of a soil is the climate. Temperatures are important. Where they are high the decay and decomposition of organic matter in the soil proceeds quickly. Where they are low the process is a slow one.

Rainfall is even more important. Whenever it rains some of the rainwater soaks into the soil. As it does so it carries tiny particles of solid material down with it, a process called eluviation. It also dissolves minerals and other plant foods in the surface layer of the soil and carries them down too. This process is called leaching. In some parts of the world, such as those with an equatorial climate, rainfall is heavy throughout the year. In these areas the soil is always being leached. As a result it is not naturally fertile. In dry periods the downward movement of soil water is replaced by an upward movement. Minerals and plant foods become concentrated near the surface, thereby enriching the upper part of the soil.

3 The third factor is the vegetation. Some plants enrich the soil they grow in. Others take out more plant foods than they put back. Grasses have shallow roots which bind the soil and take food from only the top few centimetres of the soil. Trees tend to have long roots which help to break up the soil and take food and moisture from much further down. Trees with large broad leaves (eg those in tropical rain-forests) produce a thick leaf litter which forms good humus. In contrast, trees with small spiny leaves (eg those in coniferious forests) provide poor humus.

4 The fourth factor is the relief of the land. On steep slopes two things happen. One is that some of the rain that falls there runs down the surface of the land instead of soaking into it. As it does so it carries particles of soil along with it, a process known as soil erosion. The other thing that happens is that under the action of gravity the entire soil mass, not just the soil exposed to the rain, tends to move very gradually downhill. This movement is called soil creep. As a result of soil erosion and soil creep the soils on the lower slopes of hills and in valley bottoms are thicker than those on steep upper slopes. They also contain more humus and are therefore darker in colour and richer in plant food. The soils covering the coral rock in Barbados provide an example of differences brought about by slope rather than by parent material, climate or vegetation (see page 106–7).

33

Soil horizons

The composition and colour of soil changes with depth. Often it is possible to see three distinct layers. These layers are called the A, B and C horizons. The top few centimetres consist mainly of particles of roots, twigs and fallen leaves which are big enough to be felt with the fingers and seen with the naked eye. This surface layer is called the A_0 horizon. Just underneath it is the A_1 horizon where biological activity has decomposed the plant matter into much smaller particles. This horizon usually contains so much humus that it is dark in colour. Further down still is the A_2 horizon. It is here that most eluviation and leaching take place in wet climates and that most minerals accumulate in dry climates.

Below the A horizon is the B horizon. It is here that the minerals leached and eluviated from the A horizon accumulate. In the hot, wet climatic conditions of the Caribbean, large quantities of silica and aluminium hydroxide have been washed down from the A to the B horizon. Both these minerals are white in colour. Aluminium hydroxide, better known as bauxite, is mined and exported from several Caribbean countries. In Jamaica a third mineral, iron oxide, is also present. It is this mineral that gives Jamaican bauxite its characteristic red colour.

The lowest of the soil layers is the C horizon. This consists mainly of weathered fragments of the parent rock, but it may also contain minerals leached from above. In contrast to the A and B horizons, this layer does not contain much humus, and little biological activity is going on.

The soil profile in Diagram 3.1 shows the three horizons and the subdivisions of the A horizon.

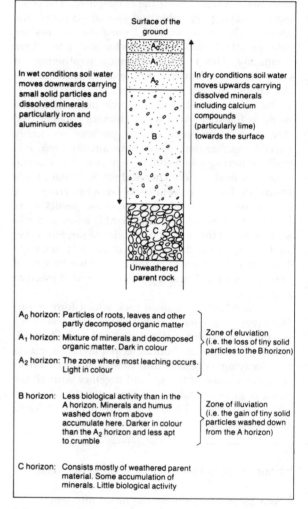

Diagram 3.1 Soil profile showing the horizons.

Soil types

Two groups of soils exist throughout the world. In one of them the soil-forming conditions are such that iron and aluminium compounds accumulate. This group is called pedalfers. The name is taken from the chemical symbols for aluminium (Al) and iron (Fe). The other group is called pedocals because these soils accumulate calcium compounds, particularly lime. (Ca is the chemical symbol for calcium.)

Among the pedalfers are the latosols (also called laterite soils) of tropical rain-forest areas. In the hot,

moist conditions that exist in these areas biological activity in the soil is very rapid. Leaves falling from the trees are decomposed soon after they reach the ground. The roots of the trees absorb the decomposed matter so quickly that little humus is formed. Beneath the soil surface chemical activity weathers most minerals, apart from silica, into oxides of aluminium and iron, a process called laterization. Owing to the high proportion of iron oxide, latosols are usually red or reddish-brown in colour. A profile of a latosol is shown in Diagram 3.2.

Latosols depend for their fertility on a heavy fall of leaves from the overlying forests. Where the forests are cleared, this fertility soon declines. The traditional 'milpa' system of shifting cultivation in Belize and other parts of Central America takes account of this fact. Under the milpa system farmers clear and burn a few acres of forest, cultivate the cleared land for a year or two, and then move on to clear another area. Secondary forest grows on the land they leave behind. The soil gradually recovers its lost fertility and in time it can again support crops. Shifting cultivation of this kind is possible only where farmers have access to enough land to enable them to move from place to place. This amount of land is no longer available in the West Indian islands and is becoming harder to find on the Central American mainland.

Podsols, which form beneath the coniferous forests of northern Canada and other high latitude countries, are also latosols. More information about podsols is given in chapter eighteen.

Pedocals form in areas where the dry season is long enough for upward-moving soil water to carry calcium compounds (mainly lime) in solution towards the surface and deposit them there. They occur in those parts of the West Indies where there is a low annual rainfall. Provided sufficient water can be obtained (eg by irrigation) they are good for cultivation. Elsewhere in the world, the chernozems of mid-latitudes (see chapter eighteen) are another group of pedocals.

Calcium-rich soils develop not only in dry areas but also where the parent material is limestone. Limestone is composed of a single chemical, calcium carbonate. As we have already seen (chapter one) it is constantly under attack by acid water. Given sufficient time, immense quantities are dissolved away. Only the insoluble impurities are left behind. These form a thin cover of clay soil known as a rendzina. Below the surface layer of humus, rendzinas have a single A and B horizon rarely more than a few inches deep. This layer rests directly on the C horizon, that is the weathered surface of the parent material. Rendzinas vary in colour from place to place. Where they are composed largely of iron oxide they are known as *terra rossa* because of their red colour.

Soil erosion

Soil erosion in the West Indies is caused by rain. Even short showers can be very heavy ones. Half a centimetre of rain may well fall in an hour. If it does, the amount of water falling on an area of land one kilometre long by one kilometre wide will weigh five million kilograms. If the soil cannot absorb all this water, some of it runs downhill. The steeper the slope, the faster the run-off, and the greater the load of soil the water can carry away.

Forests help to prevent run-off. Their leaves prevent raindrops from striking the ground with such force that they dislodge particles of soil. They also prevent some of the rain from reaching the ground at all. The roots of the trees help to hold the soil in place. Grass, too, is a good soil cover. It soaks up the rain so well that it is very unusual to see rainwater running down a grassy slope.

Some soil erosion is inevitable, even in forests and grasslands. But it proceeds much more quickly if the ground cover is removed. In many parts of the West Indies forests have been cleared, grasslands have been grazed down to their roots, and land has been left bare to await the rainy season when crops are planted. As a result soil erosion has become widespread and, in places, severe. No country has

Diagram 3.2 Profile of a latosol.

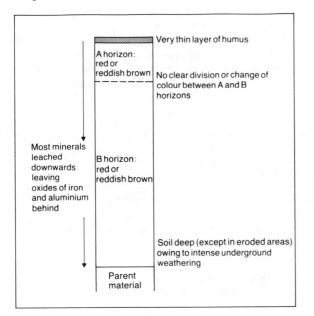

Very thin layer of humus

A horizon: red or reddish brown

No clear division or change of colour between A and B horizons

Most minerals leached downwards leaving oxides of iron and aluminium behind

B horizon: red or reddish brown

Soil deep (except in eroded areas) owing to intense underground weathering

Parent material

escaped. Some, such as Haiti, have suffered disastrously.

Two well-known areas of soil erosion in the Commonwealth Caribbean are the Scotland District of Barbados and the Yallahs Valley in Jamaica. An account of the location and rock structure of the Scotland District is given in chapter seven. Soil erosion began there when the original forest was cut. This in itself led to the formation of the first gullies. Where sugar cane was planted soil erosion continued, particularly when the ground was ploughed every few years before replanting. Where grass grew, sheep were allowed to over-graze it until the rain fell on bare soil. The resulting landscape is shown in the photograph on page 32.

The kinds of rock that compose the Scotland District have contributed to the destruction of the original landscape. The surface layer of coral limestone allows rainwater to soak through it easily. The underlying rocks of the Oceanic Series do not. As a result, water collects along the junction between the two types of rock. It acts as a lubricant so that the top layer of coral can easily slip over the rocks below, as shown in Diagram 3.3. At times huge blocks of coral break off and slip down the steep slope towards the sea.

Controlling soil erosion in the Scotland District is a slow and difficult process. No one method is sufficient. The most eroded areas and the coastline are being planted with trees. Where slopes are not too steep, sugar cane and other crops can still be grown provided that furrows are ploughed along the slopes and not up and down them. On some steep slopes terraces are being constructed. On others grass is the best soil cover, but it must not be over-grazed. In gullies the rapid run-off of rainwater is being

checked with huge wire baskets filled with boulders. Elsewhere, water is being led away in pipes to places where it can do no harm.

The Blue Mountain District in which the Yallahs Valley is set can be seen in the photograph of the Blue Mountains in chapter one. The slopes there were always steep. But while they were covered with forest they were smooth.

Serious soil erosion began in the eighteenth century when large areas of the forest were burned to make way for slave-run coffee estates. It continued after emancipation when many of the estates were sold or abandoned and the land was occupied by smallholders. These people continued the practice of clearing the land by burning it so that they could grow a variety of food crops, mainly for home consumption. Removing the ground cover in this way allowed rainstorms to wash away the soil, and in places to carve deep gullies in the hillsides. A hill farmer's land could be threatened by water pouring downhill from other farms further up the slope and by the growth of gullies on either side. There was nothing an individual farmer could do to prevent this from happening. Crop yields declined, and farming life became poorer and poorer. Then, beginning in the 1950s, the Jamaican government made an attempt to restore the area. Basing its approach on that of the Tennessee Valley Authority (see page 222) the government set up the Yallahs Valley Land Authority. One of the Authority's aims was to protect the upper slopes of the river basin from further erosion. Another was to improve conditions in the lower Yallahs valley where frequent floods carried enormous volumes of silt, pebbles, and even boulders out to sea. Quick-growing trees, including Caribbean pine and eucalyptus, were planted on the

Diagram 3.3 Erosion in the Scotland District, Barbados.

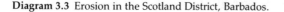
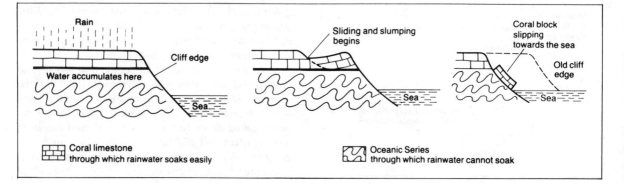

mountain summits and steepest slopes. Farmers were shown various ways of terracing their land, growing grass strips at the bottom of their vegetable plots, and planting crops which helped to prevent rainwater from streaming down the hillsides. There can be no doubt that over the period of the Authority's existence many improvements were brought about. However, full restoration was more than the country could afford. In recent years new areas have been planted in coffee for sale overseas, and smallholders are increasing their output of vegetables and salad crops for sale in Kingston. As a result, land is still being cleared by fire, and steep slopes which ought to be under forest cover are still being cultivated.

Soil pollution

The best way to preserve soil fertility is to add rotted plant matter (compost) and animal manure to the land. On some farms, known as organic farms, no other fertilizer is used. But in many parts of the world the place of compost and animal manure has been taken by factory-made artificial fertilizers, particularly nitrates. The use of these chemicals ensures high yields and enables farmers to make good profits. Unfortunately not all the chemicals are absorbed by the plants and the soil. Some soak into the ground where, in time, they make their way into rivers and into drinking water where they cannot be removed. There are fears that drinking such water over a long period may be harmful to health. One topic worth discussing is whether a government should prevent farmers from polluting their soil by using more artificial fertilizers than the land can absorb. Similarly, should a government be given the power to prevent farmers from allowing soil erosion to occur? Should land-owners be allowed to do what they like with their land, or should their use of it be controlled so as to preserve it for future generations?

Questions and assignments

1 Name one environmental condition that supports the growth of:
   a) elfin woodland,
   b) mangroves,
   c) cactus thorn scrub,
   d) epiphytes,
   e) savanna,
   f) lianas.
   In each case name one place in the West Indies where the type of vegetation is to be found.

2 Name five kinds of tree that grow naturally in West Indian forests and two kinds that have been specially planted. In which countries do the trees grow? What are they used for? (Check the index to find the answers to this question.)

3 Name two problems that can arise when forests are burned for clearing. What measures can be taken to overcome these problems?

4 What parts of the country in which you live have been preserved in forest? Why has this been done?

5 What is meant by the following terms:
   a) mechanical weathering,
   b) chemical weathering,
   c) soil creep,
   d) soil profile,
   e) humus,
   f) soil horizon,
   g) leaching,
   h) eluviation,
   i) pedalfer,
   k) pedocal,
   l) latosol?

6 Describe briefly the contribution made to the composition of a soil by:
   a) the parent material,
   b) climate (temperature and rainfall),
   c) natural vegetation,
   d) relief.

7 What is soil erosion? Name:
   a) two ways in which farming can make soil erosion worse;
   b) two places in the Caribbean where soil erosion is particularly bad;
   c) two ways in which the land in these places is being restored.

4

The Settlement and Development of the West Indies

Discovery

In the late summer of 1492, Columbus and about a hundred men set sail from Spain in three small ships in search of a new trade route to the rich lands of south-east Asia. Basing his calculations on mistaken beliefs about the size of the world, Columbus expected to arrive there after sailing only 4 000 kilometres. The true distance is about 18 000 kilometres! He called first at the Canary Islands. Then, helped by the favourable Trade winds, he crossed the Atlantic in only thirty-six days and landed on one of the Bahamas, which he believed to be part of the East Indies. Guided by some of the 'Indians' he met there, he sailed south until he reached Cuba. Then turning east he sailed along the north coast of Hispaniola where his biggest ship ran aground on a reef and had to be abandoned. When Columbus set out for home, he was unable to take all of its crew with him, and forty men were left behind in a small fort built on the shore – the first European settlers in the West Indies.

In the following year Columbus set out from Spain again, this time with a fleet of seventeen ships and over 1 200 men. Taking a more southerly course than before, he reached Dominica and then sailed to Puerto Rico and Hispaniola, where he found that his garrison had been killed by the Arawaks. Columbus spent the next two years organising the construction of a small township and looking for gold. He made one short cruise in 1494 when he explored most of the southern coast of Cuba and sailed right round Jamaica.

Meanwhile, the Treaty of Tordesillas had been signed by Spain and Portugal and confirmed by the Pope. This agreement gave Spain the right to exploit all newly discovered lands west of a line 370 leagues west of the Cape Verde Islands – that is, about longitude 50°W (see Map 4.1). This explains why Brazil was colonised by Portugal and why Barbados (59° 30'W), though discovered by a Portuguese navigator in 1536, was never claimed or settled by Portugal.

Columbus travelled twice more to the Caribbean. On his third voyage he discovered Trinidad, and on his fourth he explored much of the Central American coast.

Though he had failed in his original intention, Columbus had accomplished much for Spain. He had discovered a new world, the wealth from which was soon to make Spain the richest and most powerful nation in Europe. He had established the best sailing-ship routes to the Caribbean, using the Trade winds on the way out and the Westerlies on the way back again. He also met the peoples of the Caribbean – the Arawaks and the Caribs – of whom the Europeans knew nothing.

Arawaks and Caribs

Partly because the resources of the islands were so meagre, both of these peoples were very primitive. There were no cows, pigs, sheep, goats or horses in the West Indies, so it was impossible to make a living by herding. Diet was based on fish and cassava, so most of the people lived near the sea, and the interior forests were undisturbed. There were not enough useful plants to support an advanced agricultural economy or to maintain more than village life. Precious metals were also scarce: the few gold ornaments the Spanish found in the possession of the Arawaks were the accumulation of generations. Moreover, cut off as they were from any

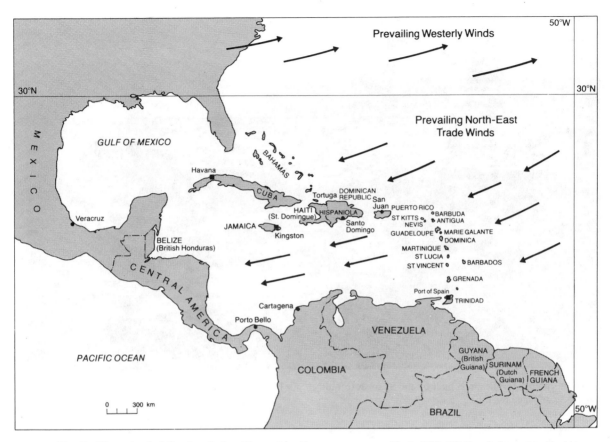

Map 4.1 The Caribbean lands following their settlement by European powers. Up to 1600 AD they belonged to Spain. Which of them were no longer Spanish by 1700 AD?

contact with the outside world, the Arawaks and Caribs had never learned to trade and there were no ports or cities. Thus, unlike the people of India and other eastern countries, the Arawaks and Caribs had no means and no wish to become traders as the Spaniards had originally hoped. What they did do was to teach Europeans how to grow cassava, sweet potatoes, arrowroot, maize, beans, and other crops in tropical conditions.

Of the two peoples, the Arawaks were more easily overcome. They were made to work to support the early Spanish settlements in the Greater Antilles and to find all the gold they could, but within fifty years nearly all of them had perished. Some had been killed in battle, others had died in slavery, but most had died of various European diseases to which they succumbed in vast numbers.

The Caribs, who inhabited the Lesser Antilles, were a more warlike people. They fought fiercely for their freedom and prevented Europeans from colonising the more mountainous islands for a long time. In Grenada their resistance was broken by the French in 1651. Those in St Vincent came to terms with the British in 1773, but few survived the eruption of Soufrière in 1812, and most of their descendants were killed by the next outburst in 1902.

The 1980 census listed no people of Amerindian descent in Grenada or St Lucia, and only 1 500 in St Vincent and 1 100 in Dominica. Thus, of the countries dealt with in this book, only Belize and Guyana have significant numbers of Amerindian inhabitants today. This is one of several examples in the world where European conquest has led to the extinction of an aboriginal people.

Sixteenth-century fortifications built by the Spanish to protect San Juan harbour from attack by the other European nations or by buccaneers.

Spain's challengers

Once the Spaniards had discovered the great riches of gold, gems and silver in Central and South America, they concentrated their energies there, neglecting the small islands altogether and using the large ones chiefly as cattle ranches.

Other European nations, especially the Netherlands, France and England, seized their chance to challenge the Spanish claim to the monopoly of the New World. They traded wherever they could, they established settlements wherever they could and they allowed and even encouraged their seamen to plunder the Spaniards wherever they could.

There were innumerable harbours where pirates and buccaneers could careen their ships and lie in wait for the Spanish treasure fleets. The buccaneers were at times even powerful enough to assault Spanish towns, so the Spaniards chose defensible sites for their towns and fortified them. Santo Domingo in Hispaniola, Havana in Cuba and San Juan in Puerto Rico were the most important bases

in the islands, and Veracruz, Porto Bello and Cartagena were amongst the most important on the mainland (see Map 4.1).

One of the Spanish rules was that no other nation could trade with her Caribbean possessions unless given permission to do so. As permission was hard to obtain, certain venturers towards the end of the sixteenth century took the risk of trading illicitly with the Spanish colonies. Their cargoes of manufactured goods, clothes, wine and slaves were so eagerly sought after that large Dutch, French and English companies were formed to handle West Indian trade and colonisation.

Colonisation began in the small islands farthest from the Spanish centre of interest. The English successfully occupied Bermuda in 1612 and St Kitts in 1624. Barbados, Nevis, Antigua and Barbuda followed in quick succession. The French landed on St Kitts shortly after the English, and the two nations shared the island. The French also took St Barthélemy, Guadeloupe, Marie Galante and Martinique, and shared St Martin with the Dutch. The

Dutch seized Saba and St Eustatius in the northern Caribbean, and Curaçao, Bonaire and Aruba in the south and began the settlement of the Guianas.

The first of the Greater Antilles fell in 1655 when an English expedition captured Jamaica. From Jamaica a few settlers ventured to the Central American coast. This settlement persisted, in spite of Spanish opposition, to become Belize. French colonists, in league with the buccaneers of Tortuga, settled in the western part of Hispaniola and in 1697 the Spaniards were forced to cede this part of the island to them. It became the French colony of St Domingue. However, Spain held on to most of her possessions, and it was not until the nineteenth century, when one by one they broke away to become independent republics, that Spain lost her power in the New World.

Agriculture and settlement in the young British colonies

The first settlers in the British West Indian islands established farms on which they grew tobacco, ginger, indigo and cotton for export, and maize, cassava and vegetables for themselves. The emphasis was on export crops rather than foodstuffs, and from the outset the colonies imported such provisions as flour, salted meat and fish as well as manufactured goods. This pattern still exists, although the output of local foodstuffs and industrial products is growing, often with special government support.

In the early days of colonisation field labour was supplied mainly by indentured workers brought from the British Isles. At first they came voluntarily, but later the supply dwindled and prisoners and rebels were shipped out to maintain the labour force. At the end of their period of service, most indentured labourers acquired land of their own and became their own masters.

For a time, tobacco was the most profitable export, but it was not long before it was unable to compete with the better quality leaf produced in large quantities in Virginia in North America. So in the 1640s, the colonists were glad to learn from Dutch traders the methods by which the Portuguese in Brazil were extracting sugar from sugar cane. The crop was an immediate success. Sugar was very profitable because of the great demand for it in Europe and North America; a demand which continued to expand as these two markets grew into great commercial and industrial communities. Sugar cane was well suited to the temperature, the rainfall, and the rainy and dry seasons of the West Indies. It withstood droughts better than most crops, and reaping was usually completed before the onset of the hurricane season. Moreover, because cane could not be grown far outside the tropics, there was little fear of competition from other areas. Sugar therefore replaced tobacco as the chief export and soon became the only product of importance in the Lesser Antilles.

The change of crop resulted in a change in the type of farming. It was found that cane was more suited to larger land holdings than most of those in existence, and to planters with plenty of money to begin with rather than those who started out with nothing. The main reason for this was that, as cane had to be manufactured into sugar as soon as it was cut, each farmer had to have manufacturing equipment of his own and the buildings to house it. These things were costly and were only worthwhile if the property was large enough to supply a lot of cane and earn a lot of money. In addition, those farmers who could afford to pay several thousand pounds for an estate could find enough money or credit to tide them through bad years. Small farmers could not, and after such disasters as a succession of droughts, hurricanes, losses at sea, or a fall in the price of sugar they were forced to sell out to their richer neighbours. Thus the land fell into the hands of a few rich planters who were then in a position to make enormous profits if they managed their properties well.

Many unskilled labourers were needed in the cane fields, but few were available. Many of the men who had served their indentures preferred to join those who had sold their properties and were emigrating, rather than stay and work in the fields. Within forty years of the first colonies being founded in the Lesser Antilles, thousands of settlers had left again to look for a better life. Some went to Jamaica after its capture in 1655; others to America and elsewhere.

It was to supply the growing demand for field workers that slavery grew to such a volume. There developed a 'triangle of trade'. Ships setting out from British ports carried cloth and other cheap manufactured goods to the coast of West Africa. There they were exchanged for slaves, who were transported to the West Indies where they were either sold on the spot or transferred to other ships for sale to the Spaniards. Some ports, notably

Kingston, had a very large trade with the Spanish colonies. On the return voyage to Britain the ships carried sugar and other tropical produce. A secondary trade grew up between the West Indies and the North American colonies. Sugar and molasses were the chief exports, and flour, salt fish and some manufactures were bought in exchange.

It is not known how many African slaves were brought to the Caribbean and to North, Central and South America from the time the Spaniards began the traffic in the early sixteenth century to the time when it was stopped in the nineteenth century, but it must have been several million. There were about 700 000 slaves living in the British West Indies alone at the time of their emancipation in 1834. By then they outnumbered the whites by seven to one. Today their descendants form the majority of the people in nearly every Commonwealth Caribbean country.

European rivalry in the Caribbean

Just at the time when the British West Indies were beginning to export sugar and were becoming commercially important (about 1650) the British enacted a number of laws designed to link the colonies more securely to Britain and keep any profits out of foreign hands. Based on the Spanish idea of monopoly, these laws obliged the British West Indies to trade only with Britain or with other British colonies. All their goods had to be carried in British or colonial-built ships. In return, the colonists were given a protected market in Britain, their sugar being charged much less duty than sugar from elsewhere. However, this applied only to unrefined sugar. Britain imposed such high duties on refined sugar that it could not be made profitably in the colonies.

This is still the case. The small quantity of refined sugar made in the Commonwealth Caribbean territories today is sold only in the territories themselves. It cannot easily compete with sugar produced by refineries built near to the market, for these have the advantage of being able to import raw sugar from countries in different parts of the world and so keep operating all the year round. Also they are better placed to make and package the various types and grades of sugar their customers want. As a result the West Indies have not been able to develop what could be a valuable sugar refining industry.

The laws Britain imposed on shipping were resented by other nations. The Dutch, who were the chief traders in the Caribbean in the early seventeenth century, were the first to suffer, and soon they were at war with Britain. The Dutch thereafter lost much of their influence in the Caribbean, though their islands of St Eustatius and Curaçao continued to act as important free ports where ships of all nationalities would call to buy wine, slaves, European manufactures and American goods. From then on, Britain's chief rival was France, often allied with Spain. The French colonists in Martinique, Guadeloupe and St Domingue not only produced more sugar than the British colonies but sold it much more cheaply and so built up a considerable trade with North America, which was legally a British market. As the West Indies became increasingly valuable, so the conflicts over the islands became increasingly fierce. Raids were carried out to devastate plantations, destroy sugar works and capture slaves in order to reduce the enemy's sugar output for years to come. Those islands of the Lesser Antilles that were weak enough to be easily captured and rich enough to be worth taking changed ownership several times with the result that their development was retarded.

The end of the West Indian sugar boom

Though each of the British sugar colonies reached the peak of its prosperity at a different time, the last half of the eighteenth century saw them all at about their richest. They were rightly described as being 'the jewels in the English crown', as they brought more money to Britain than did any other part of the world. A century later, however, all had changed. The output of sugar had dwindled in most colonies, and had ceased altogether in some.

The underlying cause of this decline was the high cost of British West Indian sugar. This resulted in part from the high duties charged on sugar entering Britain from sources outside the British West Indies. Safeguarded in this way from competition, the planters had no incentive to improve their estates. They kept large numbers of slaves who, being unpaid, knew no incentive to work except force. This was inefficient because the workers were naturally reluctant to do more than they had to, and because about one man in twelve was needed as a supervisor and did no productive work. None of the slaves had a highly skilled job. The few who worked in the factories were semi-skilled; the vast majority in the fields were unskilled and used only the simplest tools. Unskilled labour and primitive equipment resulted – as it always does – in low productivity. Labour-saving methods were not unknown, but they were disregarded by the planters because their main concern was to find ways of keeping the slaves occupied for as much of the year as possible. Nothing could have been less suited to sugar – a seasonal crop which pays the best returns to those who plant and reap it quickly. Yields were therefore low and prices high.

Another factor in the decline was the overdependence on sugar and the lack of alternative exports or even of foodstuffs for local consumption. Any fall in the price of sugar or rise in the price of imports was a severe blow to all the estates and was ruinous to the weaker ones.

As for the planters themselves, they often preferred to spend the greater part of their income on lavish living rather than on improving their estates. When times were bad they maintained their way of life by borrowing from British merchants and paying high rates of interest. Money therefore flowed out of the West Indies. They left their properties in the hands of managers who had little interest in efficient farming and every opportunity to be dishonest.

In spite of these weaknesses the British West Indies enjoyed a final short period of prosperity at the end of the eighteenth century when the slaves in St Domingue successfully revolted and set up the independent state of Haiti. Sugar exports suddenly ceased from what had been the world's largest producer, and so the American and European markets were open to British West Indian sugar for a few more years. However, the latter market was lost when in 1804 war broke out between France and Britain, and Napoleon closed the European ports to British shipping. In order to maintain the supply of sugar on the continent, Napoleon encouraged the cultivation of sugar beet. Sugar production was no longer confined to the tropics and cane sugar never regained its former importance.

The economic consequences of emancipation

The emancipation of the slaves in the British West Indies in 1834 created further problems for the sugar industry. The freed slaves resented the way the planters had bitterly resisted emancipation, and the period of apprenticeship intended to encourage them to remain as paid labourers on the estates was not successful. Wherever they could, they left to settle on smallholdings of their own. This was most common in Jamaica, Guyana and Trinidad, where plenty of unused land was still available. It was least common in such small, densely peopled islands as St Kitts and Barbados, where there was no such choice and life had to go on much as before.

For some years after emancipation Britain continued to charge much lower duties on colonial sugar than on sugar from other countries. Unfortunately for the British West Indies this policy was short lived. Large manufacturing towns were springing up in Britain and as British factory workers were paid very low wages they had to have cheap foodstuffs. In the years following 1846 the duties on non-colonial sugar were gradually reduced until there was no difference in treatment between colonial and non-colonial imports. British West Indian sugar was no longer protected. As we have seen, it was expensive. It could not easily compete on equal terms with slave-grown sugar from such rapidly developing countries as Cuba and Brazil. Many estates were sold at a fraction of their former value. Many others could not find purchasers at any price.

In spite of the difficulty of making much money from cane, it was not easy for the estate owners to find anything to replace it. Cane cultivation had been so successful for so long that it had absorbed all their capital, interest and skill. Little was known about other tropical crops, which in any case were less able to withstand hurricanes, diseases and droughts. The peasants were more adaptable. Not only did they produce a variety of foodstuffs for local markets, they often led the way in developing new export crops. Arrowroot in St Vincent, cocoa in Trinidad and Grenada, coffee, citrus fruits, spices and cotton in several islands, and bananas in Jamaica were commercially successful crops developed as much by peasants as by estates.

New immigration

On the estates the greatest efforts were still directed towards improving the sugar industry. Profits could still be made in favoured areas provided there were enough workers to handle the crop. Some places, such as Barbados, had enough estate workers.

Others, such as Antigua, Tobago and Nevis, started a sharecropping system. Still others, particularly Trinidad and Guyana, were very short of labour, and so in the 1840s a new wave of immigration began. Some people moved from the densely populated parts of the region to the more sparsely settled areas. Others came from Africa, Madeira and China, but by far the largest number came from India.

Nearly half a million Indians arrived in the West Indies in the following eighty years. They were employed for a few years as indentured labourers and could return home when their contracts had expired Some did so, but most chose to remain on the estates or to settle on smallholdings of their own. Their descendants form the larger part of the population in Guyana. In Trinidad they equal the number of people of African descent. They also form a small proportion of the population of other islands. In Guyana and Trinidad they are still closely associated with the sugar industry, but they have also contributed to agricultural diversification, particularly by cultivating rice and, more recently market garden crops.

Once assured of a labour supply, the estate owners could set about improving the methods of cultivating and processing their cane. Ploughs became common in the West Indies for the first time. New varieties of better yielding cane were planted. Steam-driven machinery was installed in a few of the bigger factories. Gradually, the industry's dependence on water and wind power dwindled, and windmills and watermills went out of use.

The quality of the sugar was greatly improved by boiling it at a relatively low temperature in vacuum pans. Where centrifugals were installed, dry crystals were extracted which could be sent overseas in cheap sacks instead of in the costly hogsheads required to carry the wet sugar which had been made previously.

These improvements were underway on some estates, notably those in Guyana and Trinidad, when the sugar industry received the greatest set-back of all. Towards the end of the nineteenth century the governments of some European countries began to subsidise their exports of beet sugar. As a result of this it became cheaper than cane sugar. The crop sold so well that by 1893 cane sugar formed only slightly more than a quarter of Britain's total sugar imports. Only the sales of British West Indies sugar in North America saved the sugar industry from complete ruin.

Heavy industry: the inside of a West Indian sugar factory.

Agriculture in the twentieth century
Sugar

Throughout the present century sugar exports from the Caribbean have had to compete with cane sugar grown in other parts of the tropics, and with beet sugar grown in the temperate zone. Faced with this competition, Caribbean sugar has seldom been highly profitable. Some countries have ceased to be sugar exporters. Others have survived only by paying field workers low wages and providing them with deplorable living conditions.

The situation would be worse were it not for marketing arrangements made between sugar exporting and sugar importing countries. The first of these was the International Sugar Agreement which came into operation shortly after the 1939–45 World War. It had two main aims. One was to regulate sugar production by allocating an export quota to each sugar exporting country. The other was to prevent prices from rising and falling sharply from year to year. Despite much effort, the second aim has never been achieved. Sometimes world prices are high. Mostly, however, they are lower than the cost of producing sugar.

Though the International Sugar Agreement has not succeded on a world-wide basis, its aims have been taken up on a smaller scale. Thus for many years most Caribbean sugar sales have been made

THE SETTLEMENT AND DEVELOPMENT OF THE WEST INDIES

Characteristics of estates (plantations)

1 Estates are large, often hundreds or even thousands of acres in size.

2 Originally they were all privately owned, usually by Europeans. Now some are owned by companies and some by the government.

3 They occupy the best farming land. Any poor land they contain is often left idle.

4 They grow one major crop (eg sugar cane or bananas). This sort of farming is called *monoculture*.

5 The crop is grown primarily for export, not for sale in local markets.

6 Because monoculture exhausts the soil, estates have to use chemical fertilisers to prevent crop yields from falling.

7 Estates also have to make use of tractors, ploughs and other large-scale farming equipment to maintain large-scale production.

8 Estates are run by paid workers with specific jobs to do (eg managers, supervisors, accountants, field labourers). Some jobs are well paid; others poorly paid. If the crop is a seasonal one (eg sugar) casual labour may be employed at harvest time. Some workers may lose their jobs in the out-of-crop season.

9 Some estates have their own processing plants (eg a sugar or coffee factory).

10 Because estates depend for their success on one major crop they are at great risk from pests and diseases that attack that crop.

11 Estates cannot easily change from one crop to another. If they fail to make a profit they may go out of production and be left abandoned.

Characteristics of smallholdings (peasant farms)

1 The farms are small. Few are over two acres in size. Many are under one acre. They tend to get smaller as the land is subdivided for use by children and grandchildren.

2 The land is usually owned by the farmer who works on it.

3 The land is seldom the best. Slopes may be steep. Soils may be thin and easily eroded.

4 Smallholdings can support only a low standard of living.

5 Smallholdings usually provide a variety of foodstuffs (eg ground provisions, vegetables, fruits, eggs, milk, and occasionally meat). This sort of farming is called *mixed farming*.

6 Smallholders may supplement their income by taking other jobs at harvest time or for one or two days a week throughout the year.

7 The day-to-day tasks of weeding and watering the crops and looking after the animals are undertaken by the family, including the children. Employing labour even to clear the land or harvest seasonal crops is very unusual. More commonly these tasks are shared with neighbouring small farmers.

8 Cultivation is done with hand tools (eg machetes, hoes, forks).

9 The main function of a smallholding is to provide the family with its basic food requirements. This sort of farming is called *subsistence farming*.

10 Surplus foodstuffs are sold in nearby markets. They may be taken there by a member of the family or by a small trader (often a woman) called a 'higgler' in Jamaica and a 'Madame Sarah' in Haiti. (See the photographs on pages 47 and 48).

11 Some of the land on a smallholding may be used to grow an export crop (eg rice in Guyana, coffee in Jamaica and Haiti, bananas in several countries). These crops are often graded and marketed by a co-operative or by a government agency.

12 By growing a variety of crops smallholders spread the risk of loss through attack by plant diseases and insect pests.

13 Smallholders can easily change their crops if they need to do so.

under special marketing arrangements with purchasing countries.

Between 1951 and 1975, Commonwealth Caribbean countries benefited from the Commonwealth Sugar Agreement. This provided a market in Britain for some 900 000 tonnes of Commonwealth Caribbean sugar a year. About two-thirds of this amount was sold at a special price called the 'negotiated price' because it was worked out by the governments of Britain and other Commonwealth sugar exporting countries. Every year the price was set at a level at which efficient sugar producers in the Commonwealth could expect to make a reasonable profit. For most of the time this price was considerably higher than the world market price.

When Britain joined the European Economic Community (EEC) new trade arrangements had to be made. These came into being early in 1975 when delegates from forty-six independent African, Caribbean and Pacific countries (the ACP states) and from the European Community signed the Lomé Convention. This convention resembles the Commonwealth Sugar Agreement it replaced in that it guarantees a market in the EEC for up to 1.3 million tonnes of ACP sugar at an agreed price. The price is, in fact, the same price that is paid to European beet sugar producers. The present quotas for Commonwealth Caribbean countries are:

Barbados	50 000 tonnes	St Kitts	15 000 tonnes
Guyana	159 000 tonnes	Trinidad	44 000 tonnes
Jamaica	118 000 tonnes	Belize	40 000 tonnes

In recent years Caribbean cane sugar has had to face competition from a new source. During the 1970s American technologists found a way of manufacturing a sweetening substance out of maize. As the United States is the world's leading maize producer, the new sweetener, called high fructose corn syrup, was soon available in large quantities. It quickly replaced sugar in canned and bottled drinks. By 1985 it had captured a third of the United States' entire sweetener market.

The United States, like Europe, has made special arrangements with Caribbean countries for purchasing their sugar. However, with the rise of the new sweetener it has reduced its import quotas. The country hardest hit has been the Dominican Republic, but Commonwealth Caribbean sugar producers have also been affected.

Marketing Caribbean cane sugar is becoming increasingly difficult. In the United States and Canada the consumption of high fructose corn syrup is rising. It can be expected to continue to do so now that a way has been found of turning the syrup into crystals. In Western Europe the competition comes

Improvements in loading sugar have matched improvements in production. Georgetown, Guyana, is one of the places in the Caribbean where it is bulk-loaded directly into ships' holds.

from beet. The European Community is now the world's largest single source of sugar. It produces far more than it can consume. Its farmers receive large government subsidies. Its sales of sugar on the world market are the chief reason why the world market price of sugar is usually very low.

Throughout this century Caribbean sugar producers have had to reduce their production costs in order to remain in business. The main way of doing so has been to concentrate output in large factories capable of processing at least a quarter of a million tonnes of cane in a season. As these factories are very costly to build and operate, they are owned not by individuals but by companies, or increasingly

these days by the government. They are set in the midst of wide expanses of cane fields, some of which usually belong to whoever owns the factory. The ownership of the rest of the land under cane varies from place to place. It may belong to other estates, or to cane farmers, a co-operative or the government.

Several square kilometres of flat land are required to grow enough cane to support a large factory. In almost all the smaller islands this is not available and sugar production has ceased. In the Commonwealth Caribbean only Barbados, St Kitts, Jamaica, Guyana, Trinidad and Belize are able to support factories large enough to be competitive.

Throughout the West Indies women undertake the tasks of taking small farmers' produce to the market.

Large-scale agriculture in the West Indies presents many problems. One is that farm work is not well paid and has no prestige. This explains why workers prefer to reap crops in America, or even in another West Indian territory, rather than in the place where they live. Many people prefer to remain unemployed if the only alternative is agricultural employment. A second problem is that there are large tracts of land lying unused or ineffectively used. A third is that more mechanisation is needed if sugar estates are to improve their efficiency, but people are reluctant to accept it for fear of unemployment. All have contributed to a decline in sugar output in recent years.

A problem of a different kind is that people living in Britain and America are tending, for health reasons, to eat less sugar than they used to. For this reason the present consumption of about fifty kilograms of sugar per person per year in Britain and America is unlikely to increase. At the other extreme there are some developing countries where the sugar consumption is only two kilograms per person per year. They are not potential markets because they are not rich enough to increase their imports of food.

Bananas

Replacing sugar cane with a more profitable crop has proved to be almost impossible. The only new export crop to have been successful on a large scale has been bananas. The first country to develop the trade was Jamaica. Since the 1950s four of the Commonwealth Eastern Caribbean States – St Vincent, Grenada, St Lucia and Dominica – have also became prominent banana exporters.

Other crops

The bulk of the export crops other than sugar, and most of the foodstuffs consumed locally, are grown on smallholdings. In all, these take up to two-thirds of the cultivated land in the Commonwealth Caribbean territories. Some small farmers are fairly well off, but the great majority live in poor conditions on tiny plots of land which they cultivate in a primitive and inefficient way. Improving their living conditions, their methods of cultivation and their crop yields are among the biggest problems facing West Indian governments today. Three of the most useful forms of help are the provision of proper titles to the

A large variety of crops are sold in local markets.

land, the establishment of land settlements, and the granting of loans for development. Others are the formation of co-operatives and other organisations to assist in producing and marketing crops, bulk purchases at guaranteed prices, and the provision of plants, seeds and fertilisers at little cost.

Equally important is the need to bring abandoned land back into cultivation. All Caribbean countries are spending large sums of money on imported foods. They cannot affort to allow land to stand idle when it could be put to good use. As Diagram 4.2 shows, the amount of unused land in the Commonwealth Caribbean islands equals the area under cultivation. Some of this land is undoubtedly suitable for farming.

Population and economic development

The rapid rise of population in the Commonwealth Caribbean in the present century is shown in Table

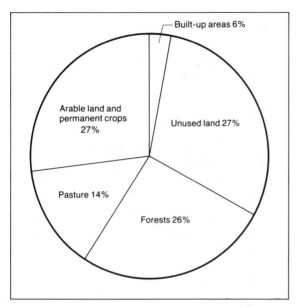

Diagram 4.2 A divided circle (pie-chart) showing the percentage of land in the Commonwealth Caribbean islands used for various purposes.

4.3. None of it is due to immigration. That had ended by 1921. Instead it is due in part to a high birth-rate and in part a sharp reduction of the death-rate.

This increase has taken place in spite of the emigration of many thousands of West Indians to other parts of the world in search of better conditions. Early in the century they went to Panama to help construct the canal, to the Central American republics to work on the giant banana plantations, and to Cuba and the Dominican Republic to work in the canefields. Later they went to the oil industries of Venezuela, Curaçao and Aruba and to the goldfields of French Guiana. More recently they have gone to Britain and the United States.

During the 1950s about a quarter of a million West Indians went to Britain where they found employment in London and other large cities. When Britain imposed restrictions on immigration in the 1960s, this movement declined, and an increase took place in the number of people going to the United States and Canada. People are still leaving the West Indies to live in both of these countries, although restrictions on numbers are in force there, too.

There can be no doubt that emigration has benefited the Commonwealth Caribbean by reducing the pressure of population on limited resources. In addition, the money sent home by many emigrants has been of great help to many families. But emigration is a mixed blessing. It tends to attract people with professional and technical skills, the very people the West Indies can least afford to lose. Emigration is in no sense a substitute for economic development.

A further consequence of emigration has been the rising demand for yams, sweet potatoes, plantains

Table 4.3 Population figures for Commonwealth Caribbean countries in the census years 1921, 1936, 1960, 1970 and 1980

Census years	1921	1936	1960	1970	1980
Antigua	29 800	41 800	54 400	65 000	75 200
Montserrat	12 100	14 300	12 200	11 500	11 600
St Kitts-Nevis-Anguilla	38 200	46 250	56 700	49 800	50 300
Barbados	156 300	192 800	232 100	236 900	247 000
Jamaica	858 100	1 290 000	1 606 600	1 848 500	2 190 300
Dominica	37 000	47 700	59 500	70 200	74 800
Grenada	66 300	72 400	88 600	93 600	89 800
St Lucia	51 500	70 000	86 200	100 600	115 200
St Vincent	44 500	61 700	80 000	86 900	98 000
Trinidad and Tobago	365 900	558 400	825 700	938 500	1 059 000
Guyana	307 400	376 100	558 800	702 000	759 600
Belize	43 300	59 150	90 400	120 600	145 300
Total:	2 010 400	2 830 600	3 751 200	4 324 100	4 916 100

and other West Indian foods in London, New York, Toronto, and other European and American cities. To begin with, sales were limited to the emigrants themselves, but since the 1970s they have been extended to the wider community. As a result, there is now a substantial export market for West Indian agricultural produce.

Urban growth

The effect of the rising population has been felt in agricultural districts where small farmers have had to divide their holdings between so many dependants that they are no longer capable of fully supporting the people. The result has been a migration (called 'internal migration') from the countryside to the towns. Indeed, urban growth has been one of the most noticeable features of modern times, and it is still going on. Today over 40 per cent of the population of Cuba and Puerto Rico, and over 30 per cent of the population of most other territories, live in urban areas.

Each territory is dominated by one town – the chief port. This has come about because the West Indies are very dependent on overseas trade and because there is rarely more than one harbour that can accommodate large steamships. Moreover, the territories are compact enough for a single port to be able to distribute imported goods quickly and cheaply to all districts by road and, in some cases, by rail. The chief port has also become the capital and the chief commercial, shopping, manufacturing, educational and entertainment centre of each territory.

The growth of capital cities has been particularly rapid. Up to the 1920s even those on the large islands were compact enough for most of the people living there to be within walking distance of their workplace. Things are very different today. What was then an entire city is now only a small part of it – an area commonly called the central business district – containing few houses and many big banks, shops and office buildings. By day the scene is one of busy activity. By night the buildings and streets are empty, everyone having left for their homes in the suburbs. Largely unplanned, these suburbs have spread shapelessly over the countryside, often over good agricultural land. They take up many times the area of the central business district and are still growing. Among them are the homes of large num-

bers of unemployed people, living in sub-human conditions in what have been called 'slums of despair'.

Details of the growth of towns, especially Kingston and Port of Spain, are given in later chapters.

Non-agricultural development in the Commonwealth Caribbean

If the standard of living of a country is to rise, its economic development must proceed faster than the rise of population. It is clear that in the West Indies considerable development is necessary even to maintain standards. This is very difficult to do where resources are so meagre. Agriculture is restricted by steep slopes, poor soils and drought to small portions of most territories. Large-scale forestry is restricted to Guyana and Belize, and in any case forestry cannot maintain an advanced economy. Large deposits of minerals appear to be limited to petroleum in Trinidad and bauxite in Jamaica and Guyana. The sea, too, has its limitations as the Caribbean is not rich in fish. Though output is expected to increase, particularly on the shallow banks between Jamaica and Belize and the continental shelf between Trinidad and Brazil, it may never be able to meet local demand. To some extent, however, fish imports are offset by growing exports of lobsters and shrimps.

One of the most valuable forms of development in the West Indies has been the establishment of new industries. These have helped to create employment, reduce imports of manufactured goods and – in some cases – to increase exports.

Industries are of different kinds. Heavy industries are those which are housed in big factories. They consume a great deal of power. They process large quantities of raw materials. In contrast to the world's leading industrial nations such as Japan (see chapter eighteen) there are few heavy industries in the Commonwealth Caribbean. Those of importance are large-scale oil refining (Trinidad), bauxite mining and processing (Jamaica and Guyana), the manufacture of alumina from bauxite (Jamaica), the manufacture of cement (Jamaica, Trinidad, Barbados, the Bahamas), the manufacture of chemicals and artificial fertilisers (Trinidad), the manufacture of steel (Trinidad) and the production of sugar (Jamaica,

Four light industries: furniture assembly; garments; light industrial components; car assembly. More women than men are employed in light industry.

Guyana, Trinidad, Barbados, Belize, St Kitts). Light industries are very different. They exist in every Commonwealth Caribbean country. They are growing in number and variety. They are housed in small buildings, consume little power, and process small quantities of raw materials.

Puerto Rico was the first West Indian country in which light industries became important. Development began in the 1950s when the government encouraged business people to take advantage of the fact that anything they manufactured in Puerto Rico could be exported to the United States without having to pay any customs duty. This is still the case. It explains why there are more light industries in Puerto Rico than in all the Commonwealth Caribbean countries put together.

Following Puerto Rico's lead, Commonwealth Caribbean governments have supported the development of light industries. They have allowed new businesses a tax-free period in which to get established. They have set up industrial parks and in some cases the factory buildings as well. They have placed restrictions or heavy duties on competing imports. They have created duty-free zones beside the major ports. Despite these forms of support, manufacturing has not grown rapidly enough to make any real impact on unemployment. One reason for this is that a lot of capital is needed to start a new industry. The West Indies have little capital to invest, and overseas investors have the whole world to choose from when seeking a location for a new factory. Another reason is that modern factories are highly mechanised, requiring only a few employees to produce a large volume of goods. A third reason is that the local market in each territory is small.

Caricom

It was the need to enlarge local markets that led to the creation of the Caribbean Free Trade Association (CARIFTA) in 1968, which developed to become the Caribbean Community (CARICOM) in 1973. Today the members of CARICOM are: Antigua and Barbuda, the Bahamas, Barbados, Belize, Dominica, Grenada, Guyana, Jamaica, Montserrat, St Kitts-Nevis, St Lucia, St Vincent and the Grenadines, and Trinidad and Tobago. Four of them – Barbados, Guyana, Jamaica, and Trinidad and Tobago – are known as

'More Developed Countries' (MDCs) and the rest as 'Less Developed Countries' (LDCs).

One of the main aims of CARICOM is to create the conditions in which its members can increase their output of agricultural and manufactured goods and sell them to each other. The better this aim is achieved in practice, the less the region will have to import from elsewhere. In order to achieve the aim, a common trade policy has been adopted for the whole community. It operates in two ways. First, as a general rule members of the community do not charge duties on goods imported from other CARICOM countries. Second, all the members charge the same duty on goods imported from outside the community. As a result, trade within the community has grown considerably and brought benefits to all members, particularly the more developed ones. However, this growth bears no comparison with that of some other Commonwealth developing countries. Hong Kong, for example, has found markets for manufactured products in all parts of the world.

Caribbean Basin Initiative

In recent years there has been some expansion of light industry in the Caribbean as a result of the United States 'Caribbean Basin Initiative' (CBI). This has been of particular benefit to the manufacturers of garments and electronic equipment. The system operates in the following way. Cloth which has already been manufactured and cut to size in the United States is stitched into garments in the Caribbean and returned to the States for packaging and sale. In a similar way, American electronic equipment is assembled in the West Indies and returned to the United States. In both cases the United States government does not charge duty on the full value of the goods. Instead, it calculates the proportion of the value that has been contributed in the West Indies, and charges duty on that.

The West Indian contribution to these industries is very small. For this reason they are sometimes called 'finishing touch' or 'screwdriver' industries.

Tourism

Before the 1939–45 World War only a small number of people in the world could afford a holiday abroad.

'New skills have led . . . to the moulding of new landscapes.' Tourists play golf beside the ruins of an old Jamaican sugar mill on land which was once under cane. What changes of land do you know of in the district in which you live?

Tourist resorts in the Caribbean were therefore few and far between. Those of most importance were Nassau in the Bahamas, Montego Bay in Jamaica, and Havana in Cuba. Since the war, despite one or two setbacks, tourism has grown rapidly to become big business in nearly every Caribbean country.

Some Caribbean tourism is internal. For example, people from all parts of the Caribbean visit Trinidad for Carnival. There are families in Trinidad who spend their holidays in Barbados. There are people from the southern Caribbean who spend a few days in Jamaica on their way to Miami.

Most tourists, however, come from outside the region. There are three main sources. One is western Europe (eg people from Britain visiting Barbados and people from France visiting Martinique and Guadeloupe). Another source is South America (eg people from Venezuela and Colombia visiting the nearby islands of Aruba and Curaçao). But by far the biggest source is North America.

Tourism has made a major contribution to employment in the West Indies. Thousands of men and women who work in hotels, apartments and travel agents rely entirely on tourism for a living. Many other workers in resort areas are almost as depend-

ent. They include taxi drivers, entertainers, musicians, restaurant staff, those who hire out cars and boats, and those who work in airline offices. Tourism also adds to the income of people in other occupations such as farming, shop-keeping and craft work.

The growth of tourism has been accompanied by a number of problems. One is the rise in the value of imported goods, including food, not only for tourists but also for those West Indians who have come to share their life-style. Another, in areas of low rainfall, is the provision of sufficient fresh water. In some countries, such as the US Virgin Islands and New Providence in the Bahamas, fresh water has to be obtained by desalination, an industrial process that removes the salt from sea water. A third problem is that of preventing drainage and sewage in tourist resort areas from polluting the sea. Social problems also arise. Some tourists display racial attitudes towards West Indians. Some West Indians are resentful of the apparent wealth of visitors taking expensive holidays. The spread of crime and drug-taking is also often blamed on tourism. A summary of the main advantages and disadvantages of tourism is shown on page 55.

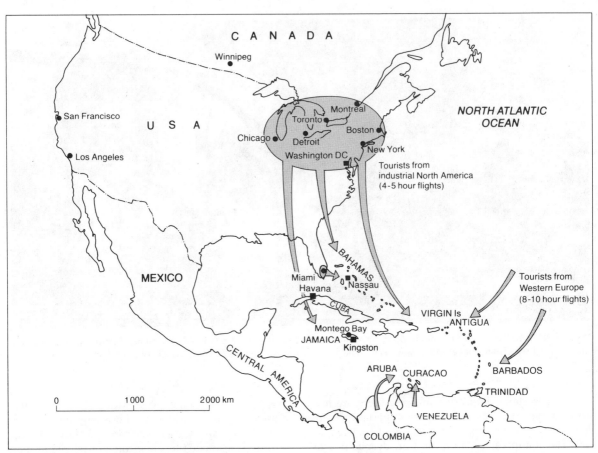

Map 4.4 Major sources of tourists to the Caribbean.

A tourist hotel in The Bahamas. In some places land that is valueless for agriculture and mining can still bring rich returns. What other examples can you think of?

North American Tourism

The following reasons explain why most of the tourists visiting the Caribbean come from the United States and Canada.

1 Together the United States and Canada have a population of about 200 million. Of these some 100 million live in the area bounded by a line joining Chicago, Washington, New York, Boston, Montreal and Toronto (see Map 4.4). This area is one of the world's most productive industrial and commercial regions. Most of the people living there earn enough to be able to spend a holiday away from home every year. In addition, many of them have at least three weeks' paid holiday a year. Mass tourism owes its existence to the provision of paid holidays.

2 Jet aircraft can fly from such cities as New York and Toronto non-stop to most Caribbean destinations in under five hours. Flight times are shorter than they are to the west coast of America, and much shorter than those from western Europe to the Caribbean.

3 By carrying 400 and more passengers at a time, modern wide-bodied jet aircraft have reduced costs to a point where Americans do not have to be well off to fly to the Caribbean. Charter flights on which a planeload of people travel together are particularly inexpensive. So are package holidays when they not only fly together but spend their holiday together at the same hotel.

4 Tourists who prefer to travel by sea can join a cruise ship at New York, Miami and other ports in the United States and spend a week or two in the Caribbean. Sailing mostly by night the ships call at a different island each day to enable passengers to go ashore for sight-seeing and shopping.

5 The West Indian islands are very attractive places for American holidaymakers. Their beaches are among the best in the world. Their inland scenery is often strikingly beautiful. Their fortifications and other historical sites are interesting places to visit. Above all, the climate is pleasant: always warm enough for people to be out of doors by day and by night; seldom uncomfortably hot. The contrast with North America is at its greatest in winter when temperatures over the northern part of the continent are often below freezing. A holiday in the sun is particularly welcome then. This explains why the period from mid-December to mid-April is the most popular time of year for American tourists to visit the Caribbean. Because the summer months are less popular, many Caribbean hotels reduce their prices so as to keep their rooms occupied then.

Some advantages and disadvantages of tourism

Advantages

Brings foreign exchange into the West Indies.
Provides direct employment
(eg in hotels and apartments).
Provides indirect employment
(eg car rental; shopkeeping).
Can lead to better understanding of other countries.
Can foster the conservation of historic buildings and areas of scenic beauty.

Disadvantages

Increases the import bill for food and other items.
Much employment is of a subservient nature.

Some employment is seasonal.

Can create social problems and hostility.

Hotel development can spoil sea views and cause sea pollution.

Geography and current events

This chapter has surveyed the developments that have taken place in the West Indies which explain the conditions in which we live today. How, then, do these conditions compare with those in other parts of the world? One indication is given by the figures for per capita income (that is the total income of a country for a year divided by the number of people living there). World Bank records show that in 1987 the world's richest country was Switzerland with a per capita income of US$ 21 000 followed by the United States (US$ 18 500). Towards the bottom of the scale were such countries as Bangladesh (US$ 160) and India (US$ 300). Most of the Commonwealth Caribbean countries lay well between these extremes. At the top came the Bahamas with a per capita income of US$ 10 320, followed by Barbados (US$ 5 330) and Trinidad and Tobago (US$ 4 220). Per capita incomes in the Commonwealth Eastern Caribbean states lay between US$ 1 000 and US$ 1 500. The figure for Jamaica was US$ 960, and that for Guyana was US$ 380. Elsewhere in the Caribbean, Puerto Rico had a per capita income of US$ 5 500, the Dominican Republic US$ 700, and Haiti, the poorest country in the region, US$ 360.

Raising the per capita income of the West Indies is one of the major tasks in the years ahead. Other related tasks are providing employment for more and more people, raising living standards, and protecting the environment for the benefit of future generations. How best to accomplish these tasks are political matters on which different people and different political parties have different views. In most of the West Indies people are being asked to support one view or another when they reach the age of eighteen and are able to vote in elections.

When making a choice between one view and another, a knowledge of Caribbean geography is a great help. Thus, if you are considering a problem facing the territory in which you live, you will need to know a) how the problem originated, b) what resources your territory possesses that can be used to tackle the problem, c) how other territories have tackled the problem and with what success, and d) what resources the other territories possess. In thinking about other territories it is not sufficient to consider only those in the Commonwealth Caribbean. For example, when considering the future development of your territory it is important for you to bear in mind the Cuban attempt to reduce the gap between the rich and the poor, and the Puerto Rican method of raising per capita income by means of industrialisation. Both have their advantages and their drawbacks, and both have their supporters and their opponents.

Until recently the people of the Commonwealth Caribbean had little opportunity to take part in the decisions that shaped their lives. This is no longer the case. Now that the West Indies have undertaken the responsibility for shaping their own destinies, great changes have been taking place in their social, economic and cultural affairs, and in regional co-operation, foreign trade and international relations. You will wish to know and understand what is happening, and you will find your geographical studies of great assistance in doing so.

Questions and assignments

1 Name three West Indian islands (or parts of islands) where the official language is Spanish, three Dutch, and three French.

2 Trace a map of the world and draw arrows leading to the Caribbean:
   a) from Western Europe, naming five countries from which immigrants came to the West Indies;
   b) from West Africa, naming two countries from which immigrants came;
   c) from two different parts of Asia, naming the countries from which the immigrants came.

3 Trace a map of the West Indies, and mark and name:
   a) three passages leading out of the Caribbean Sea;
   b) the Panama Canal;
   c) three harbours that were fortified in Spanish colonial times, two naval bases in British colonial times, and two present-day US naval bases. In each case give one reason to explain why the site was chosen for military purposes.

4 a) Name three ways in which farming on smallholdings differs from farming on large estates in the West Indies.
   b) Name one area where small farming is important, and one where estate farming is important.

c) Suggest two problems faced by small farmers and two faced by estates in the areas you have chosen.

5 Give three reasons why sugar cane became the most important crop in the West Indies in the eighteenth century. Give two reasons why it is difficult to find another crop to take the place of sugar cane.

6 a) Name two sweetening products that compete with cane sugar and say where they are grown.

b) Name two ways in which the West Indies have been affected by this competition.

c) What is the international agreement by which Commonwealth Caribbean sugar is sold at a preferential price?

7 From the information given in Table 4.3:

a) Name the countries with the highest and lowest populations at the time of the 1921 and 1980 censuses.

b) Calculate the difference between their 1921 and 1980 populations.

c) Calculate the population density per square kilometre of Barbados (430 sq km.) and Trinidad and Tobago (5 123 sq km.) in 1921 and 1980.

d) Draw a bar graph to show the total population of the region in 1921, 1936, 1960, 1970 and 1980.

e) Calculate the percentage of the total population in 1980 that lived in i) Jamaica, ii) Trinidad & Tobago, iii) Guyana, and iv) Barbados. Draw a divided circle (similar to the one shown in Diagram 5.7) to show these percentages. Then label the fifth segment 'All other Commonwealth Caribbean countries.'

8 a) Name one English-speaking, one French-speaking, and one Spanish-speaking country in the West Indies from which there has been large-scale emigration in recent years.

b) Name three different countries to which they have gone and give one reason why they have chosen to go there. (Check the index for this.)

c) Give two reasons why the West Indies benefit from emigration and two reasons why they do not benefit.

9 What is the difference between emigration and internal migration? Name one West Indian country where internal migration is taking place and give two reasons why it is taking place.

10 a) Name three differences between heavy industry and light industry.

b) Give two reasons why heavy industry is not common in the West Indies, and two reasons why light industries are growing in number and variety.

11 a) Name two differences between stop-over and cruise-ship tourism.

b) Name two parts of the world from which large numbers of stop-over tourists come to the Caribbean.

c) Give two reasons why tourist arrivals tend to fluctuate during the year, and one measure that is being taken to stop this happening.

12 Using the figures below draw and label a bar graph to compare the number of stop-over tourists who visited the following countries in 1986. The figures are given in thousands rounded off to the nearest thousand. Bahamas: 1 375; Barbados: 370; Jamaica: 664; Trinidad & Tobago: 186; Aruba: 181; Martinique: 183; US Virgin Islands: 470; Puerto Rico: 1 573; Cuba: 280.

5

Jamaica

Area: 11 424 square kilometres; population (1988): about 2 400 000; density of population: 213 per square kilometre.

Early development

In 1655 a force of 2 500 men in a large fleet of ships set out from England with orders to seize any Spanish West Indian possession which could be used as a base for the conquest of all Central America. This was the first direct challenge to Spanish supremacy in the Caribbean. Up to that time the only non-Spanish settlements in the area were the smaller islands which Spain had never bothered to occupy.

The expedition touched first at Barbados, where a further 4 000 men were recruited. Most of these were dissatisfied British indentured servants glad of the opportunity to leave the colony (see page 103). After still more men had been added to their numbers as they sailed northwards through the Lesser Antilles, an attempt was made to capture Hispaniola. It failed, so the leaders decided to try to take Jamaica instead. This time they were successful, though the Spaniards with the aid of their freed slaves, the Maroons, and with occasional reinforcements from Cuba, were able to fight on in the hills for five years before they were finally overcome. Even then the Maroons did not submit and, as their numbers were continually reinforced by escaped slaves, they resisted conquest. Some of their descendants remain to this day, living in semi-isolation in the hills in the interior of the island.

Throughout the century and a half of Spanish occupation Jamaica was poorly developed. Manual labour was scarce, for the original Arawak population – estimated at 60 000 – quickly died out, and few African slaves were imported. In any case the Spaniards never paid much attention to the island. Only a very small area was cultivated and most of the settlers made their living by rearing cattle, horses and pigs on the savannas. They sent their products to Europe and the mainland of Central America. Hides and tallow were most in demand and much of the meat was wasted.

Under the British, things changed rapidly. The island's position in the heart of the Spanish Empire was immediately exploited by buccaneers who soon turned Port Royal into a treasure-chest of Spanish booty. For the first thirty years or so, while the new colony needed their protection, the buccaneers were given official encouragement. Once it was secure, they were suppressed. Soon afterwards Port Royal, still one of the largest, richest and most riotous ports in the Caribbean was almost entirely destroyed by an earthquake in 1692. Much of it disappeared beneath the sea. Port Royal continued to be used as a naval base throughout the eighteenth century, but its other functions were transferred to Kingston, which grew up on the opposite side of the same harbour. Kingston rapidly became one of the chief centres of trade in the Caribbean. In the mid-eighteenth century it was declared a free port. Slaves, foodstuffs, cloth, ironware and other manufactured goods were landed there, transferred to smaller ships and taken to many other parts of the Caribbean. The Spanish colonists, in need of all these things, were glad to buy them in spite of their government's laws declaring such trade to be illegal.

But the greatest profits were made by the estate owners and those engaged in the sugar trade. Simply because of its size Jamaica was destined to become the richest British West Indian colony. At the beginning of the nineteenth century, a thousand estates were in operation, producing about 100 000 tonnes of sugar a year. Coffee was important too, and for a while Jamaica was England's richest overseas possession. What happened to alter this position we shall learn later.

Landforms

Jamaica, with an area of 11 424 square kilometres is the third largest Caribbean island. In fact, it is bigger than all the other Commonwealth Caribbean islands put together, and has just over half the total population.

Jamaica may be divided into three structural regions:

1 The eastern part is composed of many different igneous, sedimentary and metamorphic rocks which were folded and uplifted at the end of Cretaceous times. Since then they have been severely eroded by many rivers, of which the largest are the Yallahs, Plantain Garden, Wagwater and Rio Grande, all shown on Map 5.3. Today the landscape is one of sharp-crested ridges and deep, twisting valleys. (See the photograph on page 7 of the Blue Mountains). Standing in the midst of the highest range of all are the Blue Mountains, where Blue Mountain Peak rises to 2 256 metres.

2 Most of the rest of the island is capped by thick layers of white limestone (see Map 5.1 and Diagram 5.2). In the centre and west this has been uplifted in stages to form several distinct plateau surfaces, though they have been considerably broken up by faulting.

As limestone is soluble in water containing weak acids, it is eroded in a characteristic way. The result is called *karst* scenery, named after a district in Yugoslavia where the process has been studied most closely. All the typical karst features occur in Jamaica. Streams seldom remain on the surface for long but disappear underground to flow through a maze of caverns, reappearing only in the deeper basins or at the edge of the limestone. Enormous quantities of limestone have been dissolved away and in places, as shown in Diagram 5.2, the underlying rocks have been exposed. Where limestone still remains, as it does over at least half the island, the landscape varies from place to place. The Cockpit Country is so broken up into deep, circular arenas

and huge rocky buttresses that it is almost impenetrable and is therefore sparsely populated. Elsewhere erosion has produced a rolling upland countryside of rounded hills and hollows (see the photograph on page 61). Here conditions are better though much of the land has had to be left in pasture and scattered clumps of trees. In general, poor soils and the difficulty of obtaining water make cultivation difficult. Dense agricultural settlement exists only where deep, rich soils have been deposited in large solution-basins. Examples are the Appleton Valley in the upper part of the Black River, St Thomas in the Vale (once the bed of a lake), Lluidas Vale, and the Queen of Spain's Valley. These are shown on Maps 5.1 and 5.3. There are many more smaller ones.

Though it is not good for cultivation, limestone has other uses. It is so good for building and for road-making that besides being widely used in Jamaica, it could become a major export. More important, over much of its surface there lies a red clay containing bauxite from which aluminium is obtained. This bauxite is being mined and exported by some of the world's largest metal producing companies.

3 Surrounding the highlands is a narrow coastal plain interrupted occasionally by spurs of highland reaching down to the sea. The largest lowland area is the southern plain which extends from Kingston, where it is known as the Liguanea Plain, westwards into the parish of Clarendon.

Along most of the western and northern shores the land descends sharply to narrow coral terraces which provide evidence of recent small uplifts of the land. Elsewhere the plains are composed of mixed alluvial clays, sands and pebbles. Along parts of the coast the sea has deposited beach material in the form of spits and bars; for example, Palisadoes, and the bar enclosing Yallahs ponds (see Map 5.1).

Minerals

Bauxite

Bauxite is much the most important mineral occurring in Jamaica. It exists as a layer varying in thickness over about 2 500 square kilometres of the white limestone in the western two-thirds of the island. The best deposits lie in shallow basins at heights above 300 metres. Its origin is uncertain, but there is increasing evidence that it was produced by

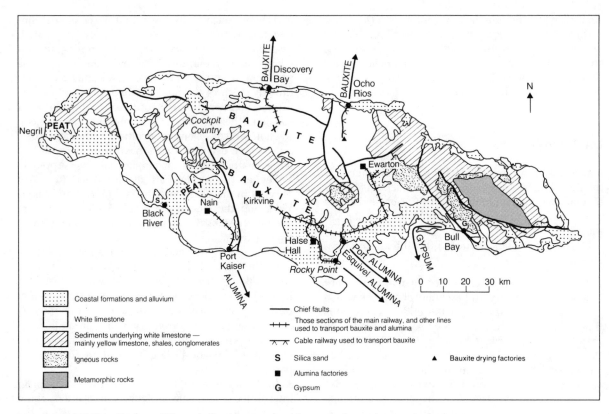

Map 5.1 JAMAICA: Geology. What relationships are there between the geology and relief?

Diagram 5.2 Sketch section from west to east across Jamaica to show the landscape and the geology.

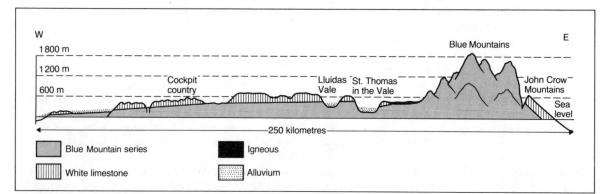

This rolling limestone upland is typical of large parts of central Jamaica. What is the land being used for? Why?

Map 5.3 JAMAICA: Main landscape features. What relationships are there between the relief and communications?

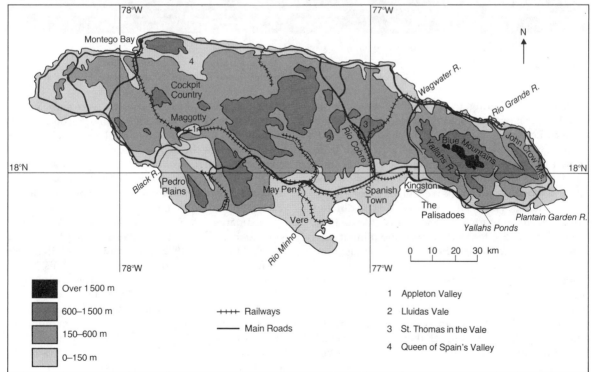

Bauxite mining in Jamaica. See also the photograph on page 209.

the tropical weathering, over millions of years, of the limestone that once covered the whole of central and western Jamaica.

Though the existence of the bauxite had been known for some years beforehand, it was not until the demand for aluminium mounted sharply in the 1939–45 World War that tests were made to see if it was worth mining. These tests showed that it differed from the ores imported by the United States from the Guianas in South America. For one thing it contained less aluminium. Six tonnes of Jamaican bauxite were needed to make one tonne of aluminium, compared with only four tonnes of the ore mined in Guyana. Because of this and other differences it was impossible to extract the alumina economically from Jamaican bauxite in any of the American factories existing at that time. However, this disadvantage was more than offset by certain favourable factors.

First, Jamaican bauxite reserves were sufficient for at least a hundred years of mining. Second, as the bauxite lay on the surface of the land, it was easy to mine. Third, as the deposits lay only 1 600 kilometres from the Gulf Coast ports, transport costs to the USA were low. Soon after the war, Canadian and American companies built special plants needed to extract alumina from Jamaican bauxite. They purchased large properties in the island and began operations. The amount of bauxite mined rose from 400 000 tonnes in 1952 to a record of over 15 million tonnes in 1974, making Jamaica the world's largest producer. Then came a decline, caused mainly by a sharp rise in the world price of oil. Because countries had to spend a lot more money on oil, they had less to spend on other goods including aluminium. As the market for aluminium declined, the production of bauxite fell. So did the price. As a result the Jamaican economy was very depressed.

To add to the problem, Jamaica, like other West Indian bauxite producers, was entirely dependent on oil power for its bauxite and alumina factories. Their needs were so large that they consumed half of all Jamaica's oil imports. As the price of oil rose, Jamaica's bauxite become more expensive and therefore less competitive in the world market. All the bauxite companies reduced their output. Some ceased operating permanently; others for a time. Some survived by means of partnership arrangements with the government.

Bauxite production continued to decline until 1985. Then, as Table 5.4 shows, it began rising again. In reading the table, you should note that:

a) In order to save space, the figures are given in thousands of tonnes ('000 tonnes). Thus the output in 1952 was 400 000 tonnes and in 1976 10 300 000 tonnes. Figures in tables are often shortened in this way.

b) A tonne (or metric ton) amounts to 1 000 kilograms.

Table 5.4 Changes in the output of bauxite in Jamaica ('000 tonnes)

1952	1958	1965	1972	1976	1982	1985	1988
400	5 772	8 500	12 600	10 300	8 300	6 200	7 900

Mining is carried out by open-pit methods, so no miners work underground. The topsoil is cleared from a few acres and the underlying bauxite is removed with huge mechanical shovels. A single deposit fifty acres in extent may yield over 5 million tonnes before it is exhausted and the land restored.

Some of the mining companies export the bauxite itself. They dry the ore in rotating ovens and load it on to ships at the north coast ports of Discovery Bay and Ocho Rios. From there it is taken abroad, mainly to the United States and the Soviet Union. Exports totalled 3.5 million tonnes in 1988. Other firms extract the alumina in Jamaica, their factories being located at Kirkvine, Ewarton, Nain and Halse Hall, as shown on Map 5.1. At the factories the ore is ground into fine particles and dumped into tanks of hot caustic soda solution under high pressure. This process dissolves alumina (that is aluminium oxide), while the unwanted residue – consisting mainly of iron oxide and silica – settles at the bottom and is strained off and dumped. The alumina is then reprecipitated from solution and heated to 1 100°C in huge rotating furnaces. It emerges as a white powder resembling table salt. About $2\frac{1}{2}$ tonnes of dry bauxite are needed to make a tonne of alumina.

The output from these factories, which totalled over $1\frac{1}{2}$ million tonnes in 1988, is taken by rail to the south coast ports of Port Kaiser, Port Esquivel and Rocky Point. From there it is shipped to Kitimat in British Columbia, to the Netherlands and other Western European countries and to the United States for conversion into aluminium. The metal itself is not made in Jamaica as the process requires large quantities of cheap electricity.

The benefits of bauxite and alumina industries are mainly financial. By paying high wages to their employees they have made poor agricultural districts more prosperous. By paying an agreed tax on each tonne of bauxite they mine plus a percentage of the price the resulting metal sells for, they have enabled the Jamaican government to undertake development projects which would otherwise have been impossible.

There are, however, certain problems and disadvantages. For one, the bauxite and alumina companies do not employ many people. For another, the high wages paid by the bauxite companies create a problem for society as a whole, as they cannot be matched by other employers. This causes dissatisfaction among workers in other sectors of the economy. A further problem of a very different kind is that of finding a use for the millions of tonnes of waste which the alumina factories dump to form large ugly lakes of red mud. The waste contains caustic soda and other chemicals which can pollute underground water supplies.

Gypsum and other minerals

On the southern slopes of the mountains behind Bull Bay a few miles east of Kingston there is a deposit of several million tonnes of gypsum. Between 100 000 and 200 000 tonnes of it are quarried each year. Some is used in the local cement industry and the manufacture of ceiling tiles and other building materials. The remainder is taken to the eastern end of Kingston harbour to await export to the United States.

Other minerals present in Jamaica include marble and phosphates, and ores of copper, lead, zinc, manganese and iron. Some of these have at times been worked in small quantities. More important is silica sand found in large quantities near the town of Black River and used in a growing glass-making industry. Petroleum has been sought for since 1952, but so far none has been discovered. However, several million tonnes of peat, which exist in swampland around Black River and near Negril are a potential source of fuel for generating electricity (see Map 5.1).

Climate

Temperature

As in the other Caribbean islands the monthly temperature range is small. Thus in Kingston the difference between the hottest month, July (27.5°C) and the coolest month, January (24.3°C) is little more than 3°C. The range between day and night is somewhat greater (8°C to 11°C), though owing to the moderating influence of the sea it is rare for day temperatures on the plains to exceed 33°C or to fall below 16°C at night.

Highland temperatures are 6°C to 11°C lower than these, and the summits of the Blue Mountains have been known to have occasional light frosts in winter.

Rainfall

The chief features of Caribbean rainfall have been dealt with in chapter two. In Jamaica the rainy season begins at about the end of April and reaches a maximum in September, October and November with a somewhat drier intervening period in June. Several factors combine to produce the summer maximum. First, as the convection currents are strongest in the hot months, the heaviest showers occur then. Thunder often accompanies afternoon downpours. Second, this is the period when the Intertropical Convergence Zone is farthest north. Rain-bearing easterly waves, moving along its northern boundary, sometimes cross the island. Third, this is the hurricane season. Though hurricanes affect Jamaica on an average only once in seven or eight years, they bring such heavy rain when they strike or pass nearby that average monthly rainfall figures are increased.

In the colder months convection currents are weaker and the air is less humid, so showers are fewer, lighter and shorter. The tendency to drought is partly offset by occasional northers blowing out from North America in winter. When a norther reaches Jamaica, the weather on the northern side of

Map 5.5 JAMAICA: Rainfall. Compare this map with Map 5.3. What relationships do you see between relief and rainfall? What other factors influence the facts shown on this map?

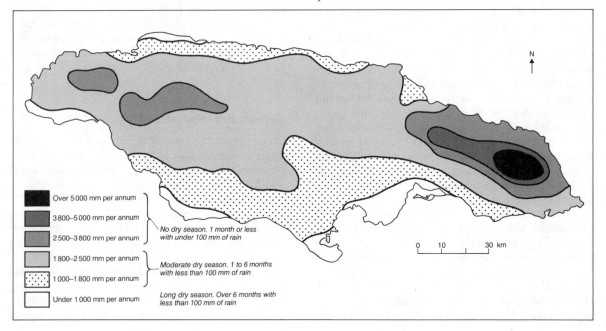

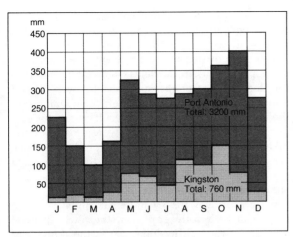

Diagram 5.6 Average monthly rainfall of Port Antonio (top) and Kingston (bottom).

the island changes dramatically. Along the north coast, temperature drops by several degrees, winds are strong, skies are grey, rain falls, and American tourists may decide to fly home. Further inland, on north-facing mountain slopes, the rain may be very heavy indeed. But the southern plains are cast in rain shadow and though the weather is cool the skies may be cloudless. These areas are also in the rain shadow when the winds are blowing from the east or north-east. As a result, rainfall is low and the dry season is long. Streams flowing down the southern slopes of the Blue Mountains are reduced to mere trickles most of the time and sometimes they dry up altogether. Several parts of the largest and driest lowlands are irrigated. For example, near Spanish Town the whole flow of the Rio Cobre River is diverted into irrigation channels where the water is used mainly for the cultivation of sugar cane. This area and the Rio Minho basin a little to the west (see Map 5.3) together account for 80 per cent of Jamaica's 100 000 irrigated acres.

Land use

As Diagram 5.7 shows, only 31 per cent of the land surface of Jamaica is used for agriculture (16 per cent for the major crops and 15 per cent for pasture). This, together with a small proportion of the forest land, is all that can be considered productive.

One reason why no more land is productive is that half of it lies above 300 metres and a third of it has slopes with gradients of more than one in five. Another is that there are large tracts of poor thin soil. This is particularly true of limestone areas where, in addition, water is difficult to obtain. But besides these handicaps, much harm has been done by man. Over large areas forests have been cut for lumber, burned for charcoal and cleared for cultivation, thus exposing the land to rapid tropical weathering. Many plantations established in unsuitable areas in the prosperous days of slavery now provide a few tenants and squatters with a meagre subsistence. In some of these areas soil erosion has become so serious that land is now very difficult to reclaim. Nevertheless attempts are now being made to do so. Two areas to which particular attention has been given are the Yallahs Valley leading southwards from the Blue Mountains to the coast and a somewhat larger area around Christiana in the centre of Jamaica. More recently, attention has been directed to the protection of badly eroded watersheds all over the island – especially to the re-forestation of sharp-crested ridges where they are found separating deep valleys.

Diagram 5.7 A divided circle to show land use in Jamaica.

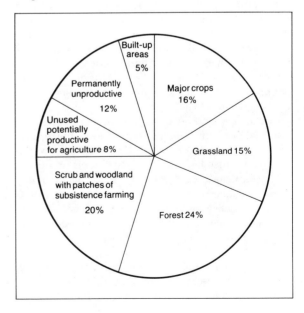

Land holdings

In the slave days the Jamaican lowlands were occupied by large sugar and cattle estates while the hills were mostly left in forest and bush. After emancipation the majority of the freed slaves left the estates and cleared small subsistence holdings for themselves in the hills. These two contrasting types of land tenure – estates and peasant holdings – still exist. Indeed, with the bauxite companies owning large properties and with smallholders subdividing their land to provide their families with a living, the distinction between very small and very large land holdings is growing. Thus in 1970, 45 per cent of the land was taken up by three hundred properties of 500 acres and over. At the other end of the scale, 78 per cent of the farms are under 5 acres in size; an area which is generally agreed to be much too small to support a family. These tiny farms take up 15 per cent of the area. Efforts are being made to eliminate both extremes and create more middle-sized farms. The problems become more severe as population increases.

Agriculture

Sugar

Reasons for the rapid decline in British West Indian sugar output in the first half of the nineteenth century are given in chapter four. It remains to be said that Jamaica, the world's largest producer in the early part of the century, suffered more severely than any other colony. There were a number of reasons for this. One was the failure of the estates to improve cultivation and processing methods while they were prosperous. Another was the cultivation of unsuitable land. A third was the dependence on slave labour which largely abandoned the estates after emancipation. A fourth was the high proportion of absentee landlords who took their profits out of Jamaica and spent them on extravagant living. These weaknesses, together with changing British economic policy, led to the collapse of the industry. This lasted for a century. Indeed, the output of 100 000 tonnes of sugar in 1805 was not surpassed until 1937.

Supported by the Commonwealth Sugar Agreement output rose to a record of 515 000 tonnes in 1965. Since then there has been a gradual decline as

Table 5.8 shows. The decline was brought about mainly by low sugar prices on the world market, the lack of investment in the factories (nearly all of which were owned by foreign companies) and lack of people to work in the fields. In an attempt to stop the decline most of the sugar estates were placed under the management of workers co-operatives in the early 1970s. However the results were not successful and the co-operatives were closed in the mid-1980s. Recent levels of sugar production have not always been sufficient to meet the Lomé quota of 118 000 tonnes (see page 46) and the local consumption of 100 000 tonnes.

By comparing Maps 5.9 and 5.3 it can be seen that sugar cane is mostly grown on the lowlands. The area under cane is declining. So is the number of factories of those that remain. Frome, in the western part of the island, is the largest in the Commonwealth Caribbean. Another, Monymusk, which stands on the irrigated plains of Vere in southern Clarendon, is almost as big and is the only one producing refined white sugar.

In addition to sugar Jamaica produces molasses and about 15 million litres of rum a year together with other spirits. Some of the bagasse is used to help fuel the factories thus saving on oil imports. Some is also used to make wallboard.

Table 5.8 Changes in the output of sugar in Jamaica ('000 tonnes)

1955	1961	1965	1971	1977	1983	1988
407	448	515	385	300	196	214

Bananas

Though the banana was introduced into Jamaica by the Spaniards in the sixteenth century, it was not until the middle of the nineteenth century that American schooners, calling at north shore ports, began to take small quantities of the fruit back with them to the United States. They sold so well that American companies were formed to handle the trade, and regular shipments began in the 1880s. The opportunity to earn a regular income from banana exports was welcomed by small farmers, and it was they who began the business to be followed, later, by estates.

The Jamaican sugar industry at that time was

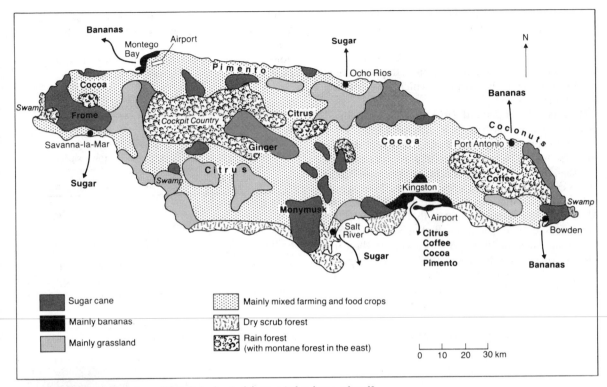

Map 5.9 JAMAICA: Land use. To what physical factors is land use related?

A fine stem of bananas. How much would this stem weigh?

unable to compete with subsidised European beet sugar, and was in its most depressed state. By 1900 banana exports had become more valuable than sugar, and they remained so, apart from a few years, until the 1939–45 World War. The peak year was 1937, when Jamaica exported nearly 27 million stems, twice as many as any other country in the world. By this time Britain had become the chief purchaser and the fruit was carried there in a fleet of fast, refrigerated ships.

Banana production in the 1930s would have been considerably greater had it not been for Panama disease. Not only did this fungus damage or kill the plants, but it infected the soil so that bananas could not again be grown on the spot for years. Several estates went out of production altogether. Output was maintained only by bringing steep hill slopes into use. These were easily eroded and soon lost their fertility. Then in 1936 a second disease – leaf spot – appeared, and soon afterwards in 1939 the Second World War began. During the war few ships could be spared for such luxuries as bananas, and exports were small. After the war there was a fairly rapid recovery in spite of Panama disease, but in 1951 a severe hurricane destroyed millions of plants. The government then helped farmers to plant a new variety of banana, the Lacatan, which was immune to Panama disease.

However, Lacatans and other recently developed varieties of bananas had their own problems. They had to be sprayed regularly against leaf-spot disease and they had to be packed carefully in order to reach overseas markets in good condition. The proportion of the crop which failed to reach the required standard was high, and exports, even before Hurricane Allen in 1980, destroyed most of that year's crop. Efforts to revive production resulted in a rise in output from an average of 20 000 tonnes a year in the early 1980s to over 34 000 tonnes in 1987. Then in September 1988, Hurricane Gilbert destroyed most of the crops and production declined again.

In contrast to sugar and other seasonal crops, bananas provide growers with a steady income throughout the year. They also give good shade for young cocoa and coffee plants before they begin to bear.

Table 5.10 Banana exports from Jamaica (tonnes)

Yearly average 1965–69	Yearly average 1970–74	Yearly average 1975–79	Yearly average 1980–84
160 000	102 000	75 000	20 000

Coffee

Jamaican coffee, first grown in the eighteenth century, soon found a ready market in Europe. One type, Blue Mountain coffee, came to be considered

Coffee in the Blue Mountains. What problems face people who live in districts as mountainous as this?

among the best in the world. Output rose rapidly and in 1814, the peak year, over 15 000 tonnes were exported. This prosperity was short lived due to the fact that coffee was a plantation crop, and soon after the slaves were emancipated the industry collapsed. Some of the land was taken over by smallholders but they allowed the land, the trees and the methods of production to deteriorate so that for the next hundred years exports averaged less than 4 000 tonnes a year.

Times were bad, for as both quantity and quality fell, so did the price of the crop. Moreover, throughout this period soil erosion went unchecked, proceeding to such a degree that some old coffee lands will never again be productive.

Coffee is of particular value as it grows well in hilly districts that is not suited to other crops. In recent years a great deal of work has been done to improve the coffee industry. Several million young plants have been given to farmers prepared to look after them properly.

A number of pulperies have been built throughout the island to process the crop. During the picking season, which lasts from August to March, ripe cherry-red berries are taken to the pulperies where they are unloaded into water tanks. The best berries sink, whereas immature ones and waste matter float on the surface and are easily removed. While the berries are still under water, a machine removes the pulp surrounding the beans. The beans are then sent to a factory in Kingston where they are dried, either artificially, using hot air, or by spreading them on a large barbecue in the sun. A few days later they are fed into a hulling machine, which strips the parchment and the underlying silver skin off the beans and polishes them. Finally, the beans are graded according to size, the largest and best being carefully inspected before they are packed into bags suitable for export. This 'washed coffee', as it is called, is exported to several countries, including Britain, Italy, Japan and Germany. In addition, some is made into instant coffee.

The famous Blue Mountain coffee is grown on small farms on the slopes of the Blue Mountains, mostly between 900 and 1 500 metres. At these heights the cooler climate causes the berries to take longer to ripen and in consequence the beans develop more of the substances which, on roasting, give coffee its flavour. The beans are processed at pulperies in the area and exported in barrels mainly to Japan.

Citrus

Most of the Jamaican citrus fruit is produced in a wide belt stretching from north to south across the centre of the island, particularly between the elevations of 300 and 750 metres. During the picking season, which lasts from November to April, all oranges and grapefruit for export as fresh fruit are sent to two factories where some are selected, wrapped and carefully packed in wooden crates for shipment to Britain and New Zealand. The rest are processed into fruit juice, canned fruit, essential oils and marmalade.

The output of citrus fruit is rising. Owing to the large local demand exports account for only 40 per cent of the oranges that are grown and for none of the limes or tangerines.

Cocoa

Cocoa, though grown in Jamaica since the earliest days of English settlement, first became important at the time of the decline of the sugar industry in the latter half of the nineteenth century. Cocoa trees replaced cane in some areas, notably the moist sheltered valleys leading up into the Blue Mountains. Exports rose to about 3 000 tonnes a year in the first quarter of the present century. During this time, however, prices fell because of the remarkable expansion in Ghana – in those days known as the Gold Coast. Few new trees were planted and, as the old ones ceased to bear, bananas were grown in their place.

Jamaica is fortunate in being free from the diseases affecting cocoa in West Africa and Trinidad. Attempts have been made to increase output. For example, plants have been given free of cost to growers in cocoa-growing areas, and large fermentaries have been built to process the cocoa properly. However, these measures have not succeeded in raising the average production above 1 700 tonnes in the 1980s.

When fermentation is complete and the beans are dry, they are sent to Kingston for blending, cleaning and grading. Local sales, which include the cocoa used to make instant drinks and confectionery, absorb about one third of the output. The remainder is exported for blending with lower-priced cocoa from the other parts of the world in the manufacture of chocolate.

Pimento

The dried berries of the pimento tree yield a spice which, because of its resemblance to the combined flavours of cinnamon, cloves and nutmeg, is called 'allspice'. Pimento thrives best amidst the pastures on the limestone highlands of the central parishes. Though it is grown a little in other parts of the Caribbean, Jamaica has an almost complete monopoly of the world's allspice trade. The leaves of the tree are also valuable as they yield pimento oil. The output – and therefore the price – fluctuates from year to year.

Ginger

Another export long associated with Jamaica is high-grade ginger. Most of it is grown by small farmers in the central hills north of Christiana where it has caused considerable soil erosion.

When the plants are dug out of the ground, the roots – shaped like a human hand – are peeled, washed thoroughly and dried in the sun. They must be handled carefully to prevent them from breaking, for broken ginger loses its value. It is sold to Britain, Canada and the United States.

Tobacco

Jamaica has a small but long established cigar industry. The tobacco is grown on small farms in the Rio Minho Valley in the south centre of the island. Great care is taken in cultivating the plants, fermenting the leaves, and ageing the tobacco for a year or more. It is then processed by hand in four factories, using imported leaf to make the wrappers. The United States is by far the biggest market for Jamaican cigars. The next biggest is the European Community.

The supply of tobacco is also sufficient to meet the requirements of Jamaican cigarette manufacturers. Another product used for smoking is marijuana (ganja). Throughout the 1970s and 80s it has been a highly profitable though illegal crop especially when smuggled to the United States and other countries.

Fruit

Many tropical fruits are grown on the island, primarily for home consumption, though increasing quantities are being flown to the United States along with flowers. In addition guava jelly and canned pineapples, mangoes and other fruits and fruit products are exported in small quantities.

Coconuts

Coconuts, grown mainly on estates along the northern and eastern coasts of the island, have suffered from disease and millions of the old trees have died. Though more resistant dwarf varieties have been planted in their place, output has fallen. For this reason, and also because of the increasing demand for fresh nuts, the island no longer provides all the copra needed by the factories making butterine, margarine, lard, edible oil, toilet soap and laundry soap.

Table 5.11 shows the relative importance of Jamaica's agricultural exports in the late 1980s.

Table 5.11 Relative value of Jamaica's agricultural exports

Sugar	55%	Citrus and other fresh fruits	4%
Bananas	10%	Yams and other root crops	10%
Coffee	6%	Green vegetables and flowers	6%
Cocoa	4%	Others	1%
Pimento	4%		

The small farmers

Throughout the period of slavery Jamaican slaves were granted a certain amount of time to grow food crops on their own small plots of land. Thus many of them gained enough experience to be able to set up on their own after emancipation. They acquired smallholdings, especially in the hills. There they grew subsistence crops and earned small sums from the sale of such things as bananas, cocoa, coffee, ginger and pimento. The rise of a stable, fairly prosperous peasantry was one of the most notable features of nineteenth-century Jamaica.

There have been further changes since then. For one thing, the rapid growth of population in the present century has led to many smallholdings being divided among too many people to provide anyone with a reasonable standard of living. For another, export, estate-grown crops again became prominent for a time. However, in recent years, with government assistance, small farmers have once again been able to obtain land. The increased demands of hotels and towns, especially Kingston, have encouraged small farmers to earn a regular income from the sale of fruit, vegetables, and animal products. They have benefited too from the construction of good roads and the improvement of marketing and cold storage facilities. Together with an increasing number of people with larger properties they are thinking more in terms of the local market than of exports. These products are of more value than all the export crops combined. They include yams, sweet and Irish potatoes, rice, several varieties of beans, plantains, pumpkins, mangoes, avocado pears, breadfruit, cassava, maize, ackees, tomatoes, cabbage and many other tropical and temperate crops.

Livestock

Though the proportions of cropland and grassland vary from year to year, they were about equal towards the end of the 1980s (see Diagram 5.7). Many properties, including some very large ones in the central parishes, specialise in cattle rearing. Altogether there are about 300 000 cattle, that is nearly three times as many as there are in all the other Commonwealth Caribbean islands combined. Their beef supplies Jamaica with about a quarter of its meat supply. The main source of meat, however, is the island's 4 million chickens. Smaller quantities come from 250 000 pigs, 300 000 goats and 5 000 sheep.

Since the erection in 1940 of a condensed milk factory at Bog Walk, milk production in the island has multiplied several times. The regular demands of the factory have encouraged small farmers to take up dairying. In addition many cane farmers make a supplementary income from milk, which is of special value to them in the out-of-crop season from July to January. Even so, the supply of dairy products is not enough to meet local requirements, and there are large imports of powdered milk, butter and cheese, mainly from New Zealand. Food imports as a whole cost considerably more than the value of agricultural exports.

Agriculture and employment

One indication of the stage of development of a country is the proportion of the labour force employed in agriculture. By mechanising their farming, highly developed countries have released many workers for other jobs, such as manufacturing and commerce.

Throughout the West Indies, though the proportion of agricultural workers is falling, it is still high. In Jamaica 44 per cent of the labour force was engaged in agriculture in 1943; 31 per cent in 1987. Those in manufacturing rose in this period from 12 per cent to 16 per cent, and those in commerce from 8 per cent to 15 per cent. Mining, in spite of the size of the bauxite industry, employed less than 1 per cent of the labour force in 1987. This shows how highly mechanised the bauxite operations are.

A serious problem in rural Jamaica is the lack of opportunities for employment. With the rise of population many people can find no work. Many others are uninterested in the jobs that do exist because they are poorly paid and offer little scope for advancement. As a result, people have been flocking into the towns. Conditions there are often worse than those they have left, but opportunities of returning to their own homes seldom arise.

Forestry

Most of the forests that once covered Jamaica have been cleared at one time or another. Today, 24 per cent of the land is classified as forest (see Diagram 5.7). However, much of this is really 'ruinate', that is poor quality secondary growth. The only areas of natural forest are in the mountains where they are difficult to reach. (See Map 5.9).

Though the forests supply only 10 per cent of the island's timber requirements, they nevertheless serve a useful purpose in preventing soil erosion. For this reason, most of the remaining forest is protected by the government from further exploitation. Other more accessible mountain areas are being re-forested, mainly with Caribbean Pine in the Blue Mountains and with mahoe and mahogany elsewhere. In some of the most beautiful places, attractive picnic sites have been established for campers and other holidaymakers.

Fishing

Several thousand fishermen make a living from beaches all round the island. Most of them operate canoes powered by outboard motors which enable them to go many miles out to sea. The shallow waters and cays off the south coast are richer than the northern waters, where, outside the reef, the sea-floor shelves steeply to great depths. Other fishermen live on cays in the Pedro and Morant banks up to 100 kilometres offshore (see Map 1.2). Their catch is loaded on to boats which visit the banks, frequently from Kingston. The annual catch of about 7 000 tonnes meets about a third of the island's needs. The main fish imports are salt cod and canned mackerel and sardines. In addition to sea fish, about 1 000 tonnes of freshwater fish are obtained each year from inland ponds specially stocked for the purpose.

Industry

Though a few industries were in existence before 1939, war-time shortages of manufactured goods showed that new industries were needed. After the war the Jamaican government, following the lead given by Puerto Rico, encouraged and protected many new industries, and Jamaica now provides a wide range of manufactured products. Most of the factories are in Kingston, where a large industrial estate has been developed on the waterfront, but some have been set up outside the capital to provide much-needed employment in the smaller towns and reduce the movement of people to Kingston.

Classification of Industry

Industries can be classified in different ways. One way is to group them into primary, secondary and tertiary industries.
1 Primary industries are those that are concerned with the first stage of production. They include mining, forestry, fishing, hunting, animal farming and crop farming. With the exception of hunting, there are examples of all these industries in Jamaica.
2 Secondary industries are those in which primary products are manufactured into more valuable goods. Examples in Jamaica are alumina (based on mining), furniture (based on forestry), frozen fish (based on fishing), condensed milk (based on animal farming), and sugar (based on crop farming).

3 Tertiary industries are the service industries such as transport, building, banking, storage, retailing, and tourism.

A second kind of classification groups manufacturing industries according to the ways that they contribute to a country's economy.

There are four such groups.

1 The first group consists of those industries that process local products and sell them abroad. They contribute to the economy by earning foreign exchange.
2 The second group consists of those industries that process local products for local sale. They contribute to the economy by reducing the level of imports. This is known as 'import substitution'.
3 The third group consists of those industries that process imported materials for local sale. They contribute to the economy by enabling the country to buy low-cost raw materials rather than high-cost manufactures.
4 The fourth group consists of those industries that process imported materials for export. These foreign-owned industries tend to move from country to country in search of cheap labour. Even so, they contribute to a country's economy by providing employment.

Table 5.12 gives examples of Jamaican industries in each of these four groups.

Table 5.12 A classification of Jamaican manufacturing industry

Process of local products for export	Process of local products for local sale	Process of imported products for local sale	Process of imported products for export
Examples	Examples	Examples	Examples
Bauxite Alumina Sugar	Cement Furniture Canned fruits and vegetables	Petroleum Chemicals Bakery products	Clothes Footwear Electronic goods
Rum and liqueurs Cigars	Condensed milk Cigarettes	Textiles Plastics	

The success of one industry can encourage others to develop. One way in which this happens is when the products of an industry are used as the basis of other industries. This kind of development is called a forward linkage. For example, citrus production in Jamaica has given rise to the manufacture of canned citrus segments, canned and bottled juices, marmalade and even animal feed from the left-over pulp. A different kind of linkage occurs when industries are set up to supply material to an already existing industry. For example, some of the chemicals needed in the manufacture of alumina used to be imported. Now they are produced locally. This kind of linkage is called a backward linkage.

In Jamaica, as in other West Indian territories, the main purpose of new manufacturing industries has been to create jobs and reduce imports, not to develop a large export business. The Jamaican economy therefore differs from that of a country like Hong Kong which exports large quantities of light manufactured goods to all parts of the world. Exports of Jamaican manufactures are, however, growing. Some movement has taken place as a result of the American Caribbean Basin Initiative designed to assist exports of new West Indian products to the USA by removing trade barriers against them.

The CARICOM countries provide another market which has benefited the Jamaican economy, but it has also created a feeling of dissatisfaction in the less developed Caribbean countries which would like to increase their own output of manufactured goods but cannot easily compete with those from Jamaica.

Some of the electricity used in Jamaica comes from five small hydro-electric stations situated on the southward-flowing Black River and the northward-flowing White River, Roaring River and Rio Bueno. If rivers are to be used for generating hydro-electricity they must provide a plentiful supply of swift-flowing water which does not vary much in volume from season to season and from year to year. There are several more rivers in Jamaica on which other small electricity-generating stations could be built. However, they are not large enough to be a major source of power, and their volume drops considerably after a long period of dry weather.

Trade

Up to the 1950s, Jamaican exports were entirely agricultural. Then bauxite and alumina grew in importance until by the mid-1970s they amounted to 70 per cent of the total. Throughout the 1980s the proportions of agricultural and non-agricultural exports changed again. The position in 1987 is shown below.

Table 5.13 Jamaican Exports, 1987

Chief agricultural exports	Per cent value
Sugar and rum	12.5
Bananas	2.8
Citrus, coffee, cocoa	3.8
Chief non-agricultural exports	
Bauxite	16.7
Alumina	31.1
Chemicals	3.0
Foods, drinks, tobacco products	9.6
Other manufactured goods	18.8
All other exports	1.7

For many years, the United States has been Jamaica's most important trade partner. In 1987, 38 per cent of the exports went to the United States and 45 per cent of the imports came from there. Other major trading partners were Britain, Canada, the USSR and Japan. Trade with CARICOM countries accounted for about 7 per cent of the total exports and 5 per cent of the total imports.

A country which relies heavily on trade must always watch its balance of payments, that is it must be careful not to spend more on imports than it earns from exports and other sources of income (such as tourism and the returns from overseas investments). The problem of maintaining the balance is difficult for Jamaica, as it is for all the West Indies. The main reason is that the price for imported manufactured goods has been rising faster than the price of the minerals and agricultural goods that are exported. In addition, the growing population and, for some, a rising standard of living has resulted in an increased demand for imported foodstuffs and for cars, refrigerators, television sets and many other manufactured goods. To prevent the demand for imports from getting out of hand, and to encourage the use of locally made products, some imports are being heavily taxed. Some goods are not allowed into the island at all.

Tourism

Jamaica became a well-known winter resort for rich Americans in the period leading up to the 1939–45 World War. The island's main attractions were its ideal winter climate, its many white sand beaches along the north coast, and its variety of lowland, upland and mountain scenery. In addition, Jamaica had the advantage of being, with the exception of the Bahamas, the closest English-speaking Caribbean country to the American continent. Because Montego Bay was easily accessible by sea and, later, by air, it became the first major tourist centre. The next phase of development took place in the 1950s and 1960s when luxury hotels and resort cottages were built on many other parts of the north coast. Ocho Rios in particular grew to rival Montego Bay in importance. Negril, on the west coast, became important in the 1970s. However, tourism has not grown at a steady pace. One reason for this is that as jet transport has cut down flight times, other more distant parts of the world have been able to capture a larger share of the luxury market. Another is that at times Americans have been uneasy about the kind of welcome they would get in a country in which so much social change accompanied new nationhood. Tourism is an unpredictable business. There are always other places where tourists can go, and any number of reasons why a hotel can be full one year and empty the next.

The growth in the number of tourists visiting Jamaica is shown in Table 5.14. In 1987 they spent nearly US$600 million and provided direct employment for 15 000 people, compared with 5 000 in the bauxite industry. Tourism also provided part of the income of other people, such as farmers, taxi drivers and entertainers.

Table 5.14 Number of tourists visiting Jamaica ('000)

1961	1965	1975	1985	1987
250	320	550	850	1 040

Population

The population of Jamaica is almost entirely derived from four immigrant streams entering the island since its capture by the British in 1655. By far the largest number came from Africa. About a million people were landed throughout the slave period, and though some of these were sent elsewhere, at the time of emancipation they outnumbered the white settlers by about ten to one. Today about 96 per cent of the population is coloured or black. Jamaica took only a small share of the indentured Indian labourers who came to the Caribbean in the last half of the nineteenth century. Their descendants now make up about 2 per cent of the total. All other groups, including Europeans and Chinese, make up less than 2 per cent of the total.

Emigration

Since the days of slavery population has risen steadily, and in recent years rapidly, in spite of considerable emigration. The first outlet for emigrants was Panama, where they worked on the canal which was begun and abandoned by the French in the 1880s and completed by the Americans between 1908 and 1914. Many Jamaicans chose to remain in Panama and a considerable number of Jamaican families are still there. Throughout this period other emigrants left for Cuba during the expansion of the sugar industry there, and for Central America – especially Costa Rica – to work on the banana estates. In the 1920s and 30s many Jamaicans went to the United States. In the 1950s the main destination was Britain, where many men and women found employment in London, Liverpool, Birmingham and other big cities. In addition, West Indian women were attracted to nursing to such an extent that many British hospitals would have to close if they left. More recently owing to immigration restrictions, the number of Jamaicans going to Britain has declined. The chief destinations now are the United States and Canada. Altogether around 160 000 Jamaicans went to live in other countries over the ten year period 1978–87.

Population density

The population is unevenly distributed over the island. This may be seen from Map 5.15 though in fact the real contrasts are not between one parish and another but between those areas which have the resources to support dense settlement and those which do not. We have already noted the contrast

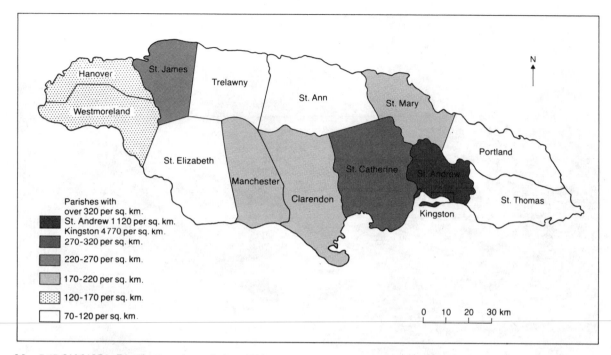

Map 5.15 JAMAICA: Distribution of population; 1980 census.

between the sparsely settled limestone uplands and the densely populated basins within them. In the Blue Mountains there is a similar contrast between the summits and the valleys, even though many precipitous slopes have been cleared for cultivation and settlement. The coastal lowlands are densely peopled, apart from a few swampy areas.

Besides going abroad, people have moved from place to place within Jamaica. This kind of movement is called 'internal migration'. As we have seen, most of the movement has been from the countryside to the towns, in particular to Kingston, Spanish Town, Montego Bay and May Pen.

Towns

Kingston was founded after the destruction of Port Royal by earthquake in 1692. It prospered immediately. Its chief natural advantages were the land-space available for building and the sheltered waterfront. It was also safe from attack, the narrow harbour entrance being protected by a fort at Port Royal on the tip of Palisadoes and another on a smaller sandspit opposite. Throughout the eighteenth and early nineteenth centuries, Kingston not only handled a large local trade, but was an important place for unloading goods from Britain and shipping them on to the Spanish colonies. For the remainder of the nineteenth century its development was retarded by the decline of Jamaican trade. Though it became the terminus of the island railway, and though the capital was transferred there from Spanish Town, Kingston was not in a prosperous condition when it was badly damaged by earthquake and fire in 1907.

When the town was rebuilt after the earthquake, it remained compact, taking up no more than three square kilometres of land. Its wharves and warehouses were confined to a short section of the harbour side. Behind them lay a rectangular network of streets, some containing the shops and government buildings, others the offices and houses. No great change took place from then until the 1920s and 1930s. Then with the development of motor transport, residential suburbs began to spread outwards into the parish of St Andrew. Map 5.16 shows

Looking towards Kingston from an aeroplane over the harbour. Note (a) the new high-rise buildings on land reclaimed from the sea; (b) the central business district extending inland from the harbour; and (c) the residential area extending . into the hills.

the extent of this development by 1950, including Stony Hill, which at that time was the only suburb in the hills.

Since 1950 Kingston has changed more than in the whole of its previous history. The old port has been closed and a new one constructed further west, with a large industrial estate behind it. A cement factory, an oil refinery, an electricity-generating station, and a gypsum-loading terminal have been built on various parts of the waterfront. A causeway built across the western end of the harbour has opened up the new housing area of Portmore where 80 000 people now live. Other suburbs have spread over all the surrounding lowlands and up into the hills beyond. Several of the lowland suburbs have been built in the form of large housing estates in which all the houses were originally of the same design. Now,

however, they display more variety because many of their owners have added extra rooms. By 1985 the built-up area covered over 100 square kilometres (more than the area of the island of Montserrat) and contained over 600 000 people. The growth over this period can be seen by comparing Maps 5.16 and 5.17.

Downtown Kingston has also changed. Many of the shops and houses there have been replaced by business offices, banks and government buildings. Indeed, the central business district occupies most of what was the whole of Kingston in 1950. Because people are moving out to the suburbs, this is one of the few places in Jamaica where the population is declining and not growing. It is crowded by day and empty at night. Nearby, however, are extremely densely peopled housing areas occupied by workers

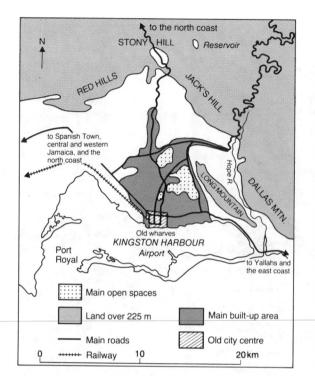

Map 5.16 Kingston, Jamaica, in 1950.

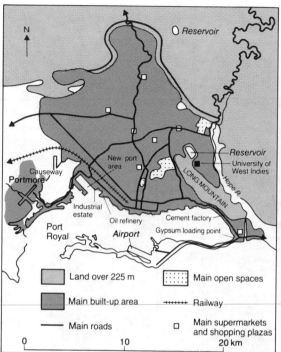

Map 5.17 Kingston, Jamaica, in 1970.

with poorly paid jobs and by thousands with no jobs at all.

As Kingston expanded, new shops of all kinds appeared in the suburbs. Along the main highways, shopping plazas were opened, each built around a parking area and containing a large supermarket, a drug store, a bank, and shops selling clothes, hardware, furniture, household goods, school supplies and a wide range of other articles. The shops in the centre of the city serve three groups of customers – city workers, people visiting Kingston on other business, and tourists.

The growth of the residential suburbs has been so rapid that serious problems have arisen. They include the disposal of garbage and the provision of water, electricity, telephones, schools, recreation grounds, and public transport. There is an immense flow of traffic and many people spend more than two hours a day travelling to and from work. Some travel in from Spanish Town, where the population has risen rapidly to 90 000 and from smaller towns along the coast east of Kingston.

None of these problems is likely to be overcome in the foreseeable future as the rate of growth of the population shows no signs of slackening. Developments already under way include the erection of high-rise buildings in downtown Kingston and certain other business areas for large organisations, the conversion of once fashionable houses in older suburbs for use as offices by small firms, and the increased use of apartment blocks for residential purposes. Also to be expected is a continuing rise in the number of unemployed, living in conditions of utter destitution. The contrast in the living conditions of the wealthy and the poor are more evident in Jamaica than in any other part of the Caribbean.

Montego Bay (70 000) began as a small port in Spanish times and grew in importance with the development of the sugar trade and, later, with the banana trade as well. Its communications with the rest of the island improved when it was made the western terminus of the railway. But it could not become a major port because its harbour was too shallow to accommodate large ships which had to

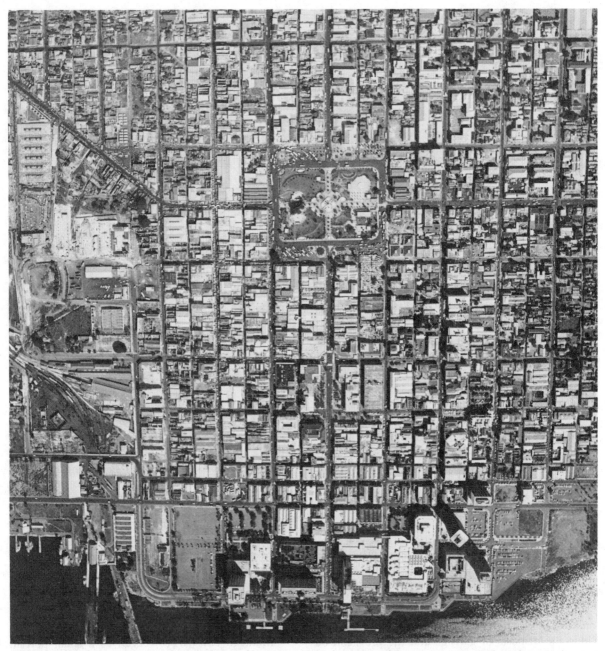

Looking directly down from the air at the heart of Kingston. Note the rectangular street pattern. Find (a) the pier shown in the photograph on page 76; (b) the waterfront area reclaimed from the sea; (c) the railway; and (d) an open-air park.

anchor some distance off-shore and be loaded and unloaded by barges.

The prosperity of Montego Bay dates from the time that tourists first began to visit the Caribbean.

It has gained a world-wide reputation as a luxury resort, and its airport is the chief point of arrival and departure for tourists to Jamaica. The construction of a deep-water harbour and freeport area has enabled

Montego Bay to increase its cruise-ship business, build a marina for pleasure boats, set up new manufacturing industries, improve its export facilities, and develop an import trade for the surrounding area. However, despite its prosperity it resembles Kingston and Spanish Town in having a shanty town population.

Port Antonio (12 000) grew to importance with the expansion of the banana trade. It is not as busy today as it was before the war, though it is still by far the leading banana exporting port. Ships docking there are sheltered from northers by Navy Island, which almost encloses the harbour mouth. Port Antonio is the eastern terminus of the railway crossing the island from Kingston. It is the most easterly of the north shore tourist resorts.

The Cayman Islands

Grand Cayman, the largest and most important of the three Cayman Islands, lies about 300 kilometres north-west of Jamaica. It has an area of 197 square kilometres, and a population in 1988 of 23 000. The other two islands, Little Cayman (26 square kilometres; population 80) and Cayman Brac (36 square kilometres; population 1 700), lie close to each other, about 110 kilometres east of Grand Cayman. (See Map 13.1).

Over two-thirds of their area is low-lying mangrove swamp and otherwise useless land. Much of the remainder is scrub forest able to withstand the drought imposed by the long dry season and the porous limestone rock which composes the islands. Agriculture is unimportant. Cotton and sugar cane cultivation have died out, and the output of coconuts has been greatly reduced by disease. Smallholders grow bananas, plantains, cassava, yams, sweet and Irish potatoes and rear some cattle for subsistence. A few larger farms specialise in dairy produce, chickens and eggs. Other occupations include lobster fishing, catching turtles (some 60 000 of which are reared in special ponds), making rope from thatch palm, and making turtle-shell ornaments.

But the prosperity of the Cayman Islands is based on none of these things, and in 1987 they were able to import 90 times as much as they exported because of sources of income that do not appear in any trade figures. One is the money sent home by Caymanians who live abroad or are employed on oil tankers and other ships. The second is the income that the government receives from the sale of postage stamps to collectors all over the world. The third and most important is tourism. The number of stop-over tourists rose from 8 000 in 1966 to about 200 000 in 1988. Three-quarters of them travelled from the United States; 10 per cent from Jamaica. Earnings from stop-over and cruise ship visitors totalled about US$100 million in 1988.

A seven-mile stretch of beach extending northwards from the capital George Town (population 8 000) to West Bay (population 7 000) is the chief tourist attraction.

The fourth and by far the largest source of income is that derived from licences and other fees paid by over four hundred foreign banks and 19 000 companies that have been registered in Grand Cayman in recent years to avoid the taxes that they would have to pay in most other countries. In this respect the Cayman Islands resembles the Bahamas. To accommodate the new business developments, the centre of George Town has been rebuilt. As can be seen on page 80 there are modern, multi-storey buildings. In addition, the old, tiny harbour has been enlarged.

The prosperity of Grand Cayman has attracted people to move there from other countries. In 1988 it was estimated that a third of the population were foreigners.

Questions and assignments

1 Name three contrasting types of scenery in Jamaica, and give two characteristics of each of them.
2 What are a) bauxite, b) alumina, and c) aluminium?
   d) Name one advantage that Jamaica has over Guyana as a bauxite mining country, and one disadvantage.
   e) Draw and label a bar graph to show the output of Jamaican bauxite in the years given in Table 5.4.
3 Using the bar graph in Diagram 5.6:
   a) Write down the average monthly rainfall figures for Port Antonio and for Kingston in a table like Table 2.4 on page 19).
   b) Using the method given on page 19, say in

The centre of George Town, rebuilt in the 1970s. What signs can be seen of (a) foreign business investment, and (b) foreign tourism?

each case which months are wet, moist and dry.

c) Say in what months the dry season in Kingston begins and ends.

4 On an outline map of Jamaica show: a) one area where sugar cane is grown; b) one area where bananas are grown; c) one area where coffee is grown.

d) Name two conditions which favour the cultivation of each of these crops.

e) Draw and label a bar graph to show the output of sugar in the years shown in Table 5.8.

5 Make lists of the manufacturing industries in the country in which you live under these headings:
a) local products for local sale;
b) local products for sale abroad;
c) imported materials for local sale;
d) imported materials for sale abroad.

6 From the information given in Table 5.12 showing the percentage value of the exports from Jamaica in 1987 write down the percentage of the total formed by: a) sugar and rum, b) other agricultural exports, c) bauxite, d) alumina, e) all the remaining exports. Draw a divided circle like the one in Diagram 5.7 to show these five categories of exports.

7 Draw and label a bar graph to show the number of tourists visiting Jamaica in the years shown in Table 5.14.

8 Draw a sketch map (similar to the one of Belize City on page 203) to explain the importance of Kingston as a port.

9 Using the following figures draw a graph to show the rise of population in Jamaica:

Year	Population	Year	Population
1871	506 000	1943	1 237 000
1891	639 000	1960	1 610 000
1911	831 000	1970	1 861 000
1921	858 000	1988	2 400 000

In what years do you think the population reached 1 million and 2 million? Extend your graph and find what you think the population will be in 1995. In what year do you think the population will reach 3 million? How old will you then be?

10 Name a town in Jamaica other than Kingston and give two reasons explaining its importance.

11 Give two reasons to account for the present-day prosperity of the Cayman Islands. Name one problem that has arisen because of that prosperity.

6

Trinidad and Tobago

Total area: 5 123 square kilometres; population (1988): about 1 270 000.

Trinidad

Area: 4 820 square kilometres; population (1988): 1 230 000; density of population: 255 per square kilometre.

Settlement and development

It was more than thirty years after Columbus discovered Trinidad in 1498 that the first Spaniards began to settle there. They found the island sparsely peopled by Arawak tribes, who, unlike the fierce Caribs on the islands farther north, could be made to work on the land. In spite of this, development was slow. There were no deposits of precious metals to attract settlers and those who established plantations met many setbacks. They were raided by English, French and Dutch marauders. Their chief export, cocoa, which they had found growing wild but had cultivated until they were able to supply all Spain's requirements, was struck by disease. Many settlements were abandoned, and by 1733 the number of Spaniards had fallen from several thousand to one hundred and fifty.

Recovery was slow until 1783 when Spain offered special encouragement to foreigners of the Catholic faith to settle in Trinidad. The French in particular took advantage of this offer, coming from Canada and from those parts of the Lésser Antilles that had recently been acquired by Britain. Others fled to Trinidad during the revolutions in France and in Haiti. The French settlers brought coffee and new varieties of cocoa and sugar cane with them and planted cotton as well. When the British took the island in 1797 they found a belt of cultivation along most of the west coast, and scattered plantations in other coastal districts and in some of the valleys leading up into the Northern Range.

The sugar industry, which had developed when Haiti ceased to export sugar after the revolution, became increasingly important. Slaves were brought in to work in the canefields but, because of the late start, there were only 21 000 slaves in Trinidad at the time of their emancipation in 1834. In contrast, Jamaica had 311 000 and Barbados 83 000 in that year. The resulting labour shortage was accentuated by the number of freed slaves who left the estates in order to establish smallholdings of their own in the unoccupied interior of the island. It was solved, after 1846, by employing indentured Indian labourers. In the seventy years that the system lasted, over 140 000 Indians went to work in Trinidad – about a third of the total who came to the Caribbean. More than three out of every four stayed when their contracts expired and, as we shall see, their descendants form a large proportion of the population today. Many people have also migrated to Trinidad from the less wealthy West Indian islands, especially from the Lesser Antilles. There were 45 000 of them at the time of the 1980 census.

Landforms

Geologically, Trinidad is not old, very little of it having been formed earlier than the Cretaceous period. At that time the southern Caribbean region was a great submarine trough in which great thicknesses of sediments were deposited by rivers flowing out from the ancient mass of the Guiana Highlands. At the close of the Cretaceous period earth movements produced the folds which are now the Northern, Central and Southern Ranges, but which were then three separate islands. During the quieter Tertiary period that followed, sands and clays, and some limestone, were deposited in the shallow seas around the islands. Then further movements occurred which lifted the whole area out of the water. In addition they exerted such pressure

Map 6.1 TRINIDAD: Geology.

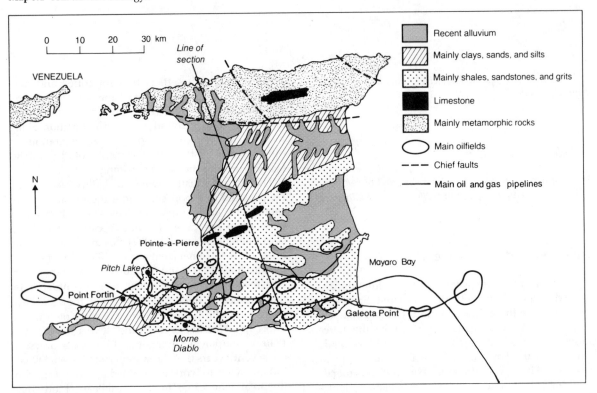

Diagram 6.2 Section showing relief and geology. The line of section is shown on Map 6.1. Heights and depths are greatly exaggerated.

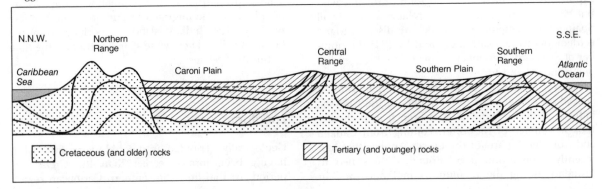

that they metamorphosed many of the rocks of the Northern Range.

Since then there has been little change apart from the relatively small earth movement that broke Trinidad off from the South American continent some 10 000 years ago. The sea passage it created between Chacachacare – the last of a series of small islands off the north-west tip of Trinidad – and Punta Peñas in Venezuela is about 11 kilometres wide.

The only true mountain system in Trinidad is the Northern Range. Though the highest peaks, Cerro Aripo and El Tucuche, rise to only 940 and 936 metres respectively, which is not high by Caribbean standards, the range forms an almost complete barrier for 80 kilometres across the north of the island. It rises so abruptly from the north shore that there is virtually no coastal plain. Much of its centre has been hollowed out by rivers which leave the range through narrow valleys. Where they emerge on the plain these rivers have deposited gravel fans, as shown in Diagram 6.3. Scenery of this kind is the typical result of river erosion in a folded mountain range.

The other two upland regions are unlike the Northern Range in that they slope gradually to the plains and present no great contrast with them. The Central Range is a broad highland mass running diagonally across the island from north-east to south-west and rising to little more than 300 metres. The Southern Range is lower still and is much narrower. Its highest peaks, the three Trinity Hills near the eastern end, do not quite reach 300 metres in height. Westwards, the range decreases in altitude and ends in the low peninsula of Cedros and Icacos Points.

The Caroni Plain which lies between the Northern and Central Ranges is lower and flatter in the west than in the east. It is drained by the Caroni River, which ends in a large mangrove-fringed swamp where it reaches the sea just south of Port of Spain. The undulating Naparima Plain in the south-west is drained by the Oropuche River which also ends in a swamp near the coast. In the east there is the Nariva Plain. Here Atlantic waves have built up a long sandbar which encloses the fresh-water Nariva Swamp.

Minerals

Petroleum

In the Tertiary rocks of the southern part of the island, and to some extent in the underlying Cretaceous as well, there are deposits of petroleum, which, though not large, are the basis of the most valuable industry in the Commonwealth Caribbean territories. Unfortunately, Trinidad is one of the most difficult countries in the world in which to find and produce petroleum in commercial quantities. The main reasons for this are:

1 In many places the underground rock structures containing it have been folded and broken so that the deposits have collected in small scattered pools. Diagram 6.5 shows why these deposits are difficult to locate and why a high proportion of exploratory drilling is unsuccessful.

Sometimes the petroleum has escaped altogether. A famous example of oil seeping to the surface is the pitch lake at La Brea. Less well known are the so-called 'mud volcanoes', a number of which occur in the Southern Range. These broad, low mounds, anything from 15–400 metres across, are formed where methane gas escapes from underground bringing up mud and traces of petroleum with it. The best known example is Morne Diablo, shown on Map 6.1.

2 Petroleum deposits in Trinidad are small and so each well can tap only a limited quantity. A well in any of the Middle East oilfields may produce over 300 times as much petroleum as a land well in Trinidad, and 60 times as much as a marine well. The island's output is therefore relatively small. In fact, Trinidad produces less than $\frac{1}{2}$ per cent of the world total.

3 In the search for petroleum over the years, 10 000 land wells have been drilled, some to a depth of 5 000 metres. Others have been drilled off the eastern and

Diagram 6.3 River erosion in the Northern Range of Trinidad.

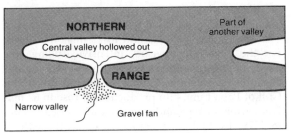

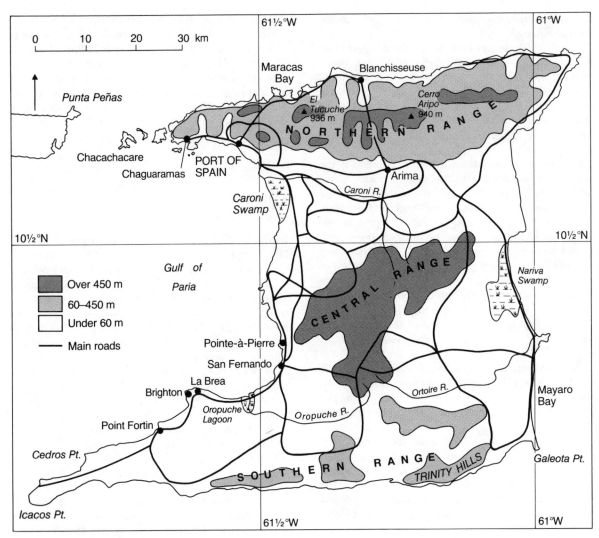

Map 6.4 TRINIDAD: Main landscape features. What relationships are there between the relief and the main roads shown on the map?

western coasts, and in the area of sea between Trinidad and Tobago. Drilling of this sort costs millions of dollars, and may – or may not – strike oil.
4 Less than half the petroleum comes up under its own pressure. The rest has to be pumped to the surface. This is a slow and costly undertaking. More expensive still are the techniques that have to be used when the first flow of oil comes to a stop. In this process gas or water are pumped in to the well so as to force more oil to the surface.
5 Trinidad produces about twenty different types of

crude petroleum, each of which needs special treatment at the refineries. This also adds to the cost of production.

Commercial production rose from 57 000 barrels in 1909 to 2 million in 1920 and to 22 million in 1940. For the next fifteen years, intensive drilling was needed to maintain this level of supply. Then output began to rise again as the first of the oilfields in the Gulf of Paria came into production. It rose to 67 million barrels in 1968 and to a peak of over 83 million in 1978. By that time marine fields to the east of

Looking over the Pointe-à-Pierre refinery towards San Fernando. In what direction was the camera pointing?

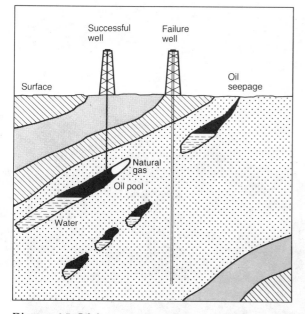

Diagram 6.5 Oil deposits collected in scattered pools, showing one of the problems of mining in Trinidad.

Trinidad were the main source of supply. Then as oil prices declined in the 1980s, output fell. The amount produced in 1987 was 57 million barrels, three-quarters of which came from under the sea. Today the main producing areas lie 30 to 40 kilometres east of Mayaro Bay (see Map 6.1). Under-sea pipelines carry the petroleum to Galeota Point where it is stored in large tanks loaded onto oil tankers for export to refineries in the United States.

Changes in the output of petroleum in recent years are shown in Table 6.6. So as to save space, the figures are given in millions of barrels (m. barrels). Thus, 83.8 stands for 83 800 000 barrels.

Table 6.6 Changes in the output of petroleum in Trinidad (m. barrels)

Year	1978	1981	1984	1987
Output	83.8	69.1	62.0	56.6

Most of Trinidad's crude petroleum is refined in the country itself. There are two refineries: a large one at Pointe-à-Pierre and a small one at Point Fortin. In the refineries the various chemicals which together make up crude petroleum are separated from one another. The products include gases such as propane, liquids such as aviation spirit, motor gasolene, diesel oil and fuel oil, and almost solid asphalt. Indeed, more asphalt is produced from the refineries than from the pitch lake.

In the 1970s, these refined products accounted for over half of Trinidad's total exports. In the 1980s however, the proportion has declined to about a third. One reason for this is that the United States has reduced its imports so as to protect its own refineries from overseas competition. Another is that the refineries in Trinidad cannot easily compete with more modern refineries in other parts of the world which produce a higher proportion of more profitable aviation spirit and motor gasolene. In addition, Trinidad's exports of refined petroleum products to other parts of the Caribbean have declined since the Bahamas, Jamaica, Antigua and Barbados built refineries of their own.

To keep the refineries working economically, the local supply of crude petroleum used to be supplemented by large imports, mainly from Saudi Arabia. With the decline in refining, these imports have declined to very low levels.

In some places, as Diagram 6.5 shows, natural gas is trapped underground together with petroleum. Where this happens the natural gas may be under sufficient pressure to force the petroleum up an oil well so that it does not have to be pumped up. Much of the petroleum from the marine wells comes to the surface in this way. In other places there are large fields of natural gas which do not contain petroleum. Those that have been tapped so far lie about 30 to 40 kilometres to the south-east of Galeota Point (see Map 6.1). Others are known to exist further east and also about 50 kilometres off the north coast of Trinidad.

Unlike the reserves of petroleum which have mostly been used up, there is sufficient natural gas to last for a hundred years. At present it is being used for three main purposes. One is to generate most of the island's electricity. The second is to serve as a fuel

Two resources in one place: rice on the surface of the land, petroleum underneath.

Railway wagons on the surface of the pitch lake.

for household purposes and for a growing number of industries including the manufacture of steel. The third is to provide the raw material for the large-scale manufacture of chemicals for export. One of the most important of these chemicals is methanol. Two others are ammonia and urea, both of which are used to make artificial fertilisers. These industries are located at Point Lisas (see Map 6.10), the largest industrial complex in the Commonwealth Caribbean. Pipelines have been laid to carry the natural gas to Point Lisas and other parts of Trinidad from the natural gas fields. The main oil and natural gas pipelines are shown on Map 6.1.

Asphalt

The world's largest source of natural asphalt is the pitch lake at La Brea. About 90 acres in extent, it lies in a shallow basin about one kilometre from the Gulf of Paria. Though one or two small patches of the pitch lake are soft and sticky, most of it is firm enough to support heavy vehicles. One type of vehicle rips furrows in the lake's surface, another type pushes the loosened asphalt into heaps, a third type dumps the material into a chain of light railway wagons, which, when full, are hauled by a wire cable up the steep slope at the edge of the lake to the factory.

In the factory the crude asphalt is tipped into huge iron tanks, and for the next eighteen hours superheated steam is piped through it to boil away all the water it contains. The resulting product, called 'dried' or 'refined' asphalt is strained and poured into hardboard drums. On cooling, it sets so hard that the drums can be shipped to all parts of the world without lids.

Refined asphalt from the pitch lake is used mostly

as a top layer on main roads where a particularly high quality, hard-wearing surface is needed, as for example, on motorways and busy intersections.

Since 1887, when operations began, over 12 million tonnes of asphalt have been removed from the pitch lake. Owing to the rate of extraction, and the fact that the asphalt is not self-replenishing, the lake surface is falling by about 10 centimetres a year.

Climate

Because Trinidad lies only 10° to 11° north of the Equator its temperature range is, if anything, less than that of the islands farther north. Temperature is lowest in January when it averages 25°C. This rises to 27°C in May just after the sun has passed overhead in the north. For the next few months it is a little cooler, but the increased humidity in this, the rainy season, makes many of the afternoons feel uncomfortably hot, although, in fact, day temperatures rarely rise above 33°C. As the sun moves south again towards the Equator, temperatures rise again and September is almost as hot as May. Relief from the heat is not so easy to find as it is in Jamaica, where the mountains are much higher and more accessible, and where there are considerable expanses of plateau more than 300 metres above the sea.

By comparing Maps 5.5 and 6.7 it can be seen that the rainfall of Trinidad is much more evenly spread than the rainfall of Jamaica. This is accounted for by the different landscapes of the two countries. In Jamaica, the high Blue Mountains stand across the path of the prevailing Trade winds. The rain-shadowed lowlands to the south of them receive only one-sixth as much rain as the mountain summits. In Trinidad, the mountains are only half as high as the Blue Mountains. Moreover, they run in much the same direction as the prevailing winds. As a result, the rain shadow effect is much reduced. Thus the driest areas in Trinidad receive at least one-third as much rain as the mountains.

During the dry season, which comes to an end in April, most of the wind comes from the east and north-east, and relief has a marked effect on rainfall distribution. For the rest of the year the winds are lighter and more variable in direction, convection currents are more powerful, and afternoon showers are heavier, longer lasting, and more widespread. They are particularly heavy in the west. In the east, on the other hand, there is a higher proportion of

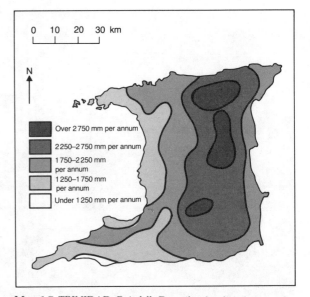

Map 6.7 TRINIDAD: Rainfall. Describe the distribution of rainfall as shown on this map.

Diagram 6.8 Average monthly rainfall of Trinidad.

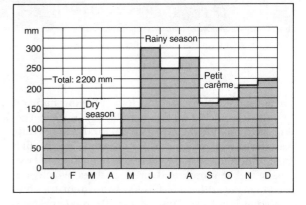

night rainfall, not only in this season but throughout the year.

The wet season, which lasts from May until December, is usually interrupted for one or two weeks in September or October by a brief dry period. The cause of this dry period, called the 'petit carême'[1], is not known for certain. The most likely

[1]'Petit carême' (Fr.) = a little Lent (as though the land were fasting).

explanation is that the Intertropical Convergence Zone and the easterly waves which are associated with much of the rainfall in Trinidad in the wet season, move to the north of the island for a short time. When this happens, Trinidad comes under the influence of the drier conditions which lie to the south of the Intertropical Convergence Zone.

Trinidad is unique in the West Indies in that it lies south of the regular hurricane paths. Only on two or three occasions in the island's history has there been any storm damage. Thus it is less hazardous to grow tree crops such as cocoa and coconuts in Trinidad than in the other islands.

Soils

In contrast to Barbados, where the most important factor governing the soil type is the amount of rainfall, the soils of Trinidad owe their nature largely to the underlying rock. The complex geology of the island has given rise to a diversity of soils within short distances. This in turn has affected agriculture. For instance, the recent decline in cocoa has been most marked in areas where the soil is least suited to the crop.

The rocks of the Northern Range produce a poor, shallow soil best left in forest. Where clearings have been made, soil erosion has occurred. Only the valleys are suitable for cultivation, and these have long supported cocoa.

In the Caroni Plain there is a marked contrast between the clays, which are fertile and intensively cultivated, and the larger areas of sands and gravels which are poor and of little use. In parts of the Central Range there are clays which form the best cocoa soils in the island. The silts and clays of the Naparima Plain are also very good, especially round the Oropuche lagoon. The sands and clays of the Southern Range are less fertile and mostly forested.

Land use

One of the most striking features of Trinidad, as seen from the air, is the way so much of it appears to be forested, especially in the highlands. In fact, as Diagram 6.9 shows, 46 per cent of the total land area is classified as forest and woodland, but it appears

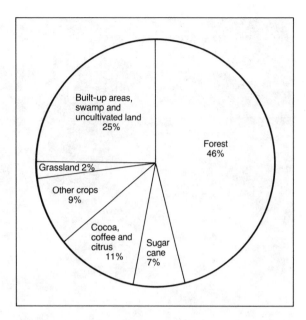

Diagram 6.9 Land use in Trinidad.

to be much more than this because of the cocoa, citrus, coffee and other tree crops grown in the country. From the air, cocoa is especially hard to distinguish from the forests because it is usually grown beneath shade trees.

Agriculture

Sugar

The sugar industry of Trinidad had not been in existence for long when it was beset by the problems that affected all British West Indian sugar producers of the nineteenth century (see pages 42–44). As we have seen, the labour shortage that followed the emancipation of the slaves was met by employing indentured Indian immigrants. In addition, costs were reduced by making use of many new discoveries to improve yields in both field and factory. Even so, towards the end of the century the owners of many small estates found themselves unable to compete with subsidised European beet sugar. They had to close their mills and plant other crops or sell out to large estates which alone could survive this period of depression. The change was a rapid one.

One of Trinidad's sugar factories. Draw a sketch map of the area in the picture to show land use and settlement.

The first central – the Usine Ste Madeleine, near San Fernando – was built in 1870. Thirty years later almost all the sugar production was in the hands of a few firms. Cane fields, once widespread throughout the island, became concentrated around the new big factories in a belt extending down the western side from the Caroni Plain to the Oropuche lagoon. Here, on flat or gently rolling land, large areas of cane could be planted. Here, too, the climate was most suitable.

Since then there has been an increasing concentration of sugar cane in this belt. Very little else is grown there today and very little cane is grown elsewhere. Changes do take place on the eastern margin, however, with the area under cane expanding in good times and contracting in poor times.

The 1980s have been poor times for sugar in Trinidad. Most of the money available for national development has been spent on developing petroleum, natural gas, and the industries that depend on them, not on sugar. Farming and production methods have become increasingly out of date. Yields have declined. Production costs have risen to the point where they are several times higher than the world market sugar price. Output has fallen from a peak of 250 000 tonnes in 1965 to under 100 000 tonnes in 1989. It might well have ceased altogether if the government had not bought the factories and

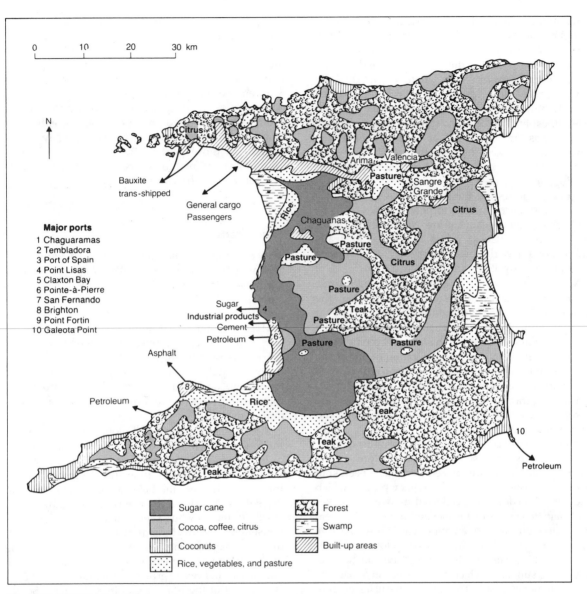

Map 6.10 TRINIDAD: Land use and major ports.

subsidised their production in order to prevent the 40 000 people engaged in the sugar industry from being thrown out of work.

Sugar exports in 1986 were 57 000 tonnes. These, together with molasses and rum amounted to a little over 2 per cent of the exports. The local consumption of sugar was about 60 000 tonnes.

Cocoa

In the late nineteenth century falling sugar prices and the rapidly expanding world market for cocoa and chocolate candy encouraged the spread of cocoa-growing in Trinidad. The area under cocoa rose from 25 000 acres in 1880 to 336 000 acres in 1913 (about equal to the total area being cultivated today). Cocoa was the island's leading export from 1900 until 1920, when 34 000 tonnes were exported. Then a decline set in. One reason for this was the remarkable increase of cocoa exports from Ghana (then called the Gold Coast). As a result, the price of cocoa fell sharply and it was no longer worthwhile to plant new trees in Trinidad. A second reason for the decline was the appearance of 'witches broom' disease which attacked many of the trees. The whole country was affected and some areas went out of production altogether.

Attempts to restore the industry have been made by carrying out research into new varieties of cocoa and selling young plants at low cost. They have not been successful. Cocoa prices have been unsteady and exports have declined, averaging 2 000 tonnes a year in the early 1980s and less since then.

Most of the cocoa is grown on small farms. Though it still takes up more land than sugar, the area under cocoa is only one-third of what it was at its maximum. Less is grown in the valleys of the Northern Range, some of which have become built-up areas, thus providing an illustration of one of the most serious problems facing the West Indies. With a rapidly rising population there is a need for increased agricultural output, but houses are spreading over the very land on which crops can best be produced.

As the price of cocoa depends partly on its quality, most growers process their beans before selling them. When the freshly picked pods have been split open, the beans and some of the juicy pulp in which they are embedded, are collected in sweating boxes and left to ferment for several days. The heat generated during fermentation partially cooks the beans and gives them their brown colour and their flavour. The beans are then spread out on trays to dry in the sun, after which they are put in a machine which removes any last remaining particles of pulp and gives the beans a smooth, shiny surface. Most of the cocoa is exported to Britain, where it is blended with less highly flavoured West African cocoa, but some is manufactured locally into chocolate and other products.

Citrus and coffee

Citrus first became important in the 1930s when many trees were planted in badly stricken cocoa areas and on some old sugar and coconut lands. Fresh grapefruit and oranges, and canned juice and segments, are exported to several countries including neighbouring CARICOM territories, especially Barbados, where very little fruit is grown but there is a demand boosted by tourists.

Coffee is another tree crop to become more prominent since the decline of cocoa. As with other cash crops, farmers have not been able to pay wages as high as those paid by the petroleum industry Output has declined to between 1 000 and 2 000 tonnes per year in the late 1980s.

Other crops

Two other crops commonly intermixed with cocoa are bananas and tonca beans. The supply of bananas is sufficient to meet local requirements. Tonca beans are exported, and are of use in the manufacture of perfumes and in flavouring tobacco.

Most of Trinidad's coconuts are grown on large estates near the sea. Output from Trinidad, and from Tobago, is insufficient to meet the needs of the industries making soap, edible oil and other foodstuffs, and there are considerable imports of copra from CARICOM countries and vegetable oils from elsewhere.

Rice is cultivated on small plots of land, mainly in the low, swampy areas of the Oropuche lagoon and on the fringes of the Caroni Swamp. It is grown in the wet season between June and December and for the rest of the year the fields are often planted with vegetables. Nearly all the rice is produced by Indian small farmers who keep most of it for their households. Many Indians with jobs such as taxi-driving, hairdressing, shopkeeping and tailoring grow a little rice as a subsidiary occupation. A small quantity of hill rice is grown in the interior. But over 80 per cent of the island's requirements have be imported, mainly from Guyana.

On the Caroni Plain not far from Port of Spain there is an abandoned sugar estate which has been divided up into holdings of one to three acres. On these holdings small farmers and their families grow about a third of the island's market garden produce, such as tomatoes, eggplants, melons, cauliflowers, cabbages, peppers, lettuce and string beans. This is some of the most intensively cultivated land in the West Indies.

Although Trinidad is self-sufficient in fresh

vegetables, large quantities of potatoes, yams and other root crops are imported from the United States and from the nearby islands of St Vincent and Grenada.

By comparing Diagrams 5.7 and 6.9 it can be seen that the proportion of pasture land in Trinidad is much smaller than that of Jamaica. Trinidad's live-stock industry is therefore comparatively small, and considerable imports of animal products are re-quired. These and other food imports, though large, could easily be paid for while petroleum exports fetched a high price as they did from 1974 until 1982. This is no longer the case, and Trinidad needs an agricultural revival. If it takes place, it will be the fourth major change in the island's economy. The first was the change from primitive agriculture to sugar; the second from sugar to cocoa; and the third was the rise of the petroleum industry.

Forestry

Apart from a few patches of savanna on the plains the whole of Trinidad was once forested. The rainy flanks of the Northern Range were clothed with tropical evergreen forest and, their summits with montane forest. Evergreen seasonal forest covered most of the rest of the island, with deciduous seasonal forest in the drier areas and thousands of acres of mangroves in the swamps. Some of these forests remain and some have been cleared for agriculture. Much more would have been cleared if the sugar industry had developed earlier, for in those days wood was the fuel used in factories. Ter-ritories developed before Trinidad all have smaller proportions of forest. Thus Jamaica has 18 per cent under forest, St Kitts 17 per cent, and Barbados vir-tually none.

Though most of the forest in Trinidad is owned by the government, timber is cut by a number of private concerns, which together produce about two-thirds of the island's requirements. Teak, mora, mahoe cedar and mahogany are among the trees most in demand for building and for making charcoal and furniture. Mangroves provide both charcoal and bark for tanning leather. Matches are made and sold to a number of CARICOM countries.

The Forest Department is carrying out a large replanting programme, especially with teak and pitch pine, Teak, one of the most beautiful hardwoods, takes many years to mature, but the constant thinning of the stands provides a certain amount every year. Pitch pine, a useful softwood, grows more quickly. It has the further advantage that it will grow in poor sandy soils. It is being used to reforest parts of the Northern Range to help prevent flash floods there.

Fishing

Fish are landed in the Cedros and Icacos areas of the south-west peninsula, and in Port of Spain, San Fer-nando, and elsewhere. In addition to white fish there is a considerable catch of shrimps. Trinidad supplies about half of its fish requirements.

Because the sea around Trinidad has been over-fished, many Trinidadian fishing boats operate in the shallow water close to the South American con-tinent, where they have sometimes got into trouble with the Venezuelan and Brazilian authorities. This is one example out of many in the world in which the rights of fishermen to approach foreign coastlines have given rise to disagreement between one nation and another. The two sides of the case, and varying opinions about the legal limits of ter-ritorial waters, are all issues worth discussing.

Industry

As we have seen, a number of large industries, in-cluding artificial fertilisers, petrochemicals and steel products, have grown up in recent years at Port Lisas. Nearby, at Claxton Bay, is the island's cement factory. Other industries in Trinidad include paints, detergents, textiles and clothing, boots, shoes and slippers, metal containers, boxes and cartons, glass bottles, pharmaceuticals, plastic goods, gramophone records, cigarettes, handbags, and many kinds of food and drink. In addition, some makes of cars, trucks, radios, television sets, stoves, air-conditioners and refrigerators are assembled. Assembly plants of this kind are examples of 'finishing touch' or 'screwdriver' industries which are being criticised by economists. These critics suggest that industries im-porting all their raw materials, paying little or no tax, exporting their profits, and paying lower wages than they would pay to workers in developed countries, are of little real value to the West Indies. This point of view is worth considering as the benefits of manufacturing should not always be taken for granted.

Location of Industry

There are seven factors which explain why manufacturing industries are located in particular places. Sometimes several of the factors operate together; sometimes one is sufficient to account for an industry.

1 The first factor is the availability of the money (known as 'capital') needed to build a factory and pay the workforce until the product makes a profit. In some countries, such as the United States, the European Community and Japan, the money comes mainly from individuals. This is private capital. In other countries, such as Russia and China, the money comes mainly from the government. This is state capital. In most developing countries, including the West Indies, the money comes mainly from abroad. This is foreign capital. Sometimes a foreign-owned company sets up a branch of its business in a developing country. Most West Indian manufacturing industries began in that way. Sometimes the money comes from overseas aid, in which case it may be provided by a single developed country such as Britain, or by the international community (eg through the World Bank). Where the money takes the form of a large loan, repaying the interest on the loan can be a severe strain on a developing country's financial resources.

2 The second factor is the work-force, that is the people needed to invent, engineer and design the product, manage the factory and organise its production, operate the machinery, undertake the office work, and market the product. Most foreign-owned companies operating in the Caribbean provide their own staff to fill senior posts until local people have been trained to take their place. In some cases the preference of one location over another may depend on the presence of cheap labour; in others it may depend on skilled labour.

3 The third factor is a market large enough and rich enough to buy the product. One reason why the United States, the European

Community and Japan are such important manufacturing countries is that they all have large populations with plenty of money to spend. In contrast, West Indian markets are small and relatively poor. A small factory employing only a handful of people may be able to supply a Caribbean country's entire needs for its product. Such a factory may have difficulty in competing with similar products made in much larger factories in other parts of the world. Its very survival may depend on being able to export some of its output (eg to other CARICOM countries).

4 The fourth factor is the presence nearby of one or more of the raw materials used in making the product. This factor is particularly important when the raw material is perishable. For example, sugar extraction and fruit canning have to take place close to where the crops are grown. The factor is also important where the raw material is so heavy that it is not economical to transport it over a long distance. For example, the West Indian cement and alumina industries are located close to the sources of their main raw material.

5 The fifth factor is the transport needed to carry the raw materials to the factory and take away the finished product. The cheapest form of transport is water. Easy access to the sea or a lake or a big river can be as important as proximity to raw materials in locating an industry. Petroleum refining is an example. The oil refineries of Trinidad, and many others elsewhere in the world, have been built close to the source of crude petroleum. But because oil tankers can carry huge loads at low cost, other refineries – such as those in Jamaica and Western Europe – have been built close to the market for their refined products. Air transport is most expensive. It is used to carry high-priced goods which weigh little and take up little space. Computers, calculators and other electronic goods are examples. Road transport is the most flexible. It is the only form of modern transport by which goods can be carried from door to door.

6 The sixth factor is the power supply. Some industrial processes, such as the manufacture of glass, pottery and chemicals, and the smelting of iron, aluminium and other metals, require a great deal of heat. For them a cheap source of fuel is essential. Some countries (eg Australia) possess large supplies of coal. Others (eg Norway) have hydro-electricity. Others (eg Britain) have petroleum. Many use all three. Generally in the West Indies, fuel is expensive. The exception is Trinidad which alone possesses large quantities of natural gas.

7 The seventh factor is government support for industry. Such support can take several different forms. For example, a government may provide an industry with free or inexpensive factory space. It may allow an industry to pay no taxes for a number of years. It may protect an industry from foreign competitors by charging a high duty on their imports or refusing them entry to the country. It may even provide cash to enable industry to survive in times of financial crisis. Many West Indian industries owe their existence to government support in one form or another.

Population

The population of Trinidad is perhaps the most mixed of all West Indian islands. There are still some traces of the Arawaks. There are small proportions of Europeans from many different countries including descendants of indentured Portuguese labourers, of Chinese, Syrians, Jews and Latin Americans. But the bulk of the population is of African and Indian descent, with each group contributing about 41 per cent of the total when the 1980 census was taken. In this respect Trinidad bears a closer resemblance to Guyana than to any West Indian island. As in Guyana, the two largest racial groups are concentrated in different areas, with less than one-fifth of the Indians living in the main towns of Port of Spain, San Fernando, Arima and Point Fortin at the time of the 1980 census. Also as in Guyana there is little intermarriage between the two groups, which retain certain distinct social patterns, have somewhat different diets and homes and tend to be found doing certain types of jobs and not others. The greatest distinction is in religion, and in 1980 there were 263 000 Hindus, 63 000 Muslims, and 606 000 Christians (over half of whom were Roman Catholics) in Trinidad and Tobago. Racial

considerations also play a part in voting in elections, though the political parties are inter-racial.

The complexity of the situation makes it hard to define. Some sociologists consider that Trinidad and the other West Indian territories are examples of 'plural societies' in which the different races mix but do not combine; they live side by side but have little in common and little desire for integration. Others dispute this, believing that there is sufficient inter-racial co-operation to create a national identity and to tackle national problems.

No matter where you live in the Caribbean, good points can be made on both sides of the case about your society. Which viewpoint do you believe to be true? What factors are helping or hindering closer integration among whatever groups exist? Do you think that, as time goes by, people will get on with one another better, or worse, than they do now?

Despite the number of people who are emigrating from Trinidad to the United States, Canada, and elsewhere, the population continues to grow. At the time of the 1960 census it was about 795 000; at the 1970 census about 892 000; and at the 1980 census about 1 039 000. By 1988 it was estimated to be 1 230 000. This gave a density of 255 per square kilometre, which was somewhat higher than that of Jamaica.

An indication of the density of population in different parts of Trinidad is shown in Map 6.11.

Constructing a Population Density Map

To make a population density map like the one of Trinidad (Map 6.11) or the one of Jamaica (Map 5.15) you need three items of information. The first is a map showing the boundaries of the administrative districts (called wards in Trinidad and parishes in Jamaica). The second and third are the area of each administrative district and its population as recorded by the census.

Once you have that information, a population density map is easy to construct. You begin by calculating the population density of each administrative district by dividing the number of people living there by the area of the district. Then you group together the districts with similar densities; for example, all the districts with less than fifty people per square kilometre, and, at the other extreme, all those with over a thousand people per square kilometre. Five or six such groupings are usually sufficient. Next you choose a different shade or colour for each group: for example, black for the highest density; white for the lowest; and shades of grey in between. Finally, you shade or colour the map and add a key to explain what the shades or colours stand for.

The result is a clear and accurate picture of the population density of a country's administrative districts. However, such a map has a big disadvantage. It does not show differences of population density *within* any of the districts. For example, a district with an overall population density of 280 people per square kilometre may contain a densely peopled town and a sparsely peopled swamp. This sort of population map cannot show such differences. Making a map which does show them is a complicated and time-consuming task. Even where the work is done by a skilled geographer or atlas maker, the result contains a certain amount of guesswork.

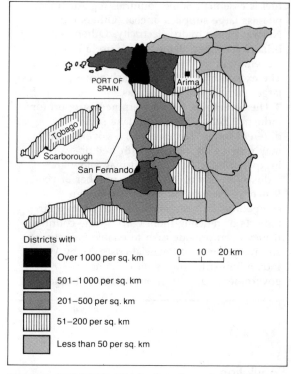

Map 6.11 TRINIDAD: Distribution of population (1980 census).

Population densities

From the map we can see at a glance the contrast between the districts with a high population density in the west of Trinidad and those with a low density in the east. In actual fact the forested mountain areas and swamps are the most sparsely settled. More people live in regions where tree crops are grown, the typical settlement pattern here being one of small villages strung out along the roads. In the sugar belt the villages are much larger. Many of them have East Indian names and are peopled largely by Indians who still form the bulk of the field labourers.

The most marked concentration of population extends from the capital, Port of Spain, eastwards along the foot of the Northern Range. Here a number of villages, which originally grew up at the valley mouths as collecting centres for cocoa, are merging together as they grow and are losing their separate identities. The biggest of these is Arima with a population of about 25 000. There are also pockets of dense settlement in the ports, all of which are situated on the sheltered Gulf of Paria. The east coast, in contrast, is sparsely settled. The long

sandbars in some places and the rough, rocky stretches in others make it almost unapproachable from the sea.

Towns

Port of Spain grew up at the only place in the island where there was both a sheltered harbour and easy overland communication with the main farming areas.

Until 1939 Port of Spain's development as a port was handicapped by the shallowness of the harbour. Large ocean-going ships had to anchor two to three miles off shore and be loaded and unloaded by barges. Then a deep-water channel was dredged to the shore, and new port facilities were built on land reclaimed from the sea. Since then the port has been further enlarged and modernised. It handles all the passenger traffic and virtually all the island's imports except crude petroleum. Exports, however, are much

A view from the central business district of Port of Spain towards the sea. Note (a) the swimming pool (part of a downtown hotel); (b) the shipping and the wharves; and (c) a new high-rise building being constructed.

less important because petroleum is exported from Pointe-à-Pierre, Point Fortin, Brighton and Galeota Point; sugar, chemicals and industrial products from Point Lisas; and cement from Claxton Bay (see Map 6.10). In addition, the bauxite carried in small vessels from Guyana and Suriname is trans-shipped into large ocean-going ships not at Port of Spain but at two terminals further west (see Map 6.12).

Immediately to the north of the port area is the central business district of Port of Spain. This has long been the island's main shopping centre. In addition, it was once the largest residential area. In recent years, however, fewer and fewer people have their homes there. Some of the downtown properties have been replaced by modern high-rise buildings occupied by offices and banks. The main government buildings are also located there. Elsewhere within the central business district, houses have been converted with little change for office and business use. This sort of change is still going on, and the central business district is expanding northwards and westwards.

Beyond the central business district lie the residential areas, very densely peopled on the eastern side, less so to the west and north. Suburbs have spread westwards to Chaguaramas and northwards over the foothills of the mountains and up into the Diego Martin and Maraval valleys. If these are included, the population of Port of Spain is over 250 000, making it the second largest city in the Commonwealth Caribbean.

Port of Spain is not a major industrial town. However, a number of light industries have been built for several miles along the road leading eastwards from the central business district.

San Fernando (40 000), the second largest town in Trinidad, is situated about 50 kilometres south of the capital. It lies at the foot and on the lower slopes of

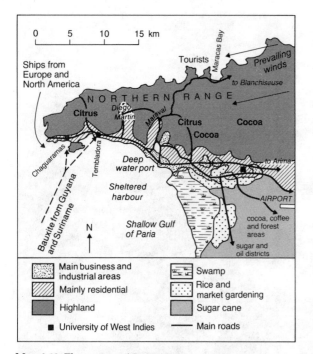

Map 6.12 The setting of Port of Spain.

a 180-metre hill which stands out boldy from the surrounding plain, as can be seen in the photograph on page 85. It began as a small fishing village and grew to prominence when the south-western part of Trinidad was developed for sugar and cocoa. With the building of good roads and a railway to Port of Spain its importance as a port and a warehousing centre both declined. Now, though the port and the railway have both gone, San Fernando is a busy, growing town. It serves as a shopping centre for the nearby sugar district surrounding the Usine Ste Madeleine, the oil refinery at Pointe-á-Pierre and the area beyond. It is also the headquarters of some government offices serving southern Trinidad. The roads connecting San Fernando and Port of Spain are the busiest in the island.

Communications

As Map 6.4 shows, main roads connect Port of Spain with most parts of the island. Only the Northern Range provides a major barrier and there is still no road running along the length of the north coast. This is a handicap to the tourist industry, for it is here that the island's best beaches are to be found. With cheap gasolene and plentiful supplies of asphalt to surface the roads, Trinidad, as might be expected, has a large number of cars. Traffic density is particularly high on the roads between Port of Spain and Arima. To relieve some of the congestion the tracks of the old railway that used to serve this area have been replaced by a road which carries express buses into the central business district of Port of Spain.

Piarco airport, about 27 kilometres out of Port of Spain, handles all the passenger and air cargo traffic in and out of Trinidad. Because it can take larger planes than the airport in Tobago it is also the main point of entry and departure for overseas visitors visiting Tobago.

Trade

Not only does Trinidad have a larger overseas trade than any other Commonwealth Caribbean territory, it is the only one where the value of exports in most years exceeds the value of imports. The major exports in 1986 are shown in Table 6.13. The figures are in millions of Trinidad and Tobago dollars.

Table 6.13 Major Exports from Trinidad and Tobago in 1986 (TT$ million)

Crude petroleum	1 986
Petroleum products	1 524
Ammonia and fertilisers	621
Steel products	238
Sugar, molasses, rum	115
Other exports	397
Total	4 881

Tobago

Area: 303 square kilometres; population (1988) about 42 000; density of population: 139 per square kilometre.

A sea passage of only 32 kilometres separates Tobago from the north-east tip of Trinidad. Yet this island, 41 kilometres long by 12 kilometres wide, shows few similarities to Trinidad. In size it is like the nearby islands to the north, but it differs from them in having no recent vulcanism.

Landforms

Running from the north-east tip south-westwards for about two-thirds of the length of Tobago are the forested mountains of the Main Ridge which rise very steeply from the north coast to a maximum height of about 570 metres. Their gentler southern slopes are deeply indented by valleys which run down to a narrow but fertile coastal plain. Though the northern slopes of the Main Ridge are made of metamorphic rocks similar to those of the Northern Range in Trinidad, the mountains are mainly composed of igneous material. This rock, which covers over half the area of the island, weathers easily to produce the most fertile soils in Tobago.

The south-western part of the island is very different. With the exception of a few small hills in the centre this area is made of a series of flat coral terraces nowhere more than 45 metres high, giving the landscape an appearance rather like that of Barbados.

Rainfall

Rainfall is heaviest on the summits and northern slopes of the Main Ridge, where in places it exceeds 3 800 millimetres a year. It decreases towards the south and south-west which is in the rain shadow and has under 1 000 millimetres a year. In the south-west the low rainfall and the porous nature of the

Looking over Little Tobago Island to Tobago. By looking at the maps on the next page, say in which direction the camera was pointing. In what ways is this sort of landscape a handicap to development?

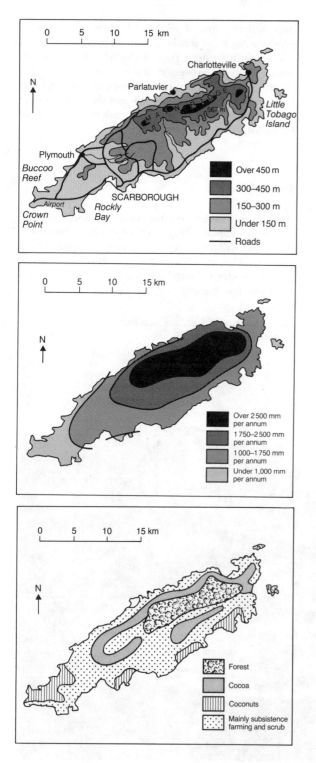

Map 6.14 TOBAGO: Relief.
Map 6.15 TOBAGO: Rainfall.
Map 6.16 TOBAGO: Land use.

coral rock makes the provision of water for coconuts and livestock a problem, particularly in the dry months – February, March and April.

Development

During the sixteenth and seventeenth centuries the prized sugar, cotton and indigo plantations of Tobago were the cause of repeated disputes between the English, French and Dutch, and the island changed hands more often than any other in the Caribbean. By the beginning of the nineteenth century sugar was by far the most important crop and the island was prosperous. But a decline set in which was intensified when the island's 11 000 slaves were freed in 1838 and a severe hurricane struck Tobago in 1847. Some sugar estates struggled on for a while by introducing the 'metayer' system under which people were allowed to cultivate small plots on the estate land provided they sent their cane to the estate-owner, who extracted the sugar and took half the crop. This could do no more than postpone the collapse made inevitable by falling sugar prices in Britain and the lack of sufficient suitable lowland in Tobago to support a large central factory. One by one the small mills ceased to operate, and many cane fields reverted to bush. By 1886 the island's exports were worth only one-tenth of those of 1839. Two years later, economic distress forced Tobago to amalgamate with the nearby richer and more powerful colony of Trinidad.

With the decline of sugar, new crops had to be established. Many estates, notably those on the windward side, gave out allotments to peasants, who in return for tending young cocoa plants were allowed to grow their own food crops until the trees came into bearing. Cocoa was also planted by immigrants from Grenada, attracted to Tobago by the sale of government-owned lands there. Today, cocoa is the outstanding cash crop. It occupies about a third of the cultivated land.

Estates on the leeward side also used the allotment system to increase their production of coconuts, which now take up more land than cocoa, though they are not as valuable. Other estates, particularly those in the centre of the island, sold or leased their land to small farmers who have since cultivated cocoa, bananas and other produce, and kept live-stock. Tobacco, another small farmers' crop, is grown in the south-west and sent for sale in Trinidad.

Although about 40 per cent of the island is cul-tivated, agriculture is not as prosperous as it could be. In some peasant areas soil erosion has become serious and yields are poor. This may be the reason why in recent years the sale of food crops to Port of Spain has virtually ceased, and at times Tobago has to buy them from Trinidad. In other areas, par-ticularly the mountainous north-east and the north coast between Parlatuvier and Charlotteville, com-munications are so poor that the exploitation of forests and the cultivation of cocoa and bananas is difficult or altogether impossible. In addition to these problems, Hurricane Flora in 1963 destroyed about half the coconuts in the island, and plant diseases are affecting cocoa and coconut trees. They have al-most wiped out the old lime industry.

The people

Unlike Trinidad, Tobago has few Indians, and nearly 95% of the population is of African descent. Num-bers are rising more slowly than in neighbouring islands because of the drift of young people to Trinidad where there are more varied opportunities for employment.

Most of the people live in the south-west, in the central belt, and along the coast. There are many small agricultural villages but the only two towns of importance are Scarborough and Plymouth. Scar-borough (2 000) is the chief market, as it has the best access to the most productive cocoa and coconut districts. Its harbour is poor, however, being reached with some difficulty through a narrow channel in a reef. Partly for this reason, and partly because Tobago is dependent on sea and air transport to Trinidad and has little direct contact with overseas markets, the town is still a small one. It does not dominate the settlement pattern as do the chief towns in the other West Indian islands.

Communications

Except in the south-west, road communications in Tobago are poor. As we have seen, this has retarded agricultural development. Some parts of the north coast are cut off to such an extent that they have to rely on an intermittent shipping service. The main shipping link, including a car ferry service, is between Scarborough and Port of Spain. The airport at Crown Point in the extreme south-west cannot take large jet aircraft. This is a handicap to the island's tourist trade.

Tourism

Tobago has been called 'Robinson Crusoe Island' from the belief that Daniel Defoe's story of that name had its setting there. This is in itself a tourist attraction and a number of small hotels have been built to accommodate visitors, most of whom come from North America and Trinidad. There is good bathing on the sheltered, white-sand beaches, fish-ing at Buccoo Reef, and most tourists make at least one trip to Little Tobago Island – 3 kilometres off-shore – where there is a sanctuary for birds of paradise, which were introduced there many years ago from the Dutch East Indies.

Questions and assignments

1 a) Trace an outline map of Trinidad leaving space for the surrounding sea. On your map mark and label i) a mountainous area; ii) an area of swamp, iii) an area where sugar cane is grown, iv) an oil field, v) a natural gas field, vi) a place where natural asphalt is obtained, vii) an oil refinery, viii) a place where petrochemicals are produced, ix) an area where market garden crops are grown, and x) a place where fishing is carried out.
   b) Give two conditions which are suitable for the growth of: i) sugar cane, ii) cocoa, iii) market garden produce.

2 Use this table to answer the following questions:

Trinidad's oil refinery products

Product	Thousands of Barrels	
	1978	1986
Motor gasolene	16 800	8 621
Jet fuel	2 200	2 470
Kerosene	4 501	607
Diesel oil	10 134	4 010
Fuel oil	45 480	18 001

a) What was the output of kerosene in 1978 and in 1986?

b) Which product increased output between 1978 and 1986?

c) What was the decline in output of motor gasolene between 1978 and 1986? What was the percentage decline?

d) What was the decline in output of kerosene between 1978 and 1986? What was the percentage decline?

e) Compare the percentage decline of diesel oil and fuel oil?

f) Give one reason to explain the overall decline in refined products over the period.

3 Name: a) three uses of natural gas, and b) two products of the petrochemical industry.

c) Compare the petrochemical industry with the garment industry under the following heads:
i) capital, ii) labour, iii) raw materials, iv) transport, and v) markets.

4 a) Give one difference between the distribution of rainfall in Trinidad and Jamaica, and one reason for the difference.

b) Give one difference between the seasonal rainfall of Trinidad and Jamaica, and one reason for the difference.

5 Using Diagram 6.8:
a) Write down the average monthly rainfall figures for Trinidad in a table like Table 2.4.

b) Using the method given on page 19 say which months are wet, moist and dry.

c) If all 12 months had the same amount of rainfall, what percentage would fall in any three-month period? What is the actual percentage that falls in the three-month rainy season and in the *petit carême?*

6 a) Name three heavy industries in Trinidad.

b) Give three reasons to explain why this is the most important area of heavy industry in the Commonwealth Caribbean.

7 a) Using the following census figures, draw a graph to show the rise of population in Trinidad and Tobago:

Trinidad and Tobago Census Figures (to the nearest thousand)

| 1871 | 127 000 | 1891 | 218 000 | 1911 | 334 000 |
| 1931 | 413 000 | 1960 | 834 000 | 1980 | 1 080 000 |

b) In what years do you think the population reached $\frac{1}{4}$ million, $\frac{1}{2}$ million, 1 million? Extend your graph and find what you think the population will be in 1995 and 2000.

8 For Port of Spain:
a) Give three reasons to explain why it is the biggest population centre in Trinidad.

b) Describe three major kinds of land use within the town.

c) Explain why the residential population of the city centre is declining.

d) Name two problems of rapid urban growth, and give two ways by which each of them might be overcome.

9 From the information given in Question 2 calculate the percentage value of each of the exports in 1986. Construct a divided circle to show those percentages.

7

Barbados

Area: 430 square kilometres; population (1988): about 254 000; density of population: 591 per square kilometre.

Development

Barbados, the most easterly of the West Indian islands, is not really a part of the chain of the Lesser Antilles as it lies in the Atlantic Ocean about 170 kilometres east of its nearest neighbour, St Vincent. Map 8.1 shows this clearly. The island was known to Europeans at least as early as 1536, at which time it was covered with forest and woodland. Today, only a few acres of this vegetation remain. They are located on part of the rim of highland that overlooks the Scotland District.

The early development of Barbados took place in two stages, each lasting for about twenty years. In the first stage, British settlers established farms on the lowlands on the leeward side of the island and along the fertile vale that runs eastwards from Bridgetown across the island. Tobacco, indigo, fustic and cotton were grown for export, and maize, yams, cassava and plantains for food. Though a few of the workers on the first farms were Amerindian slaves brought from the Guianas to teach the settlers how to grow their crops, most were white indentured servants. Black slaves formed only a small proportion of the population.

In the second stage of development the social and economic life of Barbados underwent a complete change. Between 1647 and 1667 sugar cane became the dominant crop taking up 80 per cent of the cultivated area. In the same period the number of landowners fell from 11 200 to 745 as small properties were bought up and combined into plantations. The few who increased their land holdings became rich; those who sold out had no future, and some 30 000 people left Barbados and went to live in other West Indian islands, Suriname and North America. Their place was taken by about the same number of African slaves.

The landscape and the way of life that had come into being by 1670 remained unchanged for nearly three centuries. There were cane fields on all but the steepest, driest and least fertile land along with small, densely populated villages. There was a large overseas trade consisting of the export of sugar and the import of almost everything that was needed in the island, including food, clothing and timber. The white population numbered between 15 000 and 18 000, consisting of plantation owners, managers, traders, smallholders, poor whites, and their families. And there was a growing black population which totalled 83 000 at the time of emancipation in 1834.

Emancipation brought little change to the way of life of the people. Because of the dry conditions the planters were unable to find an alternative crop to cane. They were faced with the double problem of providing work for large numbers of labourers and of overcoming the recurrent crises that struck the sugar industry throughout the nineteenth century. They did so by keeping operations on a relatively small scale, by limiting the use of labour-saving devices and by raising yields per acre.

With a population density of about 390 per square kilometre at the time of the emancipation of the slaves, and a rising population ever since, Barbados has not been able to provide adequate opportunities for employment and there have been several waves of emigration. At different times, migrants have gone to Trinidad, Guyana and Suriname, Central

America and the Panama Canal Zone, the Netherlands Antilles, the United States and Britain.

In spite of this migration and in spite of the fact that the birth-rate is one of the lowest in the region, Barbados has become by far the most densely peopled Caribbean territory. Population pressure on limited land area is one of the greatest problems in the island.

Landforms

The rocks forming the basement of Barbados are called the Scotland Series. They consist of thick layers of sedimentary rocks, mainly shales, sands, clays and conglomerates laid down in the shallow, muddy sea that must have existed in the region some 60 to 70 million years ago. Later these rocks were folded, faulted and uplifted by a great earth movement. After a considerable period they were submerged deep beneath the sea, where they were covered by deposits of a white clay-like rock known as the Oceanic Series. Finally, in the period beginning about 600 000 years ago and lasting until geologically recent times, these rocks were covered by a cap of coral formed in very shallow water. This coral is the most important rock today. It reaches a maximum thickness of 100 metres and extends over the surface of the whole island except the Scotland District of the north-east where erosion has stripped it away to expose the older underlying rocks.

The highest point in Barbados is Mount Hillaby (about 335 metres) in the north centre of the island. From here the land falls on the northern, western, and southern sides by a series of coral terraces. The edges of the terraces are old cliffs cut in the rock by the sea during the Ice Age, when the island was being uplifted by an earth movement. It is believed that some of the cliffs were formed during long cold

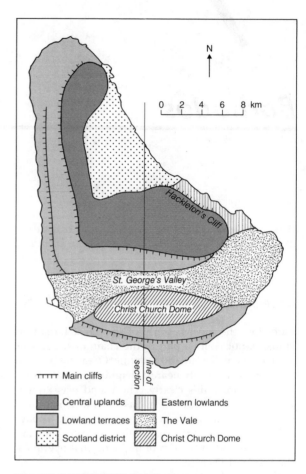

Map 7.1 BARBADOS: Main physical regions.

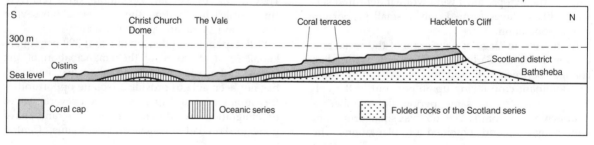

Diagram 7.2 Section from South to North through part of Barbados. The line of the section is shown on Map 7.1.

periods when the sea around Barbados was 30 to 100 metres lower than it is today, and that others were formed in warmer intervals when the sea was higher than its present level. The longest and highest cliffs are shown on Map 7.1. They are sheer rock walls up to 30 metres in height and several kilometres in length. Most of the terrace edges, however, are low, less steep, and either covered with grass or occupied by houses.

Eastwards from the highest terrace there is a great contrast. The land falls steeply for many metres and in some places by a sheer cliff to the narrow eastern lowlands and the vast amphitheatre of the Scotland District, which takes up about one-seventh of the island. In this area the streams that rise during periods of heavy rain have carved deep ravines in the soft clays while the more resistant sandstones remain as knife-edged ridges. Here, too landslides are

frequent, and at times great masses of the coral cap break off and fall on to the land below as shown in Diagram 3.3 on page 36. As we shall see in the section dealing with soils the natural processes of erosion have proceeded much more quickly since the land was first cleared for cultivation.

South of the main highland mass a broad vale runs from east to west across the widest part of the island. Southwards, again the land rises to nearly 120 metres at the summit of the Christ Church dome before dropping first to the terrace on which the airport has been built, then to a lower terrace, and then to the sea. These physical regions are shown on Map 7.1 and on the section which has been drawn from the Scotland District to the south coast (Diagram 7.2). Apart from the Atlantic coast where wave attack is too powerful to permit vigorous coral growths, there are off-shore coral reefs. If these were uplifted by a small earth movement they would form new terraces just like the others in the island.

Coral limestone has the power to absorb a lot of water, with the result that most of the rain falling on it soaks into it. In addition, the acids contained in rain and ground water have dissolved many caves and sink-holes in the rock. The water flowing down through these adds to the supply which collects underground. As it can be easily reached by wells, it forms the most important source of water for domestic purposes. A little is also used for irrigation.

Surface drainage on the coral is non-existent, except for brief periods after heavy rains. In the past, however, for reasons that are still unknown, streams must have flowed there because they carved steep-sided gullies which in places are 30 metres deep and as much across. Bridges have had to be built in some places to enable roads to cross them.

Map 7.3 BARBADOS: Relief and communications.

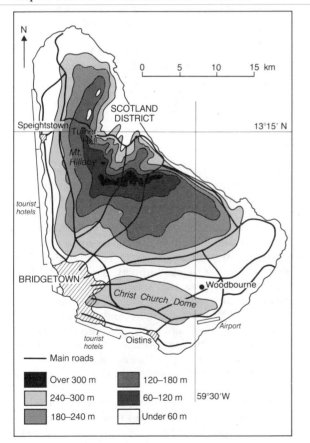

Main roads

Over 300 m

240–300 m

180–240 m

120–180 m

60–120 m

Under 60 m

Minerals

The coral limestone is a very good building material. It is also one of the raw materials used by the cement factory north of Speightstown on the west coast of the island. Another is shale from the Scotland District. Other minerals are less plentiful.

Enough petroleum was produced to supply over one-third of the country's needs in 1987. It comes from a number of wells at Woodbourne in the south centre of the island. Some of the wells are over a mile deep. It is used, together with imported crude oil, in a small refinery which makes gasolene, kerosene, diesel oil and fuel oil mainly for local consumption. For many years a small amount of natural gas has been obtained from two wells at Turner Hall and Spring Vale on the edge of the Scotland District. Recently new wells have come into production and output has increased. The gas is piped to Bridgetown and some of its suburbs mainly for domestic use.

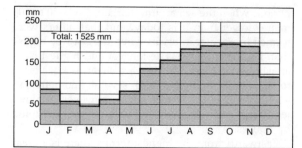

Diagram 7.5 Average monthly rainfall of Barbados.

Rainfall

The rainfall of Barbados is fairly evenly spread over the island. The wettest areas receive less than twice as much rain as the driest areas. By comparing Map

Map 7.4 BARBADOS: Rainfall.

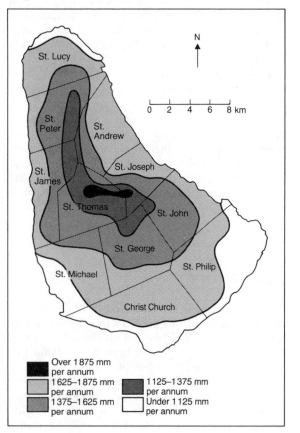

Over 1 875 mm per annum

1 625–1 875 mm per annum

1 375–1 625 mm per annum

1 125–1 375 mm per annum

Under 1 125 mm per annum

7.4 with Diagram 7.2, it can be seen that the reason for this is that no part of Barbados is high enough to be very wet. About three-quarters of the rainfall occurs in the six months from June to November. Only in the small area with over 1 900 millimetres a year is there no dry season: on the lowlands it lasts for four or five months. However, there are considerable variations from year to year. There can be twice as much rain in a wet year as there is in a dry one. Shortage of rainfall is always a cause for anxiety, as a drought or a delay in the arrival of a rainy season can seriously affect agriculture.

Soils

The most important factors determining the character of a soil are the underlying rock and the climate. Barbados shows both these relationships very clearly.

In the Scotland District the great variety of rocks has given rise to a diversity of soils, some of which are fertile, though most are so badly eroded that they will never again support good crops. Soil erosion in this area was serious before the seventeenth century ended. Gradually the cane fields went out of production, the abandoned land being used to graze sheep and goats. Uncontrolled grazing has made the situation worse, and in some places the soil has been stripped away altogether so that the underlying rock is exposed. This is shown on page 32.

Elsewhere, as we have seen, the island is covered with a coral cap and we might expect the overlying soil to be everywhere the same. But mainly because of differences in rainfall this is not so. On the highest land – that is, over 220 metres – where rainfall is heaviest, the soil is reddish or yellowish-brown in colour and supports the best cane. On the drier lowlands – that is, under 60 metres – it is black, less easy to work and usually not so fertile. In the St George's Valley, which forms part of the vale between the Christ Church anticline and the upland terraces, this black soil is much thicker than elsewhere and needs deep ploughing and draining, after which it becomes very fertile. In contrast, in the northern, eastern, and southern tips of the island it is thin. Here, too, conditions are generally dry, and these are the poorest agricultural areas in Barbados.

Mixed with the soil is a certain amount of volcanic dust, carried to Barbados by winds in the upper atmosphere during volcanic eruptions in the islands to the west. Barbados was covered with 3 to 4 centimetres of grey volcanic dust during the eruption of the St Vincent Soufrière in 1812. A further 35 tonnes per acre fell in the 1902 eruption and smaller quantities in 1979. These falls of ash improved the fertility of the soil.

Soil erosion

The early sugar planters found that the soil in their fields could quickly lose its fertility and be easily eroded. To prevent this from happening, they set up a farming system which was different from that of any other part of the Caribbean. New cane was planted in shallow holes instead of in long ploughed furrows where the soil was more easily washed away. In addition, one or more deep holes, known as 'sucks' were dug in each field to allow surplus rainwater to drain down to the underlying limestone. In recent times, machines have replaced labour on the land. Because fields are now being ploughed and not dug by hand, there are signs that some of the top soil is being washed away during heavy rains.

Because sucks are not always being kept open, there is a danger that the island's underground water supply may decrease. As we have seen all the water used by households and hotels, and for irrigation and other purposes, comes from underground. Maintaining the supply of water, and keeping it free from pollution, are difficult tasks in Barbados.

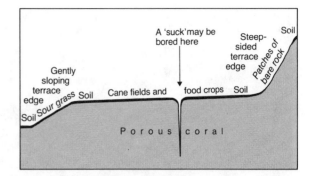

Diagram 7.6 Section across terrace to show the way the land is commonly used and drained.

Land use and tenure

Out of a total area of about 106 000 acres, some 44 000 acres were cultivated in the late 1980s, that is about one-third less than in the 1950s. Grassland took up about 4 000 acres. The remaining 58 000 acres were not used for agriculture. Some of it was taken up by urban development, including houses and gardens; some was lying unused.

Nearly 85 per cent of the cultivated land is owned by about 130 plantations, few of which are less than 50 acres or more than 1 000 acres in size. The remaining 15 per cent is taken up with smallholdings under 10 acres in size. As there are about 20 000 of these, their average area is only half an acre. These tiny plots were bought from plantations which, in order to survive, were forced to sell some of their land when sugar prices were low. The land they sold was the land they needed least. Most of it lay in areas of poor soil and low rainfall. Though it was suitable for house sites, and though in some coastal districts it has since become very valuable for tourist development, it was by no means the best land for agriculture. Even so, small farmers make an important contribution to agricultural output, producing about 10 per cent of the cane and root crops, and higher proportions of the island's vegetables, corn, peas, meat and milk. Some small farmers make all their income from their land, but most are part-time farmers with other jobs.

A Barbados plantation showing the factory and the Great House, with poor grass on a terrace edge and cane fields on the flatter ground. Draw a sketch map of the area around the factory.

Agriculture

Sugar

For over three centuries, sugar cane dominated the agriculture of Barbados. Even today there are many places in the island where cane is the only crop to be seen. The best growing areas are the upland terraces where the average rainfall is between 1 400 and 1 800 millimetres a year (see Map 7.4). Yields there remain high even in years of drought. In lower lying areas with a lower average rainfall, yields are good only in rainy years.

In recent years, sugar cane has become less dominant than it used to be. One reason for this is that only a limited amount of sugar can be sold to the European Economic Community at a good price under the Lomé Convention (see page 46). A second reason was the widespread but illegal burning of cane before harvesting in the 1960s and 70s. This reduced yields, profits and soil fertility. A third reason has been the difficulty of obtaining field labour. The wages are not high enough to attract a sufficient number of Barbadians to reap the crop,

and workers from elsewhere have had to be employed in the fields. To reduce the dependence on manpower, an increasing amount of cane is cut and loaded by machines. However, machines cannot be used in every field, and machine-cut cane produces less sugar per acre than cane that is cut and loaded by hand. Today the old and new methods can often be seen side by side, here and elsewhere in the West Indies.

Gradually the area under cane has been falling. Some of the land has been converted to other crops; some to pasture. Such crops as onions, carrots, okras, cucumbers, peppers, melons, pawpaws, yams and sweet potatoes are now grown in sufficient quantities to meet local needs, supply hotels, and be exported. Cut flowers are also important.

In the late 1980s sugar was being produced in four factories all owned by a single company in which the majority of the plantations were partners. In comparison with factories in other territories, those in Barbados are small. Though their number has decreased considerably in recent years, further reduction to one or two large modern factories is unlikely to occur, partly because of the amount of money that would be needed to build them, but mainly because the roads are too narrow to allow chains of cane carts or other large vehicles to use them for long distances. Another factory specialises in the production of fancy molasses, a high-quality product made from cane juice and sold in Canada and the United States for the manufacture of confectionery. Other products are rum, considered not only by Barbadians to be the best in the West Indies, and ordinary molasses.

All the sugar to be exported is taken by truck to the deep-water harbour at Bridgetown. Shipments, mainly to the European Economic Community totalled 70 000 tonnes in 1987. Together with molasses and rum they formed 30 per cent of total exports. Local consumption, and shipments to neighbouring islands, amount to about 15 000 tonnes a year.

Table 7.7 Changes in the production of sugar in Barbados

Years	1960–69	1970–79	1980–88
Average production (tonnes)	172 000	117 000	93 000

Cotton

Sea-island cotton has been grown on and off in Barbados for many years. It grows better than sugar cane in the driest areas, and there is a ready market for the product particularly in Japan. However, until high-quality cotton can be picked by machine, it is unlikely that output will rise to its former level when field labour was both plentiful and cheap. There were about 1 000 acres under cotton in 1987.

Various kinds of land use on the coral terraces. Compare this part of Barbados with the Scotland District shown on page 32.

Livestock

At the same time that the area under sugar cane has been falling, that under pasture has been growing. This growth has been accompanied by a rise in the number of livestock reared in the island. The government has encouraged this development. There is a ready market for meat, milk and dairy products in households and hotels. The more that can be produced locally, the less the country needs to spend on food imports. These imports are large. In the 1980s the amount of money spent on imported food has been nearly three times the amount earned by the export of sugar.

Fishing

As every source of food is valuable to this crowded island, it is fortunate that the waters around Barbados provide a fairly plentiful supply of fish. Flying fish, caught mainly between November and June, form the bulk of the catch. Besides supplying a large local demand, frozen flying fish are exported.

Though this is the biggest flying fish industry in the West Indies, it is insignificant in comparison with the cod and herring fisheries of Britain, Iceland and Newfoundland. The main reason for this is that the Caribbean Sea is not rich in fish. It contains no continental shelf like those of the west coast of Europe and the east coast of Canada on which trawlers can operate, and no up-welling currents of cold ocean water or large rivers to provide a plentiful supply of fish food.

Manufacturing

If you look at the factors that favour the growth of manufacturing industries (pages 94–5) you will see that Barbados does not possess them all. Thus, Barbados lacks the raw materials to support large factories other than those producing cement and sugar. It has no cheap source of energy: its output of petroleum and natural gas has to be supplemented with large and costly imports. The local market for manufactured goods is small. Both the cement and sugar industries depend on exports to be successful as their output is much greater than the local market can consume.

Despite these handicaps, Barbados has succeded in becoming by far the most important manufacturing country in the Eastern Caribbean. Good air, sea and telephone communications are one reason for this. Another is the presence of a large pool of educated and technically-trained workers. A third is that some American manufacturing companies have taken advantage of United States tax laws to send unfinished products, particularly electronic goods, to Barbados for completion, after which they are returned to the United States. The fourth and most important is the support that the Barbados government has given to the establishment of new industries. Several industrial parks have been established in various parts of the island, and this is where most of the island's new industries are located. Food manufacturing includes the conversion of imported copra into edible oils, lard and margarine, and the making of soft drinks, beer, biscuits and confectionery. General manufactures include furniture, mattresses, leather and plastic goods, garments, medical equipment and pharmaceuticals, transistor radio and computer parts, aluminium products, and tourist handicrafts. At Chalky Mount in the Scotland District there is a small, long-established pottery industry based on local supplies of clay. Elsewhere in the Scotland District bricks and tiles are made.

Tourism

Though Barbados had a small tourist industry before 1960, the growth of modern tourism started at about that date. By the mid-1970s the number of tourists visiting Barbados each year was about equal to the island's population. In 1977 the number rose to nearly 371 000. This was followed by a decline which

Table 7.8 Tourists visiting Barbados from 1981 to 1988 ('000)

1981	1982	1983	1984	1985	1986	1987	1988
353	304	328	367	359	370	422	451

lasted until 1986. The actual figures from 1981–88 are shown in Table 7.8. They are rounded off to the nearest thousand so that they can easily be shown in a bar-graph. If you draw such a bar-graph you will be able to see at a glance the changes that have taken place.

The figures in Table 7.8 show only those tourists who stay for a day or more in Barbados. They do not include the many visitors brought by cruise ships who land for a few hours to go sight-seeing, swimming and shopping. There were nearly 300 000 such visitors in 1988.

In the late 1980s money spent by tourists amounted to between two and three times the value of the island's exports, and over 12 per cent of the work force were engaged in tourism. The benefits are obvious, the problems less so. Nevertheless, the problems are worth considering. Four of them of particular concern to Barbados are:

1 Tourists do not arrive at a steady rate throughout the year, and there are two slack periods – one from May to June and the other from September to November – during which some employees directly and indirectly engaged in tourism lose their jobs.

2 Compared with other West Indian islands, a high proportion of the tourist accommodation consists of apartment blocks and beach houses. Unlike hotels these offer only low-paid domestic employment, with no opportunity to obtain promotion in catering, supervision and management.

3 A successful tourist industry depends on a good relationship being established between the visitors and the people they meet. New skills and personal qualities are required. If you list those that are needed by a sugar worker and by a hotel receptionist you will see how different they are, and how difficult it is for a society to make a rapid switch from agriculture to tourism.

4 Silt, pesticides and fertilisers from farmland together with sewage and dirty water from households and hotels have polluted parts of the sea around the coasts to such an extent that some of the coral reefs have been killed. As a result some of the beaches are no longer protected from wave attack. The government is having to take special measures to reduce sea pollution and prevent beach sand from being washed away.

Because the sea on the eastern side of Barbados is usually very rough, few hotels have been built there. Most of the tourist accommodation, the restaurants

and the boutiques are located in a narrow belt along the sheltered leeward coast. One area of intensive tourism extends south-eastwards from Bridgetown to Oistins. Another extends northwards from Bridgetown to Speightstown and beyond (see Map 7.3).

Population

The population of Barbados is less racially diverse than in most of the other West Indian territories. The 1980 census listed 92 per cent as black; of the remainder 3.3 per cent were white (the highest percentage of whites in the Commonwealth Caribbean), 0.5 per cent were Asian and 2.6 per cent were mixed. The small proportion of people of mixed descent shows that intermarriage between the black and white racial groups has always been infrequent. It remains so.

Some people feel that preserving the distinction is wrong and that one of the tasks of school geography is to create better inter-racial understanding. Others believe that after years of oppression and discrimination it is more important for black people to create a new identity for themselves than to form a close relationship with other races. Both opinions are worthy of respect if their intention is to improve social conditions, and both are worthy of discussion wherever you may live.

About half of the people live in rural areas, the other half in Bridgetown and its suburbs. As you will see, the photographs in this chapter show little sign of the dense rural population that actually exists. The reason for this is that there are large areas of unpopulated agricultural land and that where settlements do exist they are clustered on the edges of plantations and along the roads.

Bridgetown is the capital city, the only port, and the chief shopping, business and banking centre. Lying 800 kilometres closer to Europe than does Jamaica, it is the first port of call for many ships coming to the Caribbean. In consequence it has become the chief commercial centre in the Lesser Antilles, with a considerable re-export trade to neighbouring islands. Its deep-water harbour, a mile or so away from the city centre, can berth large ships and has facilities for loading sugar in bulk and molasses by

Downtown Bridgetown showing the busy Careenage and the end of the main shopping street.

pipeline. The old port, the Careenage, in the city centre itself is used by small vessels and inter-island schooners.

In recent years, Bridgetown has grown rapidly. This growth has taken two forms. In the centre of the city, where no spare land is available, new buildings have taken the place of old ones. So as to handle an increase in volume of business, these buildings are taller than those they have replaced. The mixture of the old and the new is still visible in the main streets of the town centre. On the margins of the city, growth has been outwards on to land that was previously used for agriculture or covered with poor pasture.

Main roads radiate from Bridgetown to all parts of the island, none of which are more than half-an-hour's drive away. Because they were built to link the rural areas with the port, their pattern resembles the spokes of a wheel and there is no easy way of travelling from north to south without passing through Bridgetown. As a result, traffic congestion in the town is a serious problem, a problem common to many capital cities.

Trade

The changing economy of Barbados is reflected in its overseas trade. In 1975, sugar, molasses and rum accounted for nearly two-thirds of the exports. By 1987 they were down to under one-third, and electronic components and clothing had become equally valuable. Throughout the 1980s, the United States, Britain and CARICOM countries were the main trading partners. The value of imports was about double that of exports. The resulting balance of payments deficit was made up by the money spent by tourists in Barbados.

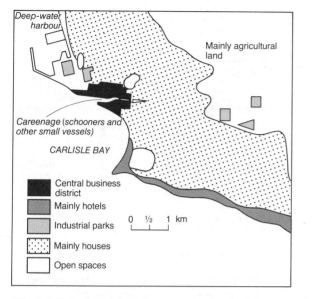

Map 7.9 Bridgetown, Barbados. Compare the harbour
with that of St George's, Grenada, see page 120.

Questions and assignments

1 a) Trace an outline map of Barbados and mark and
label: i) the Scotland District, ii) an area of
highland, iii) an area where petroleum is produced, iv) an area where natural gas is produced, v) a fishing town, vi) two tourist
areas, vii) the international airport, and viii)
the deep-water harbour.

b) Name two similarities and two differences
between the Scotland District and the rest of
Barbados.

2 Using Diagram 7.5:

a) Write down the average monthly rainfall
figures for Barbados in a table like Table 2.4.

b) Using the method given on page 19 say which
months are wet, moist and dry.

c) What percentage of the total rain falls between
the end of November and the beginning of
June?

3 a) Where does Barbados obtain its fresh water
supply? Explain how it gets there.

The deep-water harbour at Bridgetown showing the sugar warehouse (the largest of the buildings) and a number of
factories housing light industries. Beyond the harbour is the central business district of Bridgetown. In which direction
was the camera pointing? Which of the ships is a tourist liner?

b) Name two problems that affect the provision of pure drinking water.

4 Use the information given below to answer the following questions.

Production of sugar in Barbados, 1983–88 (thousands of tonnes)

1983	1984	1985	1986	1987	1988
82.8	100.4	100.2	111.1	83.4	83.3

Export of sugar from Barbados, 1983–87 (thousands of tonnes)

1983	1984	1985	1986	1987	1988
73.5	85.9	83.4	98.6	70.2	68.1

a) In which year was most sugar produced and in which was least produced?
b) In which year was most sugar exported, and in which was least exported?
c) What was the average production of sugar from 1983 to 1988?
d) What was the average export of sugar from 1983 to 1988?
e) Draw one bar graph (like the one in Diagram 5.6) to show both the sugar production and the sugar exports for the years 1983 to 1988.
f) Name two crops which some farmers are growing to replace sugar cane, and two difficulties they face.

5 Barbados has been described as a one-crop economy. To what extent is this description true?

6 Use the information given below to answer the following questions.

Tourist arrivals in Barbados by country of residence, in 1981 and 1987

Country of residence	1981	1987
United States of America	74 472	175 093
Canada	69 897	64 349
United Kingdom	72 090	79 152
Other European countries	29 621	23 019
Trinidad & Tobago	43 838	25 303
Other CARICOM countries	43 051	39 053
South America	8 576	3 498
Other countries	11 046	12 392
Total	352 591	421 859

a) What was the increase in the total number of tourists between 1981 and 1987?
b) Which country contributed most to the increase? How many more tourists came from that country in 1987 than in 1981?
c) From which country was the decrease biggest? What was the size of that decrease?
d) List the countries in rank order in 1981 (ie from the country sending the most tourists at the top down to the country sending fewest at the bottom). Do the same for 1987. Are there any differences between the two lists?
e) What percentage of the total came from the United States in 1981 and in 1987?

8

The Commonwealth Eastern Caribbean States

The Commonwealth Eastern Caribbean states were at one time divided into two political groups. In the south, *Grenada, St Vincent, St Lucia* and *Dominica* formed the colony of the Windward Islands. In the north, *Montserrat, Antigua-Barbuda-Redonda*, and *St Kitts-Nevis-Anguilla* formed the colony of the Leeward Islands. The first of the islands to become independent was Grenada in 1974. The others to have done so are St Vincent and the Grenadines, St Lucia, Dominica, Antigua and Barbuda, and St Kitts-Nevis. The special case of Anguilla is considered on page 147. Montserrat has not become independent, but it has joined the independent countries in forming the *Organisation of Eastern Caribbean States* (OECS). The aims of the OECS are to support inter-governmental co-operation, remove obstacles to inter-island travel, and create closer economic and political links.

Physically, the islands are of two kinds. Antigua, Barbuda and Anguilla are largely or wholly made of limestone and are low-lying; the rest are volcanic and mountainous. Economically, there is one island (St Kitts) which is still dominated by sugar cane, four islands (Grenada, St Vincent, St Lucia and Dominica) which rely heavily on banana exports, and the rest in which agriculture appears to be dying out.

All the islands also have some features in common. The suggestion that poverty was the chief of them was made many years ago. It should be noted that when the discussions were being held which led to the formation of the Caribbean Community, the Eastern Caribbean islands were recognised as being the less developed countries (LDCs) of the Commonwealth Caribbean. Agreements were made by which the more developed countries (MDCs) consisting of Jamaica, Trinidad and Tobago, Barbados and Guyana, should assist the LDCs in several ways. One of them was

that the MDCs should cease to give special protection to over fifty types of light industry to encourage them to begin operating in the Eastern Caribbean. Another was to provide financial assistance for LDCs.

The kinds of development needed by the LDCs and the extent to which assistance should be provided by the MDCs, are matters to consider when you are reading the rest of this chapter. The problems to be overcome in fulfilling the aims of the OECS should also be borne in mind.

The islands will be described in the order given at the beginning of the first paragraph.

Comparisons and contrasts in the Commonwealth Eastern Caribbean States.

Comparisons
All are small in area.
All have small populations.
All have only one major town.
All have a tropical climate.
All lack rich natural resources.
All are short of capital for development.
All have small internal markets.
All import more than they export.

Contrasts
Some are mountainous; some are low-lying.
The low-lying islands are made of limestone.
The mountainous islands are volcanic.
The mountainous islands have a high rainfall.
The low-lying islands have a low rainfall.
Agricultural exports are important in some islands. In others they are not important.

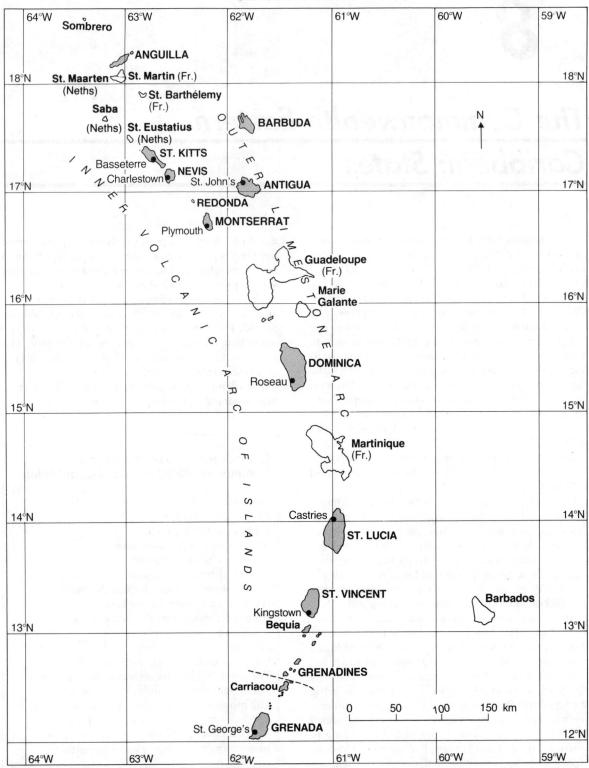

Map 8.1 THE COMMONWEALTH EASTERN CARIBBEAN STATES: This map includes some of the neighbouring islands including the French territories and the Netherlands Windward Islands.

Grenada

Area: 344 square kilometres; population (1988): about 98 000; density of population: 285 per square kilometre.

Landforms

Grenada lies at the southern end of the arc of volcanic islands, and apart from a little limestone in the north it is wholly volcanic. It differs from its northern neighbours in that its mountains are older and considerably more eroded than those of St Vincent but rather younger and higher than those in the northern part of St Lucia. The only remaining traces of former volcanic activity in Grenada are a few cold mineral springs.

The main mountain mass lies in the south centre of the island. It consists of a number of ridges surmounted by several peaks which rise to over 610

metres. Several of these contain old crater basins. One is occupied by a large crater lake, Grand Etang, 530 metres above sea-level. It is shown on page 1.

Lying to the north of these mountains is a younger, higher and narrower ridge which rises to about 840 metres in Mt St Catherine. It is flanked by numerous spurs. Close to the north-east coast there are two more crater lakes, Lake Antoine and Levera Pond.

The mountains rise steeply from the west coast and descend somewhat more gently to the east. The only lowlands are those in the north-eastern and south-western tips of the island. The south coast is very rugged and deeply embayed.

Settlement and development

The first successful attempt to colonise Grenada was made by the French in 1650. They quickly overcame

Map 8.2 GRENADA: Relief and communications.   Map 8.3 GRENADA: Rainfall.   Map 8.4 GRENADA: Land use.

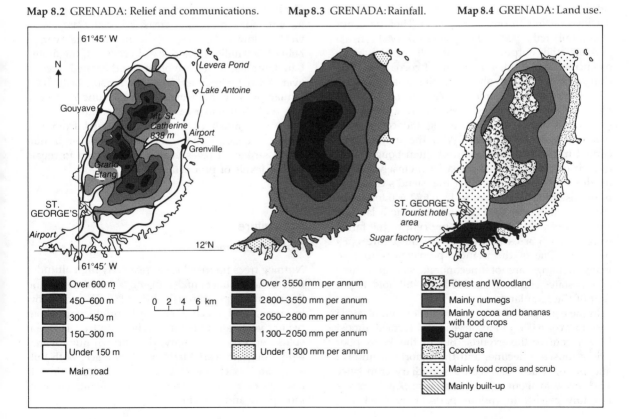

Carib resistance, an easier operation in Grenada than in the more mountainous islands of Dominica and St Vincent. Their first crops, tobacco and indigo, were supplemented by sugar, cocoa, cotton and coffee before the island was captured by the British in 1762. Under the British the population increased rapidly as many settlers migrated there from the Leeward Islands and elsewhere, and many slaves were brought in to work on the estates. Sugar soon became by far the most important crop. Cane took up most of the lowlands, while cocoa, provisions and small quantities of other crops were grown in some parts of the highlands.

After emancipation, many of the freed slaves left the estates. Some emigrated, mainly to Trinidad. Others settled in the highlands, where there was plenty of unoccupied, reasonably fertile land not too steep for cultivation. An attempt was made to replace them with indentured labourers from Malta, Madeira, Africa and India. This did not prevent the output of sugar from falling from over 4 000 tonnes in 1846 to under 1 000 tonnes in 1881. But it did give Grenada the largest Indian population in the Lesser Antilles. In recent years their numbers have declined, mainly through emigration. Their descendants numbered 2 800 at the time of the 1980 census.

While the output of sugar fell in the post-emancipation period, the output of cocoa rose. The change was brought about by the estate-owners, who encouraged labourers to plant cocoa on small plots of land by allowing them to grow their own food crops there, and by buying the cocoa trees when they began to bear. With the money they earned in this way the labourers often bought land of their own and planted cocoa for themselves. One result of this system was that the island's cocoa exports rose from 170 tonnes in 1846 to 2 600 tonnes in 1881. Another was that Grenada became a land of smallholders. By 1890 over 80 per cent of the farms were under 5 acres in area. Today the figure is 89 per cent. One of the island's problems is that so many holdings are of uneconomic size at a time when estates of more than 200 acres still hold 40 per cent of the farm land.

In the early part of this century the output of cocoa rose to over 6 000 tonnes a year and formed almost 90 per cent of the exports. But in the 1920s poor prices caused a decline, and the exports of nutmeg and mace, which had been a subsidiary crop since 1843, grew to about equal importance. Apart from a few tiny patches in various parts of the lowlands,

sugar cane became confined to a small area a few kilometres south of St George's, where a small sugar factory was built in 1935 to process all the crop.

The population density, which was over 80 per square kilometre at the time of the emancipation of the slaves, had more than doubled by the beginning of this century. In spite of the fact that the proportion of cultivated land in Grenada was higher than that of all the other islands except Barbados and St Kitts, there was considerable pressure on the land. Many people emigrated to Panama, Curaçao, Aruba, Trinidad and elsewhere, and for many years the population remained stable at about 60 000. Since then, however, most outlets have been closed to migrants and numbers have increased. The population density of 285 per square kilometre in 1988 was the second highest in the West Indies.

Climate

The main features of the climate of the Eastern Caribbean have been explained in chapter two. As for Grenada, the coastal areas, especially the south-western lowlands, receive least rainfall, the average being 1 500 millimetres a year. In contrast, the mountain summits, which are often cloud-capped, receive over 4 000 millimetres. The dry season lasts from January to May, the wet season from June to December, with November as the wettest month.

With so much of its income derived from tree crops, Grenada suffers severely whenever a hurricane strikes. It takes years for the island to regain former levels of production.

Agriculture

Nutmegs and mace

Nutmeg trees flourish best at relatively high altitudes where the annual rainfall is over 2 000 millimetres and the mean temperature is below 24°C. They are slow to grow, and reach their peak production about twenty years after planting. When the fruit is ripe it splits and exposes a shiny, dark brown nut covered with a delicate scarlet latticework of mace. Both nutmegs and mace are in demand as spices. Mace is also used to some extent in the manufacture of toothpaste and perfumes.

Separating nutmegs and mace.

The nuts are allowed to fall to the ground where, about once a week, women collect them in large baskets and bags. They are immediately taken to collecting centres where the mace is stripped off carefully because it fetches a higher price if it is unbroken.

From here the mace is sent to one of the island's processing centres (the largest of which are at Gouyave on the west coast and Grenville on the east) where it is stored in wooden bins for a few months and turns yellow in colour. Then it is cleaned and packed in plywood tea-chests for export. As for the nuts, they are spread in a thin layer on wooden shelves for six to eight weeks until their kernels are fully cured. Just before shipment the shells are broken open and the kernels are extracted and graded according to size. They are exported in sacks, mostly on the banana boats going to Britain.

Though nutmegs are grown in other West Indian islands and in other tropical countries, only Grenada and Indonesia are major exporters. The price of nutmegs on the world's markets therefore depends largely on the amount available from these two areas. This explains why, when a hurricane in 1955 reduced the volume of nutmegs from Grenada to only 5 per cent of what it had been previously, the price rose so much that the value of exports was only halved. It was not until 1975 that yields from new trees brought production up to the pre-hurricane level. In 1988 nutmegs and mace formed 44 per cent of the island's exports.

Cocoa

The decline in cocoa production which began in the 1920s went on into the 1940s when many of the trees became affected by 'witches' broom' disease. The turning point came after the 1939–45 World War when a beginning was made in clearing the worst stricken areas and replanting them with disease-resistant plants giving four times the yield per acre. Further replanting to replace old trees has been taking place in recent years and output is expected to rise.

Though cocoa is grown as high up as 370 metres and as low as 60 metres, the most productive areas lie in a horse-shoe shaped belt on the northern, western and eastern slopes of the mountains. The belt is broken in the south where the dry season is longer and more marked than elsewhere.

Except that cocoa is seldom grown under shade, cultivation and processing methods are similar to those in Trinidad. Windbreaks are common in order to prevent the wind from blowing the flowers off the trees; and for these, rows of mango trees are often used. About 70 per cent of the output comes from farms over 50 acres in size, most of which have their own fermenting, drying and mechanical polishing facilities. The remainder comes from smaller farms which usually send the wet beans direct to cocoa dealers to be processed.

The beans are graded before being exported. Only the best are used to make chocolate. The rest are used to make cocoa butter. Cocoa accounted for 10 per cent of the exports in 1988.

Bananas

Until the 1955 hurricane, bananas were only a minor export from Grenada. The rapid development that followed was due to the fact that in re-establishing fields of cocoa or nutmegs, farmers planted bananas between the seedlings. In the case of cocoa, they acted as a shade crop and an income-earner for three or four years; in the case of nutmegs they provided an income for ten years or more while the trees were still young and unproductive.

In 1980 another hurricane did considerable damage to the banana crop. Since then production has not risen to former levels and in 1988 bananas accounted for only 14 per cent of Grenada's exports.

Other crops

The sugar industry in the south-west of Grenada is of interest because it is one of the last remaining examples in the Commonwealth Eastern Caribbean. Some of the cane is grown on two estates belonging to the company operating the sugar factory, some by sharecroppers who cultivate estate land and pay the company a third of their earnings, and some by small farmers who also grow a wide range of food crops.

Output of sugar is very small, seldom reaching 500 tonnes a year. Most of the island's sugar requirements are imported from Trinidad. Most of the rum made in the factory is bought by hotels and used to make rum punch. There are also some smaller distilleries in other parts of the island.

Coconuts are grown, particularly along the east coast (see Map 8.4). Some are exported; some made into edible oil and soap. Among the spices produced are pimento, cloves, ginger and cinnamon. Among the many tree crops are mangoes, grapefruit, guavas, avocados and breadfruit. The export of fresh fruit and vegetables, mainly to Barbados and Trinidad, formed 25 per cent of the total exports in 1988.

Recent developments

During the period of the People's Revolutionary Government (1978–83) there was a policy to reduce Grenada's dependence on the export of cocoa, nutmegs and bananas, and to raise the consumption of locally produced foodstuffs. Farmers were encouraged to grow more fruit and vegetables for local and overseas sale. To assist them, roads were built to provide better access to their land, and low-cost fertilisers were made available. Factories were built to process such products as cocoa, coffee, mango chutney, juices, jellies and jams. Attempts were made to bring idle land back into production, thereby increasing output and providing more agricultural employment. The biggest single development was the construction of a new airport, with Cuban help, at the south-western tip of the island. Its main purpose was to attract more tourists. The existing airport had two disadvantages. One was that it could not take large jet aircraft. The other was that it was situated a long way from the capital and the most

attractive tourist areas (see Map 8.4).

Following the American invasion and the change of government, the airport was completed. Tourism is growing. So is the production and export of light manufactured products, particularly garments made from imported fabric. There is a large factory at which baking flour and animal feed is made from wheat imported from the United States and Canada.

Towns and communications

The capital, St George's is situated on a deep, sheltered inlet, part of which is an old, submerged volcanic crater. The inner part of the harbour, known as the Carenage, has long been used by schooners and other sailing-ships. More recently a wharf has been built to accommodate ocean-going vessels, as, for example, those loading bananas. Nearby there is a marina for visiting yachtsmen who form a high proportion of the island's growing tourist industry.

Map 8.5 St George's Harbour, Grenada.

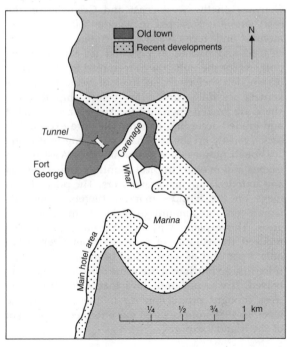

St George's Grenada, showing the harbour, the wharf and the marina. In what direction was the camera pointing? Compare the picture with Map 8.5 and describe the site of the town.

St George's is connected by road to all the coastal districts of Grenada. The west coast road enters the town through a short tunnel which has been built through the promontory on which Fort George stands.

Carriacou and Petit Martinique

Though most of the Grenadines (see Map 8.1 and pages 125–6) are politically part of St Vincent, two of them – Carriacou (33 square kilometres) and Petit Martinique (22 square kilometres) – belong to Grenada. Carriacou, with a population of about 5 000, is a farming and fishing community producing cotton and a wide range of food crops.

St Vincent and the Grenadines

Area (including the Grenadines): 389 square kilometres; population (1988): about 110 000; density of population: 283 per square kilometre.

Landforms

With its jumbled array of peaks, ridges and ravines, St Vincent almost rivals Dominica as the most mountainous island in the Lesser Antilles. Indeed, the interior range is so high and so steep that the island is the only one that is still not crossed by road.

St Vincent is entirely volcanic in origin, being mostly composed of ash and other fragmented material, though there are some lava flows in places. The northern end of the island is dominated by Soufrière. Part of the irregular rim of its main crater – which dates from an eruption in 1817 – reaches a height of 1 200 metres only three kilometres from the sea. Soufrière is one of the two active volcanoes remaining in the Caribbean. Like its partner Mt Pelée in Martinique its outbursts are infrequent but explosive. The eruption of 1902–3 killed 2 000 people and devastated nearly a third of the island. The previous explosion of 1812 was even more violent. It created the crater lake which still exists at the foot of rock walls which fall for 300 metres (see Map 8.6).

Soufrière was quiet until 1979 when two lava streams burst out and flowed down to the sea. Dust

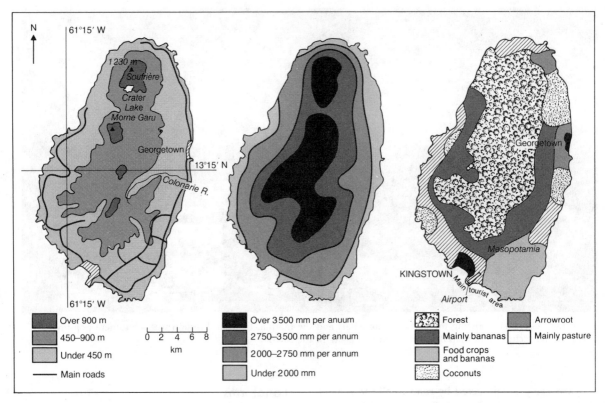

Map 8.6 ST VINCENT: Relief.   **Map 8.7** ST VINCENT: Rainfall.   **Map 8.8** ST VINCENT: Land use.

and ash were thrown high into the air, destroying all the vegetation around the volcano. Considerable damage was done to bananas, cocoa and coconuts over a much wider area. Many people had to leave their homes and move to safer parts of the island. About 1 500 livestock died during that time.

Though Soufrière is so young, some deep narrow gullies have already been cut in it by the streams which flow off its slopes after heavy rains. They radiate like the spokes of a wheel.

South of Soufrière there is a broad trough and then the land rises again to another volcano – Morne Garu, 1 070 metres. Form here a sharp-crested ridge runs to the southern end of the island. Many spurs breaking away from this central ridge run down to the coasts where they end in high cliffs. Erosion has proceeded further in this older area than in the north. Each stream has carved a ravine in its upper course and deposited an alluvial fan where it leaves the hills.

The mountains drop steeply towards the west coast. On the eastern side there is a series of well-defined natural terraces indicating that the land has been uplifted in stages. These terraces, moulded by erosion into a rolling landscape, support some of the best agricultural land in the island. Flat land is very limited in extent. Indeed, only 5 per cent of the island has slopes of five degrees or less.

Settlement and development

Because St Vincent was one of the Carib strongholds, it was one of the last of the Lesser Antilles to be colonised. In fact, in order to gain a foothold there at all the early French and British settlers had to make treaties with the Carib inhabitants. In 1773, ten years after the island became British, the last of these treaties allotted special reserves to the Caribs, the largest of which was in the north-east of the island. Few of these people survived the 1812 and 1902 eruptions of Soufrière, but there are some descendants of the Black Caribs, a race which sprang from a mixture of Carib and Negro stock. Their numbers are small because most were deported in 1796 after an unsuccessful uprising. Their later story is told in the chapter on Belize.

During the eighteenth century cotton was extensively grown in St Vincent but after the island became British, sugar cane became the foremost crop. Many slaves were brought in to work on the estates and there was a slave population of 23 000 by the time of emancipation. After emancipation many of the newly freed people left the estates, bought small plots of land, and set up on their own as small farmers. Some Portuguese and Indian indentured labourers were brought in to work in their place, and the descendants of those who did not emigrate again form a small proportion of the population today.

In the second half of the nineteenth century St Vincent shared in the general decline of the West Indian sugar industry. A further setback occurred when the eruptions of Soufrière at the beginning of the present century destroyed much of the best cane land. The industry managed to struggle on in a small way until 1962 when the last surviving factory was closed. Efforts to revive the industry proved too expensive. They came to an end in 1985.

The decline of sugar following emancipation was matched by a rise in the production of arrowroot. This plant, brought to the island by the Caribs, was known to them and the early settlers both as a food and as a cure for the wounds caused by poisoned arrows. Later, when arrowroot starch became widely known as an easily digested food for invalids, there came a growing demand for it from abroad. The opportunity to sell arrowroot enabled many small farmers to make a living for themselves, and many estates to find a substitute for cane. St Vincent obtained a near monopoly of the world's market, and for a century arrowroot was the island's leading export. Though this might seem a favourable position to be in, arrowroot prices were never high and the bulk of the population remained desperately poor. Since then there has been little improvement in living conditions. Exports of arrowroot have declined, and the only major expansion has been that of bananas. With the exception of Haiti, St Vincent is the poorest country in the Caribbean.

Climate

The rainfall of St Vincent is heavy, very little of the island having less than 2 000 millimetres a year. The mountainous interior, which receives over 3 800 millimetres, is the source of many streams. One of them – the Colonarie River – provides hydro-electricity. Several others are put to use by the arrowroot factories, where plentiful supplies of pure water are required. St Vincent suffered from hurricane damage in 1980 and again in 1986.

Land use and tenure

The steep slopes of Soufrière and the central ridge have been left in forest. It is of little economic value but it does help to prevent soil erosion and landslides. Altogether just over half of the total area is forested. On the lower edge of the forest there is a narrow zone of shifting cultivation where food crops are grown on tiny patches of land. The best farming land lies below a height of 300 metres on the western, eastern and southern sides of the island. Slopes are gentler there and soils are richer than they are elsewhere. Many of these slopes have been terraced to prevent soil erosion. About one-third of the island is used for agriculture.

Since St Vincent became independent all but a few of the old colonial estates have been broken up into holdings of five acres or less. As a result nearly all of the agriculture is now undertaken by small farmers. In most places cash crops and subsistence crops are intermixed. This helps to spread the risk if one of the crops fails. It also maintains plant cover on the ground and prevents soil erosion.

Agriculture

Arrowroot

Arrowroot, a plant which grows to a height of 1 to 2 metres, is cultivated for the sake of the starch in its rhizome (popularly called the root) which may reach a length of 45 centimetres. It is planted on sloping ground and when it is ready for harvesting in October the labourers begin at the bottom of the fields and work their way uphill, the last of the crop being reaped in May. Immediately the plant is dug

Carrying arrowroot into a factory.

up the rhizome is broken off and the shoot of the plant is buried in the ground. It grows into a new plant which is itself ready for harvesting about a year later. After three or four years of this, this field is ploughed and replanted with pieces of rhizome.

The rhizomes are carried by truck to one of the island's three factories. There they are pulped and carried in a plentiful supply of pure water through a series of sieves which extract the coarser fibre. The remaining suspension of starch particles in water is allowed to stand in vats until the starch settles to the bottom. Then the water is drained off and the starch is dried and sent to Kingstown where it is graded, ground into a fine powder, and exported mainly to Britain and the United States.

During the 1980s the output of arrowroot has declined greatly. One of the reasons is that much of the best arrowroot land was planted with sugar cane when the attempt was made to revive the sugar industry. Another is that the manufacturing process is out of date and inefficient. Even though the wages paid to the workers are low, arrowroot starch made in St Vincent is unable to compete with that from

Brazil. A further reason is that other products have taken the place of arrowroot starch and so the demand for it is small. In the early 1970s, arrowroot formed 15 per cent of the exports. By 1980 it was down to 4 per cent, and in 1986 it was only $\frac{1}{2}$ per cent.

Bananas

Since regular shipments to Britain began in the 1950s, bananas have been the largest single export. In the mid-1970s they brought in about half of the island's income. Since then, although output has risen, bananas form a smaller proportion of the exports. They amounted to 31 per cent in 1986. The reason for this is that food crops have become prominent exports in the 1980s.

Bananas differ from the crops previously grown in St Vincent in that they need a great deal more care, both in the field and afterwards. The changes already brought about in the island by the development of the banana industry include changes in farming methods, the surfacing of more main roads in order to prevent fruits from being bumped and bruised, the boxing of all the fruit, and the building of new port facilities at Kingstown to enable the fruit to be loaded directly on to ships.

Other crops

The chief coconut producing area is the north-east of the island. Some nuts are exported and copra is used to make cooking oil, laundry soap and animal feed in a factory at Arnos Vale (on the outskirts of Kingstown).

Some cassava is grown. The starch is extracted at the arrowroot factories and some of it is exported. Sweet potatoes, which because of their short growing season are good money earners, are exported in considerable quantities to Trinidad. So are plantains, eddoes, pumpkins, carrots, peppers, groundnuts and yams. The biggest single producing district is the fertile Mesopotamia area in the south central part of the island not far inland from Kingstown. Some ginger, nutmegs and mace are grown and exported.

Food imports are of less importance to St Vincent than to any of the other Eastern Caribbean islands.

Livestock and fishing

Animals are kept to provide meat, milk and eggs. Some cattle, sheep and goats are exported and there is a ham and bacon factory that exports some of its products.

In addition to a small fishing industry, whales, porpoises and blackfish (which look like a cross between the two) are harpooned off St Vincent and the Grenadines for their meat and blubber.

Population

The rapid increase of population (or 'population explosion' as it has been called) is particularly noticeable in St Vincent. It has resulted in a population density of about four people to every cultivable acre, and in virtually half the total population being under sixteen years old (this is below the age at which they can be expected to contribute to the economy). The southern one-third of the island is much more densely populated than the northern two-thirds.

Towns and communications

Kingstown, the capital, has grown up on a large sheltered bay. Before the rise of the banana industry its port facilities were primitive and ships had to anchor off shore. Today with its suburbs, it has a population of about 25 000. There is a modern deep-water pier where cargo ships can load and unload directly. Wheat bought in bulk-carriers from the United States and Canada is made into baking flour and animal feed both for local consumption and for export. Rice from Guyana is processed in a modern rice mill. There are also special facilities at Kingstown harbour for tourists who arrive on cruise ships. The town is connected by road to all the coastal districts except the extreme northern tip of the island. Unlike two other very mountainous islands – Dominica and Montserrat – it has been possible to locate the airport near the capital. However, as the airport is unable to take large jet aircraft, tourism is restricted. In 1986, 84 000 tourists visited Grenada and the Grenadines, including cruise-ship passengers. In the same year St Lucia had 174 000.

A small but successful industrial estate has been set up in Kingstown where garments, plastic and paper goods, toys, sporting goods and other light manufactures are made and a variety of electrical products are assembled. Some are exported to Trinidad, the United States and elsewhere.

Trade

Largely because of the amount of vegetables and fruits that are sent to Trinidad, over half of St Vincent's exports went to CARICOM countries in 1986. Next came Britain which took one-third of the exports, mainly bananas. Most of the imports come from the United States, Britain and CARICOM.

The Grenadines

The Grenadines are a group of over forty small islands and many more rocks and reefs standing on a shallow submarine volcanic ridge which extends south-westwards from St Vincent almost to Grenada (see Map 8.1). Apart from Carriacou and Petit Martinique, they all belong to St Vincent, though some are privately owned. The area of those belonging to St Vincent is 67 square kilometres; the population about 8 000.

The main occupations are growing provisions – chiefly corn, groundnuts, cassava, peas, yams and sweet potatoes – and rearing of livestock. Settlement is dense on cultivated land, but agriculture has suffered because slopes are steep and the volcanic soils have been severely eroded. In consequence people have left the islands to become seamen and to migrate to other countries. The bays, beaches and reefs of the Grenadines are all tourist attractions. In recent years hotels have been built on several of the islands, including Bequia, Palm Island, Petit St Vincent, and Mustique. Many of the visitors arrive by yacht; others by cruise ship. Still others make use of the small plane service that connects some of the islands with Grenada and St Vincent.

St Lucia

Area: 616 square kilometres; population (1988): about 145 000; density of population: 235 per square kilometre.

Landforms

The volcanic island of St Lucia may be divided into two physical regions:

1 The south and centre of the island is young and mountainous. A number of peaks rise to over 600 metres and the highest of all, Morne Gimie, reaches to almost 960 metres. Extremely steep slopes are common in the region. This is especially true of the pitons, which are the resistant lava plugs left standing like pinnacles when the rest of the volcanoes have been weathered away. Two of these, Grand Piton and Petit Piton, both of which rise from the sea to over 750 metres, are among the most remarkable and best known scenic features in the West Indies. They are shown on the front cover of this book.

Many ridges radiate outwards from the region, those running westwards terminating very close to the sea. The southern flanks of the mountains lie buried beneath an outflow of volcanic mud, ash and boulders which slopes down to the sea like a giant fan. It has given rise to fertile soils on which most

of the island's cocoa is grown.

Hot sulphurous streams, and the large active fumarole near Soufrière from which sulphur was once dug for export, show that vulcanicity in the southern part of St Lucia has not entirely died down. At present this fumarole – like the others in the Lesser Antilles – emits mainly hydrogen sulphide gas. If this were to be replaced by sulphur dioxide, it would be an indication of potential danger. The underground water at Soufrière is so hot that it could serve as a source of energy (geothermal energy). Plans have been made to use the heat to generate electricity.

2 The older northern half of the island has been so worn down by erosion that the outlines of the old volcanoes are no longer traceable. The backbone of this region is a central ridge about 300 metres in height which, with its offshoots, is surmounted by numerous pitons, the highest of which is La Sorcière, 675 metres. There are also many lower individual hills. In contrast to the gorges of the south, the rivers in this region flow in wide flat-bottomed valleys.

Settlement and development

The first European attempt at settling in St Lucia was made by the British in 1638, but the Caribs living there were too powerful, and they were forced to withdraw. A few years later the French succeeded. From then until 1803 St Lucia was one of the most disputed lands in the Caribbean and it changed hands no less than fourteen times. French influence there is still very marked. It shows in the place-names, the patois, and in some of the laws, especially those relating to the ownership of property.

The contests of the eighteenth century retarded the development of St Lucia. Thus sugar cane did not supersede the early crops – tobacco, cotton and ginger – until a century after it had become the mainstay of Barbados, Antigua and St Kitts. However, sugar did in time become the most important export. By 1830 over eighty sugar factories were in operation and over 13 000 slaves were at work. Then in the difficult years that followed, the output dwindled again. Shortage of labour was the chief problem; the freed slaves preferring to find their own employment or to emigrate to the gold-fields of French Guiana and elsewhere. Over 2 000 Indians

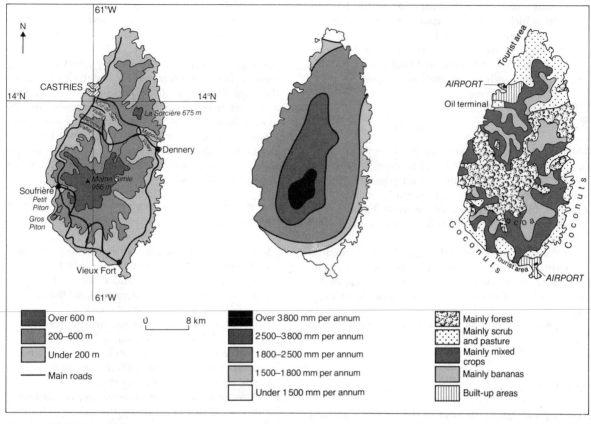

Map 8.9 ST LUCIA: Relief. **Map 8.10** ST LUCIA: Rainfall. **Map 8.11** ST LUCIA: Land use.

were brought to St Lucia to take their place as field labourers but they soon found other employment. Most of the estates were broken up into smallholdings. Towards the end of the nineteenth century several new sugar factories were erected. None has survived. Limes were introduced and exported for many years, but disease caused a decline in the 1930s. Cocoa exports also increased, but most of the land was given over to subsistence crops. Shifting cultivation became common and soil erosion inevitably followed.

The lack of interest in commercial farming was due to better paid employment being constantly available for hundreds of workers in Castries. The large, deep sheltered harbour there was selected as the chief coaling station in the West Indies. Coal, imported from the United States and from Britain, was stored on a wharf and loaded on to ships which tied up there for refuelling on their voyages from Europe and North America to South America and the Pacific. As the loading operation was never mechanised, the coal had to be carried aboard a bag at a time.

From the 1880s to the 1920s this coal brought in over a half of the island's income and it was common for a thousand ships to call at Castries in a year. But in the 1930s, as fuel oil replaced coal, the trade declined and disappeared.

The unemployment and depression which would otherwise have followed were averted because labour was needed to build the United States Army and Navy bases at Vieux Fort and Gros Islet. Soon after they were closed, Castries was destroyed by fire and workers were needed to rebuild the capital. When this outlet for employment came to an end in the 1950s, St Lucia turned increasingly to agriculture

127

as a source of income, in particular to the banana business which grew very rapidly at that time. Since then new forms of employment have been created by the rise of tourism. As in Antigua the closing of an American base has benefited tourism by providing the island with an international airport.

Rainfall

Over most of St Lucia the rainfall is heavy and there is no really dry season. This can be seen by referring to the tables of rainfall figures on page 19, one of which shows the average monthly rainfall for Castries, by no means one of the wettest places. The low-lying northern and southern tips of the island have the least rain.

In contrast to its easterly neighbour, Barbados, drought is seldom a problem in St Lucia. Instead, especially on the older and more eroded soils in the northern half of the island, the combination of steep slopes, heavy showers of rain and recklessly cleared land create a situation where landslides can easily occur.

Land use

Although about 40 per cent of the land is classified as forest and woodland, only the rain-forest in the inaccessible mountainous districts is in good condition today. The remainder is secondary woodland which has grown up on land that was cleared for agriculture until soil erosion caused its abandonment. The northern tip of the island is very badly eroded and supports only scattered patches of thorny scrub.

Prosperous agriculture in the northern half of the island is limited to the alluvial flats, most of which are in banana estates. The southern part of the island is more fertile. There is no landslide problem and peasant farming is more successful. About 45 per cent of the total area can be cultivated. A further 5 per cent is pasture, and the remaining 10 per cent is built-up land.

Agriculture

Banana exports began in the 1920s, declined in the 1930s because of Panama disease and ceased during the 1939–45 World War when there were no ships to carry the fruit. After the war a new start was made with disease-resistant bananas. Half a million stems were exported in 1955; over 3 500 000 in 1961. When the sugar industry ceased shortly afterwards, large areas of land were released for banana cultivation in the large and fertile Roseau and Cul de Sac valleys, and there was a second wave of expansion. In 1965, over 6 330 000 stems were exported, the ships being loaded at Castries and Vieux Fort. They formed 90 per cent of the total exports, thus adding another monoculture economy to the Caribbean – the first to depend on bananas.

Monoculture

Monoculture of any kind gives rise to problems.
1 One of them is that if the same crop is grown year after year, the pests and diseases that attack that crop become strongly established. For example, bananas are attacked by nematodes. These microscopic worms feed on the roots of banana, weakening the plants so that they yield poorly. Changing the crop from year to year – a practice called crop rotation – keeps pests and diseases in check.
2 A second problem of monoculture is that the entire economy depends on the price paid for the crop. It even depends on the weather. Thus, when Hurricane Allen struck St Lucia in 1980, banana exports ceased for seven months. There was no other crop which could earn money for the island during that period.
3 The economy depends on a secure market for the crop. The market for bananas is not secure. From 1992, new regulations in the European Economic Community may mean that Eastern Caribbean bananas will have to compete on equal terms with bananas produced in other parts of the world.

Despite such setbacks as the 1980 hurricane and the 1987 drought, banana production has risen throughout the 1980s. In some years it has almost equalled the combined output of the other three Eastern Caribbean producers – Grenada, St Vincent and Dominica. The 1988 output of 128 000 tonnes formed over 75 per cent of St Lucia's entire exports.

Though coconuts are a minor crop compared to bananas, the output of 4 000 tonnes of copra a year is the largest in the eastern Caribbean. Nearly two-thirds of them are produced on farms over 100 acres in size. Some are exported to Barbados for processing. Most are made into coconut oil in a factory at Soufrière. Another product is laundry soap.

Cocoa is grown in most parts of the island and especially in the south-west. Small quantities of beans are exported. Oranges, grapefruit, and a smaller quantity of limes are grown. So are plantains, coffee, nutmegs and a variety of tropical fruits.

Fishing

Fish – particularly dolphin and flying fish – are landed on many beaches especially at Vieux Fort in the south of the island. The peak season is from January to June. Like the other Eastern Caribbean islands, St Lucia is not self-sufficient in fish. Raising the production substantially will depend on two things. One is the provision of bigger boats that can

travel further and stay at sea longer than the canoes used at present. The other is the provision of cold storage facilities to prevent fish spoiling unless they are sold to customers within a few hours of their being landed.

Tourism

With the opening of a new international airport near Vieux Fort so that visitors can fly in directly from London and America, and the building of a number of large luxury hotels, St Lucia has become the largest tourist centre in the Commonwealth Eastern Caribbean south of Antigua, not counting Barbados.

Tourism and agriculture are so different from one another that it is no easy task to integrate them in a single economy so that both prosper. Antigua has not succeeded in doing so, and Barbados is having its problems. In theory it would seem that with luxury hotels spending so lavishly on food, the local

Part of the sheltered harbour of Castries. Note the old, eroded volcanic landscape in the distance; the liners docked beside a wharf which has been built specially for tourists; the large new Government buildings at the head of the harbour, and the houses spreading up from the harbour into the foothills.'

production of meat, milk and a wide variety of fruits and vegetables should flourish. In fact, in Antigua and Barbados this is not the case. Opportunities for employment in tourism have turned people against taking up a farming career. It remains to be seen whether tourism will stimulate the production of more foodstuffs in St Lucia. A considerable area of unused agricultural land could be used for this purpose. A point for discussion is the role you think a government could usefully play in making a country more self-sufficient in foodstuffs. Is a government right to use taxpayers' money to subsidise farming? If so, how should the money be used? If not, are there other ways of encouraging farmers to grow more crops and raise more animals for local consumption?

Manufacturing

Though St Lucia has no major manufacturing industries, a number of light manufactures are produced and some are exported. Garments are the most important, followed by the assembly of electrical and electronic goods. In 1982 a large American-owned oil transhipment terminal began operations on the coast not far from Castries (see Map 8.11). It makes a small contribution to the island's economy by paying a royalty to the government and by providing some employment.

Towns

Castries (35 000), Soufrière (5 000) and Vieux Fort are the three chief towns. Castries, which stands at the head of one of the best and most sheltered harbours in the West Indies, handles most of the island's overseas trade. The centre of the town, built on a small alluvial flat, was largely destroyed by fire in 1948. It was rebuilt on modern, planned lines, and the present central business district – with its warehouses, offices, shops, department stores, banks and blocks of flats – is more easily distinguished from the surrounding residential area than that of any other West Indian town.

Though relatively small, Vieux Fort – at the opposite end of St Lucia from Castries – has developed as a banana exporting town, a shopping centre, and a fishing port.

Dominica

Area: 751 square kilometres; population (1988): about 80 000; density of population: 106 per square kilometre.

Landforms

Though many of the islands of the Lesser Antilles are mountainous, Dominica is undoubtedly the wildest and most complex of them all. It is such a mass of peaks, ridges and ravines that in proportion to area it is more rugged than Switzerland.

In the north the volcanic pile of Morne au Diable (860 metres) forms a blunt peninsula ending in high northward-facing cliffs. There is little flat land in this region apart from that behind the town of Portsmouth and this tends to be swampy.

The centre of the island is a maturely eroded highland. Probably the remnants of an old plateau, its summits rise mostly to about 450 metres, though some ridges and isolated peaks rise to 600 metres. Its is dissected by the gorges of many streams and by the relatively wide basin of the Layou River. On top of the plateau stand two young, inactive volcanoes. The one in the south is the Morne Trois Pitons (1 424 metres), a mountain surmounted by three high pitons similar in shape to those shown on the front cover of this book. The one in the north is Morne Diablotin (1 420 metres), from which high ridges radiate to the north, south and west. Those in the west reach almost to the coast. To the east, however, the descent is more gradual.

South of the Morne Trois Pitons and Micotrin (1 220 metres) is the basin of the Roseau River which falls by a series of cataracts to the capital. Farther south still there is another complex volcanic mass of intermediate age, the highest peak of which, Watt Mountain, rises to 1 225 metres.

By world standards these mountains are not high. Indeed, half the island lies below 300 metres. It is steepness of slope rather than altitude which gives Dominica its particular character and makes transport and agriculture so difficult. Remoteness in such a country is not a matter of distance but of difficulty of access. Even though Roseau is only 30 kilometres in a direct line from the larger of the two airports on the east coast (see Map 8.12) the journey by car on the narrow, winding road takes two to three hours.

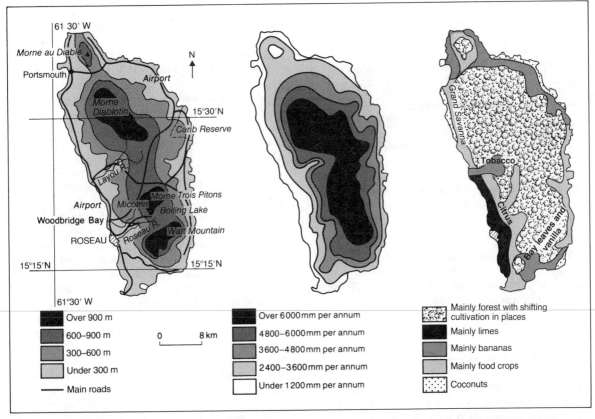

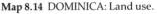

Map 8.12 DOMINICA: Relief.   **Map 8.13** DOMINICA: Rainfall.   **Map 8.14** DOMINICA: Land use.

Hardly any non-volcanic rocks have been found in Dominica, and the numerous fumaroles and hot streams indicate that there is still some subdued volcanic activity there. So does the boiling lake in the Valley of Desolation. The surface of the lake is frequently broken by jets of boiling water which may spurt up three metres and more. The steaming, sulphurous fumes emitted from the lake have killed much of the surrounding vegetation. Dead trees stand between occasional clumps of ferns, and coarse grass and dead logs cover much of the ground.

Rainfall and vegetation

Rainfall varies considerably from place to place, but in no district is it scanty. Over 80 per cent of the island has at least 2 000 millimetres a year (see Map 8.13) and even the sheltered leeward side of the island can expect rain on two days out of three. The mountain peaks get over 7 500 millimetres a year. June to November are the wettest months and February to May are the driest. The average monthly rainfall at Roseau, one of the driest places, is shown in Diagram 8.15.

About 70 per cent of the island is forested, the highest proportion of forest in the West Indies. The high mountains are covered with elfin woodland, but below 1 000 metres this changes to tropical rainforest which in Dominica is particularly luxuriant. On the sheltered western side below 300 metres there is a deciduous forest where trees shed their leaves towards the end of the least rainy months. Lower down beside the coast there is a narrow belt of thorn bush and scrub. In one area close to the coast a recent lava flow has given rise to such poor soil that it supports only grass.

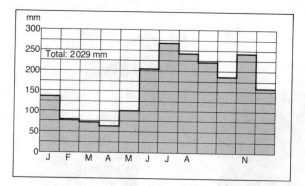

Diagram 8.15 Average monthly rainfall of Roseau.

Though the lumber industry is still small, several varieties of timber, including white and red cedar, balata and mahogany are taken to saw mills near Roseau and exported in small quantities.

Settlement and development

Because the rugged and forested interior of Dominica provided a refuge for the Caribs, Europeans were unable to settle in Dominica for two centuries after its discovery. Then French settlers gained a foothold. They began the cultivation of several crops, of which coffee came to be the most important. Though Dominica later came under British control, French influence is still to be seen in the place-names and heard in the patois.

When coffee declined in the nineteenth century, sugar took its place. However, the island never became a large sugar producer, and in recent times the output has almost ceased as there is not enough flat land to grow the cane required to support a modern factory. Cocoa became important about the beginning of this century. Then West African competition caused a decline. Limes were introduced about 1870. Because they could grow in higher, more exposed areas than sugar or cocoa, they soon became the mainstay of the economy. By 1920 lime products accounted for 80 per cent of the island's exports. For a time Dominica was the world's leading producer. However, setbacks occurred in the 1930s, when a process was discovered in Europe for manufacturing citric acid synthetically and when diseases and hurricanes destroyed many trees. Most of the lime plantations on the windward side of the island were abandoned. Since then there has been a slow and intermittent recovery.

Several attempts were made before the 1950s to establish banana growing in Dominica, but they were not successful. Now with banana boats calling every week and preferential prices being paid for bananas in Britain, cultivation is widespread and bananas form the bulk of the exports. Thus Dominica has had several periods of relative prosperity, each based on a different crop.

Dominica is the only West Indian island to have an area set aside for the Carib population. Several hundred people, few of whom are of pure Carib descent, live in a reserve some 3 000 acres in size (see Map 8.12). It stretches along 13 kilometres of the windward coast and up into the ridges behind. They cultivate food crops and catch fish. They have lost their old language but they have retained their traditional craft of basket making.

Because the development of the island was retarded for so long and because so little of it was suited to plantation agriculture, relatively few slaves were employed there. In consequence the population was never large and the island is still considered by some to be under-populated. It is true that Dominica is the only Commonwealth Eastern Caribbean state in which a large proportion of the resources are still undisturbed, but it is hard to see how an increase in population could create any overall economic benefits.

Agriculture

Farming conditions in Dominica are so difficult that only one-fifth of the total area is agricultural land, and not all of that is farmed in any one year. Most crops are confined to river valleys and alluvial flats. Estates take up about half of this land. The remainder is farmed by smallholders.

Bananas

Since the rapid expansion of banana farming in the 1950s, bananas have dominated the island's export economy. In the late 1980s they took up 50 per cent of the cultivated land and formed over 40 per cent of the exports. As in St Lucia, so much emphasis on one crop gives rise to problems. Pests such as nematodes, and diseases such as leaf spot, are costly to control. Yields are low, only one-fifth of those in Honduras. Risks are high. Hurricanes, such as those in 1979 and 1980, can wipe out production for months. Transport is difficult. Good road surfaces cannot be maintained where slopes are so steep and rainfall so heavy. To prevent the bananas from being badly bruised in the trucks that take them to the coast for shipment, they have to be carefully packed in the field. As soon as they are cut, the separate hands of bananas are placed on absorbent pads. These pads are treated with fungicide to keep them from spoiling. The bananas in their pads are then packed into cartons before beginning their long journey to Britain. This process, called field packing, is practised throughout the Eastern Caribbean states.

Part of the Layou Valley. In what ways does a landscape like this hinder development?

Citrus

Dominica is the only Eastern Caribbean country where citrus fruits are important. Oranges and grapefruit are grown on estates, packed in a government factory and exported to Britain in the same ships that carry the bananas. The biggest sales are between August and November when the South African crop is over and the crop from Israel is not ready for reaping. Dominican oranges and grapefruit also find a ready market in CARICOM countries. In addition, some canned grapefruit juice is exported.

Most of the limes are grown on estates in the south-west of the island below a height of 300 metres. A few are exported as fresh fruit to other West Indian islands, particularly to the neighbouring islands of Martinique and Guadeloupe, and to those such as Antigua and Barbados with tourist industries. But the bulk of the crop is converted into lime juice and lime oil which brought in 2 per cent of the foreign earnings in 1985.

Coconuts

Coconuts are another subsidiary crop. They are sometimes interplanted with bananas. Their advantage over bananas is that they can be processed into manufactured products. No such linkage is possible with bananas. Most of the coconuts are made into laundry and toilet soap for export to CARICOM countries. Some are made into coconut oil and animal feed. In the late 1980s, coconuts and coconut products, including soap, formed about one-third of the island's exports.

Other crops

Bay oil is extracted from the leaves of bay trees (few of which have been deliberately planted) and exported, mainly to the USA. A small amount of sugar cane is grown to supply an old mill and rum distillery near Roseau. The supply is supplemented by shipments of molasses from Montserrat.

Shifting cultivation is common among the peasants and extends into parts of the forest. Some fruit and vegetables have at times found a market overseas, especially in the Bahamas, but production of food crops has tended to decline with the rise of bananas.

Other commodities

Dominica has only a few of the modern light manufacturing industries that are being set up on industrial estates in CARICOM countries. However, it has a small but successful craft industry. This involves the manufacture of straw goods, especially floor mats. They are exported to a variety of countries, including Barbados, Bermuda and the United States Virgin Islands. Other small industries include the making of cigarettes, pipe-tobacco and cigars – from tobacco grown mostly in the Layou valley – and the making of soft drinks.

The island's fast flowing streams are suitable for small hydro-electric stations. Three-quarters of the island's electricity is generated in this way.

Tourism

Dominica lacks the white-sand beaches and the certainty of prolonged sunshine that most tourists look for when taking a Caribbean holiday. However, the island is attractive to tourists with an interest in natural phenomena (eg the boiling lake), plant collecting, bird watching, mountain climbing, hiking and camping. As a result, tourism is growing.

Towns and communications

Roseau (17 000), the capital, is situated on a small alluvial fan created by the Roseau River on the western coast. Only small ships can tie up at the jetty. Larger ones load and unload at the Woodbridge Bay deep water port in the north of the town. Portsmouth (4 000) has a much better harbour, but banana ships have to be loaded by lighters. Most of the other settlements have been built on small, isolated alluvial flats and in all about 90 per cent of the population lives within a mile of the sea.

Set as it is between the French islands of Martinique and Guadeloupe, Dominica is isolated from the other Commonwealth Eastern Caribbean states. However, the ruggedness of the terrain has been a bigger handicap to development than has isolation, and the construction and maintenance of roads are difficult problems. Long stretches of the coastline are so rugged that there is no continuous coastal road.

Montserrat

Area: 84 square kilometres; population (1988): about 12 300; density of population: 146 per square kilometre.

Landforms

Montserrat, which lies about midway between Guadeloupe and Nevis, is part of the inner volcanic arc of the Lesser Antilles (see Map 8.1). It consists of three main volcanic masses. That in the north is the oldest. It has been reduced by erosion to rounded hills, the highest of which – Silver Hill – rises to about 400 metres. In the south, the Soufrière Hills, which rise at their highest point to 912 metres, and South Soufriere, which reaches 760 metres, are recent steep-sided volcanic cones deeply incised by ravines. They contain fumaroles which emit sulphurous fumes that have killed off all but the most resistant vegetation nearby. In general, however, their upper slopes are wooded and their lower, more gently sloping shoulders are in pasture and vegetable cultivation.

Development

During the period of slavery sugar estates occupied the best agricultural land, and in 1789 there were 6 000 acres under cane; double the area under crops today. In the financial crises which followed emancipation the landowners resorted to sharecropping rather than sell their land. Whenever conditions improved they employed labourers again. Even so, the area under cane declined. Sea-island cotton took its place. If cotton is to grow well, the fields have to be kept free from weeds. The result is that the land is very susceptible to erosion.

Rainfall

The Central and Soufrière Hills rise high enough for their summits to be cool and wet. The east coast, exposed to the drying influence of the Trade winds, is somewhat drier than the west coast. The northern, and to a lesser extent the southern parts of the island, are drier still

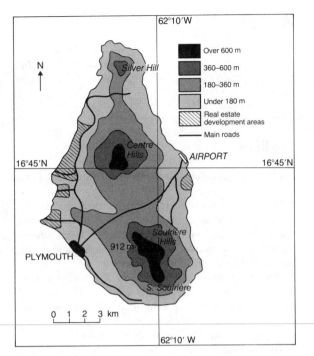

Map 8.16 MONTSERRAT: Relief.

Map 8.17 MONTSERRAT: Rainfall.

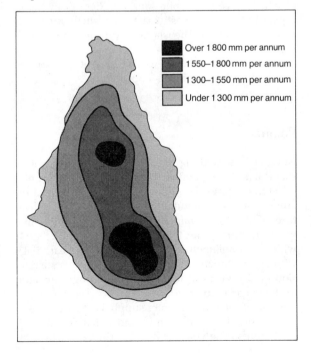

Agriculture and industry

Fruit and vegetables

Only some 3 000 acres – that is one-eighth of the island – is farmed. Sugar cane has virtually disappeared, and fruits and vegetables are the most important crops. Most are grown for local consumption, but small amounts are sometimes exported. Peppers have been sold mainly to Britain, tomatoes at various times to Canada, Bermuda, Puerto Rico, St Thomas, Florida, and elsewhere, depending on the transport available. Other crops to have been exported on occasion include carrots, onions, sweet and Irish potatoes, pumpkins, bananas and mangoes. But again because of the lack of transport, sales have been limited, and confined mostly to the neighbouring island of Antigua.

Transport is, in fact, the chief problem hindering further development. Like all small islands, Montserrat does not buy or produce enough to attract much shipping, but until ships do call regularly there is no incentive to produce more. At present, the only regular large-scale opportunity for exporting produce is provided by inter-island ships.

Limes, introduced about the middle of the nineteenth century, were once an important export. Some are still grown, mostly by a few estates on the leeward side of the island, but because climatic conditions proved to be not particularly suitable and because trees have been damaged by hurricanes, diseases and insect pests, the output has declined.

Some cotton continues to be grown. The area under cotton expands and contracts from year to year, but it is never large. In recent years the crop has been used to manufacture clothes for sale to visitors and to CARICOM countries but without much success.

The other resources of Montserrat are very small indeed. Some timber – chiefly cedar – and some shingles and charcoal are exported and there is a small boat-building industry. With over 5 000 cattle in the island there is usually no shortage of locally produced meat and milk. Some animals are occasionally exported to the French West Indies and Antigua. Industry is limited to a few modern light manufactures including electronics assembly and the making of plastic bags and paper products, processing cotton, making blocks and tiles for house building, retreading tyres, and making soft drinks.

The result of all this is that exports are minute, even considering the small size of the island. Thus

135

in 1988 locally produced exports amounted to only about 9 per cent of the value of imports. Over three-quarters of the exports were accounted for by a single item – the assembly of electronic components.

Part of this enormous trade gap is met by the money that is sent home by people who have left Montserrat to live in other countries. Emigration has gone on for many years. As a result there are at least three times as many people from Montserrat living overseas as there are on the island itself. Also as a result the population of Montserrat has remained at about 12 000 since the 1960s. Montserrat is the only island where the population has not grown in recent years.

Tourism

Another part of the trade gap is met by tourism. Though the number of tourists visiting Montserrat is only about a tenth of the number visiting Antigua, their contribution to the economy is considerable. In addition, well over 1 000 acres of land in various parts of the island (shown on Map 8.16) have been bought by real estate companies and developed as residential areas for Americans to live when they retire. Because Montserrat does not possess the same mass market attractions as the most popular tourist resorts, visitors to the island have special reasons for going there. Among them are the restful atmosphere, the friendliness of the people, and the inland scenery. Tourist development has brought with it a rise of employment in the construction in-dustry and in domestic service. It has also led to some of the island's most fertile land being taken out of production and converted into a golf course. (The photograph on page 53 could as easily have been taken in Montserrat as in Jamaica.) It seems strange that such land can be of more value in an unproduc-tive than in a cultivated state, but wherever there are wealthy people looking for relaxation it is possible for a golf course to earn more money per acre than a farm.

The only town and only port in Montserrat is Plymouth (3 000). Plymouth lies on the south-west coast where the sea is sheltered by the Soufrière Hills and where water is deep enough to allow ships to come close to the shore.

Roads extend some distance to the north and south of the town, but none encircle the island.

Antigua

Area: 280 square kilometres; population (1988): about 83 000; density of population: 296 per square kilometre; area of dependencies (Barbuda and Redonda): 162 square kilometres.

Landforms

Antigua is divided into three distinct structural regions:

1 The area south-west of a line joining Five Island Harbour and Willoughby Bay consists of the eroded remnants of old volcanic mountains. These steep-sided hills rise to over 300 metres, the highest point, Boggy Peak, reaching 400 metres.

2 Stretching from north-west to south-east across the centre of the island is a narrow clay lowland about 16 kilometres in length and 5 kilometres in width. It is flat or gently undulating country, rarely rising more than 15 metres above sea-level.

3 The northern part of Antigua is composed of a rolling limestone upland which rises fairly steeply from the central plain to heights of over 100 metres.

The coast is rugged and contains many bays, some of which have fine white sand beaches. Elsewhere, especially on the west coast, are small areas of mangrove swamp. The island is surrounded by coral reefs.

There is little mineral wealth in Antigua. Some clay is dug to make bricks and pottery.

Rainfall

Antigua is something like Barbados in being a low island with a low rainfall. The annual average is only 1 150 millimetres, less than half that of Dominica or any of the other mountainous islands. Another fea-ture of Antigua's rainfall is its uncertainty. Some years are much drier than others. For example, 1981 with 1 450 millimetres of rain was a wet year; 1983 with 567 millimetres was a dry one. It was a succes-sion of dry years in the 1960s that brought an end to the sugar industry.

Some of the island's water supply is obtained from underground; some from ponds, reservoirs and catchments. The volcanic hills are the best source of

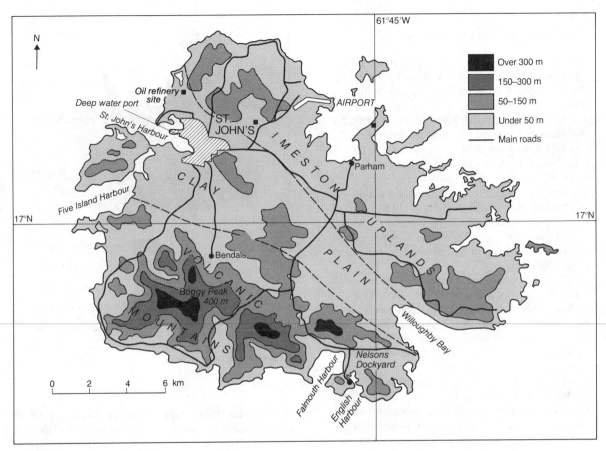

Map 8.18 ANTIGUA: Relief and communications.

water. Unfortunately, because of the generally low rainfall and the unpredictable droughts the supply of water is not always enough to meet the needs of households and hotels. The problem is greatest between December and April. This is the dry season. It is also the time when water consumption is highest because of the number of tourists visiting the island.

Development

The history of Antigua resembles that of Barbados and St Kitts in that there was a brief period when smallholders cultivated tobacco, cotton and indigo, followed by nearly two centuries of slave-worked sugar estates. By the middle of the eighteenth century, there were 35 000 slaves but only 2 500 white people in the island. The original forest cover had been largely removed to make way for cane, which was grown everywhere, even on top of the volcanic hills. Throughout this period there was so much specialisation in this one industry that the inhabitants had to rely on imports for practically everything they needed, even for the bulk of the food supply. Thus the depressions which struck the British West Indian sugar industry in the nineteenth century were felt particularly severely in Antigua. The better-situated lowland estates struggled on in spite of greatly reduced profits, but marginal land went out of use altogether and in many places it has never been cultivated since. The remains of many old stone windmills that once crushed the cane are still to be seen in the hills standing amidst brush and thicket now cropped only by goats.

Changes of land use in Antigua

It is possible to deduce that major changes have taken place in land use in Antigua by studying the photograph on page 139. The reasoning is as follows:

1 Antigua was originally covered with forest. As the photograph shows no sign of the forest, it must all have been deliberately cleared. The only common reason for clearing forest land is to enable the land to be cultivated.

2 No one would go to the trouble and expense of clearing all the land in sight, including the hilltops, unless the crop to be planted there was a very profitable one. Therefore, at some period of its history, Antigua was planted with a very profitable crop.

From the photograph we cannot tell for sure what crop it was, though we can say that it was unlikely to be a tree crop, such as cocoa, because there are no trees to be seen today. In fact, the crop was sugar cane. Had the remains of an old windmill appeared in the picture, we could have deduced this too.

3 While the land was under forest it was protected from erosion. The gullies you see in the hillsides must therefore have been formed after the forest was cleared; that is during the period in which the land was under cultivation. Such big gullies would have taken many years to form. Therefore the land was under cultivation for many years. Throughout that time it seems, agriculture remained prosperous enough for the crop to be grown right up to the tops of the hills.

4 For some reason (we cannot tell from the photograph what it was) the crop being grown ceased to be profitable. As a result, cultivation on the highlands and much of the lowlands was abandoned. This took place some time ago; long enough for scrub vegetation and bushes to have grown up on the hillsides where the cultivation used to be. The period of agricultural prosperity is therefore long past.

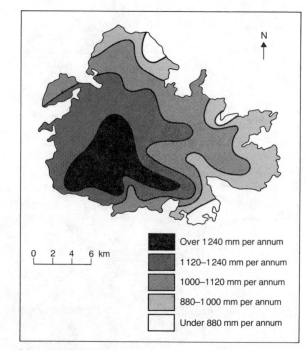

Over 1 240 mm per annum

1 120–1 240 mm per annum

1000–1 120 mm per annum

880–1 000 mm per annum

Under 880 mm per annum

0 2 4 6 km

Map 8.19 ANTIGUA: Rainfall.

After their emancipation in 1838 many of the freed slaves wanted to obtain land of their own. Very little was available because the proprietors were reluctant to sell their estates despite their declining value. For that reason there was no great development of peasant farming in the nineteenth century. Nor was there demand for wage labour. With the failure to find an alternative to cane, a shortage of locally produced foodstuffs, and a population density of 150 per square kilometre, the island inevitably entered a period of depression. This was made worse when the naval station at English Harbour was abandoned in 1899. Throughout the sailing-ship era it had been the chief British naval base in the Caribbean, but with the coming of steamships its strategic importance ended and it fell into decay. The old fortifications, shops and harbour works of Nelson's Dockyard have been restored. They are one of the island's tourist attractions.

During the first half of the present century there were three major developments:

1) The manufacture of sugar gradually became concentrated in one central factory.

2) The dependence on one export crop was lessened to some extent by the introduction of sea-island cotton.

3) With government assistance many abandoned properties were bought, split up, and sold or rented

English harbour, Antigua. In what direction was the camera pointing? What can you tell about the present function of the built-up area (Nelson's Dockyard)? What evidence is there that it is not a flourishing settlement?

to small farmers, most of whom grew cane and cotton for cash and food crops for subsistence. Being able to live on a piece of land of their own brought with it a feeling of independence that was lacking in a totally estate economy like that of St Kitts. But the uncertainty of the water supply prevented people in Antigua from farming intensively, and living standards therefore remained low. Many people emigrated. They went to Cuba, Panama and the United States, to the banana plantations of Central America and to the oil refineries of Aruba and Curaçao.

More recent developments have been of a different nature. As we have seen, the island's sugar industry was brought to an end by drought in the 1960s. Since then low prices and labour shortages have prevented recovery. Today the economy is dominated by tourism which provides over three-quarters of the island's income.

Land use

With the decline of sugar cane and cotton, export agriculture ceased to exist. Many of the old estates

were abandoned and have been taken over by the government. Today about 70 per cent of the island's total area is taken up by woodland, scrub and grass. On much of it flocks of goats and sheep are allowed to graze with little or no control. Less than 10 per cent of the land is cultivated. Small farmers use it to grow a variety of crops for households and hotels. Carrots, onions, sweet potatoes, tomatoes, cucumbers, and pineapples are all important. Tree crops, grown in the wetter areas, include limes, avocados, and mangoes. As in Montserrat, golf courses now occupy some of the land which was once agriculturally productive.

Tourism

The development of tourism began in the 1950s, putting Antigua years ahead of the rest of the Eastern Caribbean. There are several reasons why Antigua was able to lead the way. For one thing, by the 1950s the island was already well-known to the American public because of the publicity given to a group of millionaires who had bought several square kilometres of land in the east of the island and built their homes there – a development known as the Mill Reef Club. For another, the island already possessed a big airport, built originally as part of an American military base and later made available for commercial purposes. In addition, Antigua had two geographical advantages over the islands in the volcanic chain. One was that it possessed a deeply embayed coast with white sand beaches where luxury hotels could do big business. The second was that, being relatively low-lying, it had a drier, sunnier climate than the volcanic islands, and fine weather is what tourists want for their Caribbean holidays.

Nearly half of the tourists who visit Antigua come from the United States. For them and for Canadians as well, the months between December and April are most popular. Britain and other European Community countries are another important source, particularly in the school holiday months of July and August. By reducing their room rates in those months, hotels are able to attract more tourists and spread their business more evenly throughout the year. The monthly figures for 1984 are shown in Table 8.20. Note that as they are in thousands 10.4 stands for 10 400 tourists.

Table 8.20 Tourists visiting Antigua in 1984 ('000)

Jan	Feb	Mar	Apr	May	Jun	Jul	Aug	Sep	Oct	Nov	Dec
12.2	13.2	12.6	13.2	8.6	8.2	10.4	10.2	6.4	9.0	12.1	13.0

People hold conflicting opinions on the benefits of tourism to the West Indies. Some claim that the economic benefits are sufficient in themselves. Others point out that tourism contributes to a rise in the cost of living and to so great an increase in the price of property that local people can no longer afford to buy a piece of land of their own. Some believe that only tourism can provide the employment opportunities that are so desperately needed by young people. Others say that the kinds of jobs that are available contribute little to the development of personal dignity. Yet another group of people is concerned about the effect that casino gambling (which is permitted in Antigua) and night clubs are having on the moral values of society.

If you live in a tourist area, make a list of people in various occupations who could be asked for an opinion. Find out what they say, and discuss their views. Are there noticeable differences of opinion between old people and young people, between men and women, and between those who make a living from tourism and those who do not? What agreements and differences exist among yourselves.

Manufacturing

Antigua was one of those West Indian islands which, like Jamaica and the Bahamas, set up an oil refinery based entirely on imported crude petroleum. While it operated, its products formed the island's leading export. It also supplied local needs, including jet fuel for the planes landing at the busy airport. However, it became unprofitable and was closed in the mid 1970s.

Antigua produces a range of light manufactured goods including men and women's garments, paper and plastic products, corrugated iron sheets, stoves, refrigerators, solar water heaters, paints, furniture, batteries and retreaded tyres. Some of these are sold abroad, particularly in CARICOM countries.

Towns and trade

The capital, St John's, owes its location to its sheltered harbour and its ease of access to the central lowlands. It is the only port and, with a population of about 30 000, the only town of any size. The volume of its trade is much smaller than that of the banana ports of Castries, Roseau and Kingstown further south in the chain of Eastern Caribbean islands.

In the mid 1980s manufactures made up 80 per cent of the island's small export trade; agricultural products only 3 per cent. The cost of imports was three times the value of the exports. About 30 per cent of the imports were food products, showing how far Antigua is from being able to supply its own requirements.

Barbuda

Area (including the lagoon): 160 square kilometres; population: about 1 000.

Extending northwards from Antigua is a shallow, submarine bank on which – some 38 kilometres

Port development at St John's, Antigua. The containers in the foreground are waiting to be loaded on to ocean-going ships at the modern deep-water port. The old port can also be seen. It is still used by smaller vessels.

away – stands the island of Barbuda. Two-thirds of the island is a flat, monotonous plain only a few feet above sea-level, but in the east, a series of steep-sided, flat-topped coral terraces rise to just over 60 metres. There is a narrow belt of sand-dunes round most of the coast. Everywhere the soil is shallow and much bare rock is exposed.

The rainfall is low, averaging 900 millimetres a year, and severe droughts are common. When rain does come, it often falls in heavy showers and the heavy, impermeable clay pan which lies beneath the thin layer of topsoil causes the plain to become waterlogged. In these conditions no large trees can grow, and the vegetation consists of low woodland and bush with patches of savanna in the south-east.

Agriculture has never been developed on a large scale, and today it is limited to the production of food-crops – mainly corn yams, groundnuts, pumpkins and peas – and the rearing of livestock for local consumption. The only significant export consists of lobsters which are caught in the large shallow lagoon on the western side of the island and flown out to Antigua. So far the tourist industry is only a small one.

Owing to emigration and the number of Barbudan men who leave the island in order to make a living as seamen, the population of the island has not increased but remained fairly constant. The only village – Codrington – stands at the head of the lagoon.

About 40 kilometres south-west of Antigua is *Redonda* a small volcanic island one mile long, one-half of a kilometre wide and 300 metres high. It is of no economic significance.

St Kitts-Nevis

Area: 269 square kilometres; population (1988): about 45 000; density of population: 167 per square kilometre.

St Kitts

Area 176 square kilometres; population (1988): about 35 500.

Settlement and development

The small party of colonists who landed in St Kitts in 1624 were the first British settlers in the West Indies. They gained a precarious foothold and a year later welcomed French help to drive the Caribs out of the island and defend it from Spanish attack. St Kitts was then divided between them, the British occupying the middle and the French the two ends of the island. With so much rivalry between the two nations this arrangement was not successful for long, and the island changed hands several times.

In the early days the settlers came as smallholders to grow food crops for themselves, and tobacco, cotton, ginger and indigo for export. Population increased rapidly, the total for St Kitts and Nevis reaching 20 000 by 1640. This growth came to a halt around 1650 when sugar cane was introduced. Indeed, as the sugar estates grew in size, many of the smallholders chose to emigrate rather than work for other people on land that had once been their own. Their place was taken by African slaves who increased in numbers from 3 000 in 1707 to 24 000 in 1774.

When emancipation came in 1838, the freed slaves had little opportunity to make a new life for themselves. They owned no land, and found the estates unwilling to sell them any. They lived in houses belonging to the estates, and they could be turned out if they ceased to work in the cane fields. Some were able to rent small patches of land, usually on the unused upper margins of the estates. Others emigrated to places such as Trinidad and Guyana, where land was plentiful. Most had little choice but to remain as a low-paid unskilled labour force on the estates. With workers available, and with good land, plentiful rainfall, and some of the best soils in the West Indies, the sugar industry was able to continue to dominate the economy and to hold back the social development of the mass of the people.

As time went by, the factories became larger in size and smaller in number until, in 1911, a single factory was built to mill all of the island's cane. Gradually, too, the field operations became more efficient. As a result, sugar production rose from about 11 000 tonnes reaped from 7 500 acres in 1908, to about 50 000 tonnes reaped from a little over 13 000 acres in 1960. Since then, however, the area under cane, and the output of sugar, have decreased.

Landforms

St Kitts may be divided into two parts, the high main body of the island and the relatively low south-eastward-pointing peninsula.

The backbone of the main body of the island consists of three groups of young, rugged volcanic peaks, all of which rise to at least 800 metres. The youngest and highest group in the north-west is dominated by Mt Liamuiga, 1 150 metres, a dormant volcano with some fumarole activity in its crater. Like Verchild's Mountain a little farther south, it contains a crater lake. The mountains which rise steeply above 330 metres, are composed of volcanic ash, cinders and some boulders. Around their base is a more gently sloping apron of volcanic ash dissected by deep ravines called 'ghauts' or 'guts'. There is a basalt lava flow ending at Black Rock on the north-east coast. There is also some limestone which is quarried for local use at Brimstone Hill.

The older and lower southern peninsula ends in a triangular knot of volcanic peaks, the highest of which rises to 360 metres.

Rainfall and vegetation

The land above 360 metres receives a heavy rainfall, probably over 2 250 millimetres a year. In heavy rains the streams running down the flanks of Mt Liamuiga are liable to flood. The mountains are largely covered with palm brake and rain-forest which extends down to about 220 metres in places, though most of the land between 220 and 300 metres has been cleared for cultivation.

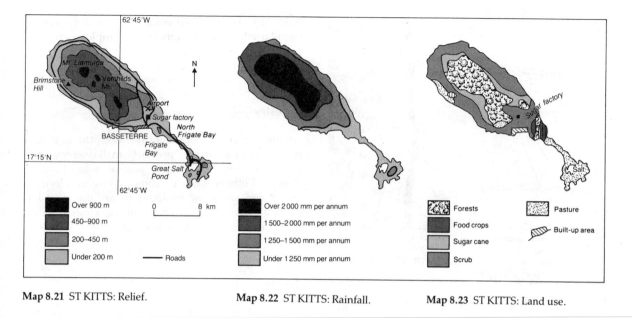

Map 8.21 ST KITTS: Relief.　　**Map 8.22** ST KITTS: Rainfall.　　**Map 8.23** ST KITTS: Land use.

The driest area is the southern peninsula, parts of which have as little as 1 000 millimetres a year and a dry season of four to six months. Most of it is covered with low shrubs and cacti, though in the flatter and less rocky places it has been cleared for pasture.

Most of the cane fields receive on average between 1 250 and 1 800 millimetres of rain a year.

Agriculture

Sugar

As can be seen from Map 8.23 the cane fields of St Kitts form an almost continuous belt around the main body of the island. They stretch from close to the coast into the hills where, as is shown clearly in the photograph on page 145, gradients are too steep for cane cultivation. St Kitts is the only state in the Commonwealth Eastern Caribbean where sugar cane remains the dominant crop. Even in St Kitts it survives only with difficulty. One problem is that the cost of producing sugar is far higher than the price paid for it on the world market. Output therefore depends on the existence of a large guaranteed market which pays a higher than world-market price. Such a market exists only in the European Economic Community. The American market is rapidly declining because cane sugar is being replaced by high fructose corn syrup made in America itself. Another problem is that wages for field labour are lower than those paid to people working in light industry and tourism. As a result, field labour is scarce. Recently there have been some years when some of the cane has been left unreaped.

To prevent the sugar industry from collapse, the government has bought nearly all the land under cane. It also owns and operates the island's sugar factory. The average annual ouput in the 1980s has been about 32 000 tonnes. About 5 000 tonnes is used for local consumption and export to nearby islands. The rest is sent to the major markets. Sugar accounted for about 40 per cent of total exports in the late 1980s.

Other crops

Several attempts have been made in the past to grow alternative export crops, but experiments with cocoa, citrus, tobacco and rubber have all failed. Peanuts became the most important subsidiary crop in the 1970s. Sea-island cotton has been successful at times but output is now restricted to Nevis.

143

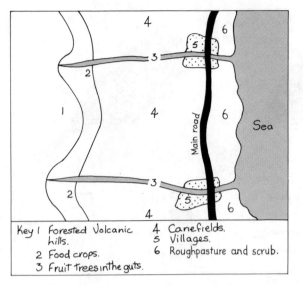

Key
1 Forested volcanic hills.
2 Food crops.
3 Fruit trees in the guts.
4 Canefields.
5 Villages.
6 Roughpasture and scrub.

Map 8.24 ST KITTS: Sketch map of land use.

Food crops are grown mainly between the upper limits of the cane fields and the lower edge of the forest, and mangoes, breadfruit, avocados, and other fruit trees are thickly clustered on the sides of the guts from the upper forests almost down to the sea. A rough sketch of this land use is shown in Map 8.24. In addition, many cane fields which have yielded three or four ratoons are ploughed and planted in vegetables. However, the production of fruit and vegetables is less than the requirements and there is a considerable import, especially from Nevis.

Tourism

Prior to the 1970s, tourism was of little significance in St Kitts. Since then several areas have been developed, and tourism now contributes more to the economy than sugar does. The most important hotel area is Frigate Bay which has the attractions of white sand beaches and a marina. The airport nearby (see Map 8.21) has been enlarged and modernised so as to take large jet aircraft. Some places near the eastern Atlantic coast have been set aside for retirement homes. There are nature trails in the highlands. Stop-over visitors numbered 65 000 in 1987 and there

were 31 000 cruise-ship visitors. Tourism provides a popular alternative to agricultural employment, particularly for women.

Industry

Another recent development has been the manufacture of light industrial products in Basseterre. The products vary from year to year as some factories close and others open. Clothing, footwear, electrical goods and electronic components are the most important. Their export, mainly to the United States, brings in more money than sugar.

Towns

Basseterre (16 000), the capital and only town of any size, is situated on a bay on the south-east coast of St Kitts. It is a busy port. Besides handling all the imports and exports of St Kitts it acts as a distributing centre for merchandise to neighbouring islands, including such non-Commonwealth ones as Saba, St Martin and St Eustatius. There is a regular motorboat service to Charlestown, the chief town of Nevis.

Most of the other settlements in St Kitts are situated in the lower courses of the guts where they widen out a mile or so from the sea.

Nevis

Area: 93 square kilometres; population (1988): about 9 500.

Settlement and development

For a long time the development of Nevis was very similar to that of St Kitts. There was a period of settlement by British smallholders followed by a much longer period of slave-run sugar estates. The slave population numbered 10 000 in the late eighteenth century.

The divergence between the two islands began soon after emancipation. With poorer soils and

Basseterre, St Kitts. Compare this volcanic landscape with that of Castries (page 129).

Nevis. What can you tell about the geological history of the island from this picture?

steeper slopes than those of St Kitts, the sugar industry of Nevis was less able to withstand the depressions which occurred in the second half of the nineteenth century. Many landowners introduced sharecropping to try to preserve their once profitable estates. But with each economic setback more and more estates went out of production.

For a time, sea-island cotton, also grown on a sharecropping system, occupied much of the cultivated land. This, too has declined. There is much less land being cultivated today than there was 200 years ago.

Landforms

Nevis is an almost circular island about 10 and 13 kilometres across. The centre is dominated by one symmetrical volcanic cone, Nevis Peak, which is about 1 000 metres high. There are also some subsidiary peaks, including Mt Lily and Saddle Hill which rise to over 300 metres in height. Because the volcanic activity was more explosive than in St Kitts, the material contains many more stones and boulders. The fields, even those on the lowlands, have had to be cleared of great quantities of rocks before they could be cultivated.

Rainfall

The rainfall varies from just under 1 250 millimetres a year on the sheltered south-western lowlands to over 2 300 millimetres at heights above 600 metres. Nevis Peak is commonly enveloped in cloud, especially during the afternoons.

Occupations

The decline of agriculture applies to every crop in the island. Both sugar cane and sea-island cotton have virtually disappeared. The output of coconuts and copra, is small. Some estates have been bought

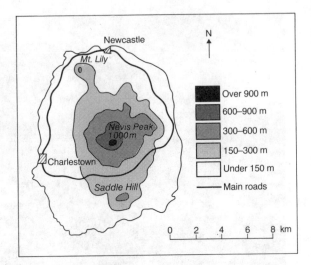

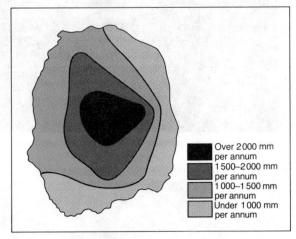

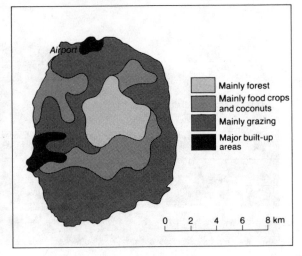

Maps 8.25, 8.26, 8.27 NEVIS: Relief (top); Rainfall (middle); Land use (bottom)

146

by the government and leased or given away to smallholders who grow sweet potatoes, yams, corn and other food crops. But most of the land has reverted to scrub, grazed at random by goats, sheep and cattle. As a result, soil erosion has become severe in some areas.

Because St Kitts is short of locally-produced foodstuffs, it provides a ready market for those grown in Nevis, and there is a brisk daily trade between Charlestown (population 1 200) and Basseterre. Some charcoal is made in Nevis and this, too, is sent to St Kitts.

Mainly because Nevis does not possess an international airport or white sand beaches its tourist business is different from that of St Kitts. Instead of appealing to the mass market, Nevis seeks to attract tourists who are looking for quiet holidays in small hotels and who are interested in the island's scenery and history.

Nevis has a few light manufacturing industries and a small boat-building industry.

Anguilla

Area: 96 square kilometres; population (1988): about 7 100; density of population: 74 per square kilometre.

Anguilla, which lies about 100 kilometres north of St Kitts, is some 26 kilometres long by $2\frac{1}{2}$ to $6\frac{1}{2}$ kilometres wide. Like Barbuda it is a low-lying coral island, rising at its highest to just over 60 metres. About one-third of the area consists of the edges of the coral terraces exposed as bare rock ribs. Over a larger area the soil is too thin for cultivation but supports scrub suitable for low-grade grazing. The remainder of the island has patches of quite fertile soil.

The rainfall, of about 1 000 millimetres a year, is both low and unreliable.

Anguilla and St Kitts have little in common. Whereas in St Kitts a few large landowners own a lot of land, and the economy is based on sugar, in Anguilla most of the land holdings are small and there is no commercial agriculture. Sugar was exported at one time, but the industry died out shortly after emancipation. Later, sea-island cotton was grown as a cash-crop, but today agriculture is limited to a few subsistence crops (eg corn and peas) and to the rearing of sheep and goats, some of which are sent for sale in the island of St Maarten, one of the Netherlands Antilles.

With some of the finest white sand beaches in the Caribbean, extensive coral reefs and rich marine life, Anguilla has a rapidly expanding tourist business. In addition to the hotel visitors there are a large number of day trippers who travel over by ferry from St Maarten.

There is a large catch of lobsters, fish and turtles. Some are sold locally but most are exported to St Maarten which has a large tourist business. Other sources of income on Anguilla are boat building and the money sent home by the large numbers of emigrants now living off the island in the Virgin Islands, the Netherlands Antilles, Britain and elsewhere in the world.

The long distance between Anguilla and St Kitts, the different social structures of the two islands and the low level of Anguilla's economic development compared with that of the nearby American Virgin Islands, were some of the reasons for Anguilla's decision in 1969 to separate itself politically from St Kitts. Anguilla is now self-governing under British administration.

Questions and assignments

1 Make a list of the Commonwealth Eastern Caribbean countries in descending order of area.
   a) Which of these countries is the largest and which is the smallest?
   b) What is their total area? How does the total area compare with that of i) Barbados, ii) Jamaica?
2 Make a similar list in descending order of population.
   a) Which country has most people and which has the least?
   b) What is the total population? How does the total compare with i) Barbados, and ii) Jamaica?
3 a) Name one island from the northern part of the chain and one from the south.
   b) Under the following headings, write one sentence to show a similarity or difference between the two islands: area, relief, rainfall, natural vegetation, agriculture, population, tourism.

4 Using the information given below, answer the following questions.

Volume of banana exports (to the nearest thousand tonnes)

Country	1981	1985	1988
Dominica	27	34	70
Grenada	12	8	9
St Lucia	43	73	128
St Vincent	30	40	62

a) What were the total banana exports of the four countries in 1981, 1985 and 1988?

b) How much greater was the total output in 1988 from that of 1981?

c) What country contributed most to the increase?

d) Describe in one sentence the change in the output from Dominica between 1981 and 1988. Do the same for St Lucia.

e) What was Grenada's percentage of the total in 1981 and in 1985?

f) Calculate the percentage of each of the countries in 1988. Draw a divided circle (pie chart) to show these percentages.

g) Name two problems which banana farmers in these countries have to face, and one measure that is being taken to overcome each of them.

5 Choose three products, one from each of the following groups:

Group 1: Arrowroot, ginger, nutmeg, sea-island cotton.

Group 2: Cocoa, coconut, coffee, tobacco.

Group 3: Bananas, grapefruit, limes, pineapples.

For each crop chosen:

a) state precisely the location of one producing region in the Caribbean area;

b) state the conditions favouring production in the region named;

c) give details of methods of cultivation, harvesting and preparation for sale.

6 Using the information given in Table 8.20:

a) Calculate the number of tourists who visited Antigua in 1984.

b) Draw and label a bar graph to show the monthly figures.

c) What percentage of tourists visited Antigua between the beginning of November and the end of April? Give two reasons to explain why this is the peak season. Give two further reasons which might explain the second peak in June and July.

7 Using the information given below, answer the questions that follow.

Percentage of foodstuffs imported by hotels in one Eastern Caribbean country in 1984

Meats	86
Seafood	19
Dairy products	99
Vegetables	35
Fruits	7

a) What percentage of each of these five categories of foodstuffs was produced locally?

b) Draw bar graphs like the one below to show the percentages of imported and locally produced foodstuffs

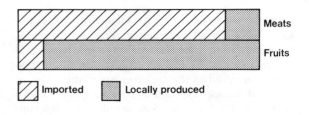

c) Name two problems that farmers face in trying to raise their output to meet the needs of hotels.

d) 'A high proportion of the money spent by tourists in Caribbean countries does not stay in those countries.' Give two reasons why this statement may be correct.

9

The French West Indies

Area: 2 792 square kilometres; population (1988): about 670 000; density of population: 240 per square kilometre.

Martinique and *Guadeloupe* (with its dependencies) are all that remain of the former extensive French possessions in the West Indies, though France still retains French Guiana in South America. The political development of the two islands has been very different from that of the Commonwealth Eastern Caribbean States. Instead of proceeding to independence they are part of the French nation. One outcome of this is that they are entitled to receive the same social welfare benefits as the citizens of mainland France. Indeed, the main revenues of the islands come from French taxpayers. Another outcome is that migration to France is unrestricted. Many people have taken advantage of this opportunity. Large numbers of French West Indians are living in and around Paris.

Martinique, with an area of 1 100 square kilometres, and a population of about 330 000 in 1988, lies mid-way between Dominica and St Lucia. Like those two islands, Martinique is mountainous, its volcanic interior rising to over 900 metres in several places. Unlike them it contains an active volcano, Mt Pelée, 1 430 metres high.

The last major eruption of Mt Pelée took place in 1902. Early in the year it began to emit smoke and there were occasional falls of ash. The eruptions increased in intensity, breaking through the sides of the mountain because the main vent was blocked by a solid plug of lava. In April, outbursts of lava, mud and ash destroyed several sugar estates and killed several hundred people. The climax came on the morning of 8 May 1902, when there was an explosion and a blazing mass of ash, lava and gas burst out of the southern face of the mountain. Burning,

melting and smashing everything in its path it overwhelmed the town of St Pierre. When the cloud cleared a few minutes later, it revealed only the shattered relic of the town. Of the seventeen ships in the harbour only one escaped to tell the tale. 'We have come from the gates of Hell,' said the captain when he reached St Lucia. 'You can inform the world that not a soul remains alive at St Pierre.' Out of 30 000 inhabitants there were two survivors. One was hidden in a cellar. The other was a prisoner protected by the thick walls of his cell.

The catastrophe, one of the most famous in the world, was so different from other eruptions recorded up to that time that it gave its name to a new type, the Peleean type, of eruption. After it was over, activity continued on a more moderate scale for several months. In addition, the lava plug

Map 9.1 MARTINIQUE: Relief.

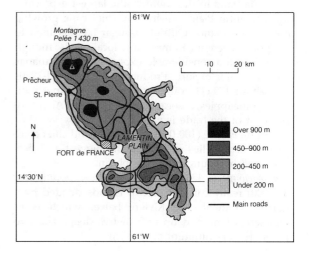

149

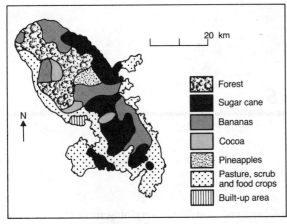

Map 9.2 MARTINIQUE: Land use.

Pointe-à-Pitre, Guadeloupe. In what ways is this French West Indian scene (a) similar to and (b) different from that in the country in which you live?

blocking the main vent of the volcano was pushed slowly upwards until it projected 100 metres or more above the rim of the crater. Exposed as it was to heavy rains and severe weathering, it was soon worn away.

Between 1929 and 1932 minor eruptions occurred again. St Pierre, which by this time had been rebuilt on a smaller scale, was untouched. No lives were lost, but for a time the road from St Pierre to Prêcheur was blocked by a lava flow and a layer of ash.

Mt Pelée is a young and slightly eroded cone. Elsewhere the mountains of Martinique are broken by deep valleys which allow roads to penetrate into the interior and to cross from coast to coast. There is not much flat land in the country, the largest expanse – the Lamentin Plain – being the chief cane growing area in the island. Output of sugar has declined to the point where it can meet only local needs, though there is still a considerable export of rum. Bananas are the major export. Production in the mid-1980s was about 170 000 tonnes a year. Other exports include pineapples, avocados and flowers. About 70 per cent of the trade is with France.

Fort de France (100 000), the capital and chief commercial centre, lies on one of the biggest and best sheltered harbours in the Caribbean.

Guadeloupe (1 430 square kilometres, population: 337 000) really consists of two islands divided by a narrow channel, the Rivière Salée, which is 6½ kilometres long and up to 5 metres deep. The two parts are very different in character.

The western part, Basse-Terre, belongs to the volcanic arc of the Lesser Antilles and is traversed by a forested mountain range which is almost inaccessible from the western side. Its highest peak, La Soufrière, 1 480 metres, erupted in 1797 and in 1836, when heavy showers of ash fell over the surrounding area. This was repeated on a smaller scale in 1976 when a new crack appeared in the mountain. Many people left their homes for a time and went to the eastern side of the island for safety. Today, sulphurous smoke and steam rise from small vents in the crater and flames can be seen at times. Hot streams on the flanks of La Soufrière are another indication of its dormant vulcanicity.

In contrast, Grande-Terre, the eastern part of Guadeloupe consists of a low limestone plateau eroded in the south into a typical karst landscape with steep-sided wooded hills and ridges rising to between 60 and 100 metres.

The higher, wetter part of Basse-Terre is particularly suited to tree crops such as coffee, cocoa and vanilla, whereas the lowlands to the east are in sugar cane and those to the south, where the rainfall

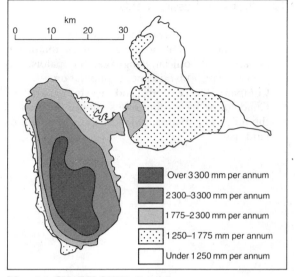

Map 9.3 GUADELOUPE: Rainfall.

Over 3 300 mm per annum
2 300–3 300 mm per annum
1 775–2 300 mm per annum
1 250–1 775 mm per annum
Under 1 250 mm per annum

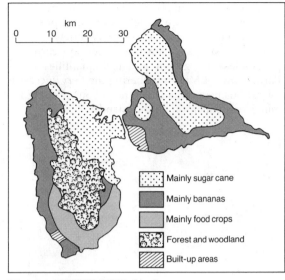

Map 9.4 GUADELOUPE: Land use.

Mainly sugar cane
Mainly bananas
Mainly food crops
Forest and woodland
Built-up areas

is higher, are in bananas. The farmland of Grande-Terre is mainly under cane with a small area in pineapples. In 1986 nine factories produced 66 000 tonnes of sugar. In addition, the island produced a large quantity of rum. Together, sugar, bananas and rum brought in about 95 per cent of the national income. The main areas of smallholders' food crops are the west coast of Basse-Terre and the east and south of Grande-Terre.

Each part of the island has its own large town. Basse-Terre (25 000) is the capital, but because it lies on the less productive side of the island and because it has only an open roadstead to accommodate ships it is smaller than Pointe-à-Pitre (80 000). Pointe-à-Pitre is the chief commercial centre and nearly all the imports and a large proportion of the exports are loaded and unloaded there. Like Martinique, Guadeloupe has a growing tourist business both from stop-over visitors arriving by air and from those who spend a few hours ashore from cruise ships.

The dependencies of Guadeloupe are Marie Galante, Désirade, Les Saintes, St Barthélemy, and St Martin – the northern part of a small island of which the rest belongs to the Netherlands. Together the dependencies have an area of about 270 square kilometres and a population of 30 000. Marie Galante is very similar to Grande-Terre. The chief products are sugar and cotton. Désirade is a long limestone

Map 9.5 GUADELOUPE: Relief.

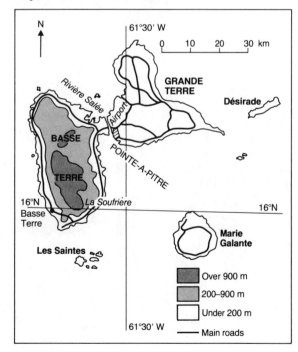

Over 900 m
200–900 m
Under 200 m
Main roads

block on which some cotton and maize are grown and some animals are raised. Les Saintes produce a small amount of sugar and coffee. A variety of crops, including bananas, tamarinds, cotton, corn and pineapples, are grown in small quantities on St Barthélemy. St Martin is sharing the very successful tourist business of its Dutch neighbour. Fishing is a minor occupation on all the islands.

Questions and assignments

1 Compare the islands of Martinique and Dominica by writing one sentence on each of the following: a) area, b) official language, c) patois, d) government, e) landscape, f) population.

2 Compare the eastern and western parts of Guadeloupe by writing one sentence on each of the following: a) area, b) landscape, c) rainfall, d) land use.

10

The Netherlands Antilles

Area: 993 square kilometres; population (1986): about 280 000; density of population: 282 per square kilometre.

Six small Caribbean islands belong to the Netherlands. Three of them – *Aruba, Bonaire* and *Curaçao* (the 'ABC' islands) – lie close to the shores of Venezuela (Map 17.1). The other three – *St Eustatius* (Statia), *Saba* and *St Maarten* (the 'S' islands) – lie hundreds of kilometres away between St Kitts and the Virgin Islands (Map 11.1).

The Dutch who occupied these islands in the seventeenth century were not seeking rich agricultural lands. One of the things they wanted was salt for their North Sea herring fisheries. This they found in St Maarten and Bonaire. They also wanted bases from which they could trade with other Caribbean territories. These they established on Curaçao and Statia, which became two of the richest transshipping ports in the region, handling large numbers of slaves and vast quantities of European goods. When Statia was captured by the British in 1781 and everything stored there was auctioned, the goods fetched about £4 000 000, even though prices in such circumstances were not at their best. Though the island was restored to the Dutch, it never recovered, and the population has dwindled from 20 000 to about 1 500.

Curaçao, with an area of 444 square kilometres and a population of about 174 000 in 1986, is the largest of the Netherlands Antilles. From 1917 to the mid 1980s the island's economy was dominated by oil refining. The crude petroleum was imported from the oilfields around Lake Maracaibo in Venezuela. It was refined in a large refinery at Willemstad, the island's capital. The refined products were then shipped to the United States and to a smaller extent the West In-

dies. The trade was so big that Willemstad was one of the world's busiest ports.

The building of new refineries in the United States and in some of the Caribbean islands brought an end to the prosperity of Curaçao in the 1980s. The Willemstad refinery would have been closed if the Venezuelan government had not agreed to lease it. Curaçao is now rebuilding its economy on tourism. Many of the visitors are from Venezuela.

Aruba (193 square kilometres; population: 69 000), has had a similar history. The oil refining industry there began in 1925 and came to an end in 1985. Tourism is expanding. Both Curaçao and Aruba have good ports and offer visitors a wide of variety of duty-free goods. They are therefore visited by many of the ships taking tourists on Caribbean cruises.

As the rainfall of the two islands is only about 500 millimetres a year a drought occurs from February to September. There are no streams or rivers either so agriculture is of little importance. However, some fruits and vegetables are being grown by drip irrigation so as to supply hotels and reduce imports.

Bonaire has not shared in this prosperity and its population has remained small – 10 500 on 288 square kilometres. Agriculture is restricted by the lack of rain, and, as in Curaçao, Aruba and St Maarten, fresh water has to be distilled from the sea. The old salt industry has been modernised, and there is a small tourist trade and a local clothing industry.

The three northern islands are much smaller. St *Maarten* (34 square kilometres, population: 24 000) is only the smaller southern portion of an island, the rest belongs to France. Recently it has developed a large and prosperous tourist business based on beautiful beaches and an international airport.

Saba (13 square kilometres) gives the appearance of being a single extinct volcano, but more probably it consists of several separate cones. These rise sharply from the sea to a height of nearly 900 metres. Most of the 1 000 people live in the village of Bottom which lies in a central hollow, 220 metres above sea-level. In this hollow yams, potatoes, beans, christophines and other crops are grown on smallholdings.

Population of the Netherlands Antilles in 1940, 1960 and 1980 (figures given to the nearest hundred)

Year	Aruba	Curaçao	St Maarten	Other	Total
1940	30 600	67 300	2 000	9 800	107 900
1960	56 900	125 100	2 700	7 800	192 500
1980	64 800	162 400	14 800	11 300	253 300

Questions and assignments

1 a) Give three reasons why the natural conditions in Aruba and Curacao have made development difficult.

  b) Name two sorts of development that have taken place there.

2 To what extent is it true to say that the Netherlands Antilles have been successful despite having an adverse natural environment?

3 Use the information in the table to answer the questions that follow.

a) Name the three islands not listed here.

b) Calculate the percentage increase in the population of Aruba between 1940 and 1960. Suggest one reason for the increase.

c) Suggest a reason for the decline in the population of the three unnamed islands over the same period.

d) Calculate the percentage increase in the population of St Maarten between 1960 and 1980. Suggest a reason for the increase.

e) Draw a bar graph to compare the populations of Aruba and Curaçao in 1940, 1960 and 1980.

11

The Virgin Islands

The Virgin Islands are a group of seven main islands and a large number of islets and cays that lie to the east of Puerto Rico. Apart from St Croix, they are the summits of a submarine continuation of the range that forms the backbone of Puerto Rico. Some islands are owned by the United States, the rest by Britain.

The United States Virgin Islands

These were purchased by the United States from Denmark in 1917 mainly so that America could control the Anegada Passage into the Northern Caribbean. Their total area is about 380 square kilometres and their population in 1988 was about 106 000 – that is 279 per square kilometre.

The largest islands are St Croix (217 square kilometres), St Thomas (72 square kilometres), and St John (52 square kilometres). The last two are of rugged build and rise to about 520 metres and 400 metres respectively. St Croix has a range of hills along the north coast which rise to about 365 metres, but the rest of the island is fairly flat.

In slave days the islands had a prosperous sugar trade. Afterwards they declined until, in recent years, they have been developed by American big business. Development has taken two forms. One is tourism. Attracted by the sunny climate, the excellent bathing beaches, the duty-free shopping in Charlotte Amalie, and the National Park which takes up 70 per cent of the area of St John, over 1½ million tourists visit the US Virgin Islands each year. Out of these the largest number arrive on cruise ships and spend a few hours on land, shopping and sightseeing. Many others make use of the direct jet service which links St Thomas with Puerto Rico and several American cities. Some arrive by yacht; the United States Virgin Islands being the nearest tropical 'playground' for Americans who live on the eastern seaboard and are rich enough to own, or charter, a boat.

The second development is that of industry, centred mainly in St Croix. Manufactures include rum, perfume, pharmaceuticals, textiles and the assembly of electronic equipment and watches. For a time there were also two heavy industries. One was alumina, based on bauxite imported from Suriname and West Africa. This was closed in 1985. The other was a very big oil refinery, now operating in only a small way. None of the industries in the US Virgin Islands owe their existence to the presence of natural resources. Instead, they depend on tax concessions and other advantages they possess by being regarded as part of the United States.

These developments have attracted many immigrants from the British Virgin Islands and other parts of the Eastern Caribbean. At the same time there has been a movement of islanders with American passports to the United States mainland. As a result only a quarter of the people living in the US Virgin Islands were born there.

St Thomas, the chief tourist centre, supports about half the population. St Croix has most of the remainder. The capital and chief town is Charlotte Amalie (35 000) on the south coast of St Thomas. In the main shopping street of Charlotte Amalie the old Danish buildings have been preserved so as to maintain an attractive old-world appearance. Inside, however, they show few signs of their origins. They have been air-conditioned, lavishly decorated, and stocked with millions of dollars' worth of up-to-date, duty-free, luxury goods.

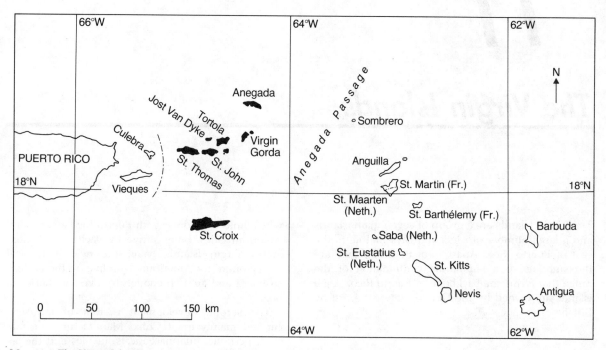

Map 11.1 The Virgin Islands and their neighbours.

The British Virgin Islands

The British Virgin Islands consist of Tortola (54 square kilometres; 10 000 people), Virgin Gorda (21 square kilometres; 2 000 people), Anegada (39 square kilometres), Jost Van Dyke (10 square kilometres) and a number of small islets which bring the total area to about 153 square kilometres. Apart from Anegada, a limestone block nowhere over 10 metres in height, the largest islands are mountainous and rugged, Tortola rising to a maximum height of 536 metres and Virgin Gorda to 417 metres.

In the days of slavery the British Virgin Islands had prosperous sugar and cotton industries, but since then all the estates have been broken up. The land has been taken over for small-scale shifting cultivation and grazing, and soil erosion is widespread. No cotton and very little cane is grown there today and no sugar is manufactured, though there is a small export of rum, mainly to St Thomas.

The small patches of fertile soil that still remain on the hill-crests and in the valley-bottoms support a variety of food crops and fruits. Some of these, especially bananas and sweet potatoes, are sold to the United States Virgin Islands. Parts of the steeper hill-slopes and valley-sides are covered with scrub and secondary woodland which are of little use except for making charcoal and small boats. Most of the rest of the land is used for grazing.

The most recent development has been in tourism. Though the business is small compared with that of the United States Virgin Islands, it is the only one of importance. There is, in particular, a flourishing yacht-chartering business. By providing job opportunities that were formerly non-existent, tourism has helped to reduce the number of young people emigrating to the United States Virgin Islands and elsewhere in search of work. It has also attracted some immigrants. However, as in other parts of the Caribbean, the growth of tourism has been accompanied by a rise in land values and by a decline in agricultural production.

Questions and assignments

1 Answer the following by referring to Map 11.1
  a) Name the Virgin Islands shown on the map.

St Thomas. What signs of tourism can you see? What reasons explain the number of yachts?

b) Which one of them is i) farthest north, ii) farthest south?

c) In what two ways does the map show which direction is north?

d) Is St John east or west of St Thomas? How do you know from the map?

e) What is the approximate direction of St Croix from Sombrero, NE, SE, SW, NW?

f) What is the approximate direction of Sombrero from Antigua, NE, SE, SW, NW?

g) What is the approximate distance between i) St Croix and Anegada, and ii) St Croix and Antigua?

2 Compare the US Virgin Islands and the British Virgin Islands by writing a single sentence about each of the following: a) area, b) government, c) population, d) tourism, e) industry. Give one reason to explain the difference in tourism and then one reason to explain the difference in industry.

12

The Bahamas

Area: about 13 900 square kilometres; population (1988): about 240 000; density of population: 17 per square kilometre.

Landforms

The Bahamas are an archipelago of about 700 islands and many more small cays and rocks which lie east of Florida and extend southwards almost as far as Hispaniola. Many of them are little known and scarcely peopled. Even their area is not known for certain. Estimates suggest that the islands take up about 13 900 square kilometres of land, about ¼ million square kilometres of sea. Seldom more than 60 metres high, the islands stand, together with many coral reefs, on a shallow submarine platform which is divided into two banks (see Map 12.2). Few passages are deep enough to take shipping. However, some do exist. The biggest lies outside the coral reef which runs along the east coast of Andros. Known as the Tongue of the Ocean it is over a mile in depth. Americans are using it as a test area to track nuclear submarines.

The base rock is limestone, overlain in many areas by sand derived originally from sea shells. Some rocks are still loose and sandy; others have been hardened by age. In upland areas the action of acid rain has pitted the limestone with small holes and dissolved sink holes which lead down to underground caves. A number of other karst features are present though on a smaller scale than in Jamaica. The lowlands often contain brackish swamps. In four islands – Grand Bahama, Abaco, Andros and New Providence – there are 'pine barrens', that is, large stretches of pine forest.

Two minerals are of importance: salt and aragonite. Salt is made by evaporating sea water in the sun in Inagua – one of the most southerly and driest islands. To obtain pure salt the evaporation process is carefully controlled so as to separate out the other chemicals that are present in the sea. Most of the output is supplied to chemical companies in the United States. Some is used for de-icing roads in winter in North America. This in itself is a good indication of the contrasts in climate between the Bahamas and the American continent.

Aragonite is dredged in the shallow waters of the banks near Bimini. This very pure form of limestone sand is used in several industries including the manufacture of cement, glass, iron and steel, and agricultural fertilisers. In the mid 1980s the exports to the United States averaged between 3 and 4 million tonnes a year.

Climate

More than anything else, the Bahamas owe their livelihood to the differences that exist between their climate and that of North America. The average monthly temperatures of Nassau and New York are shown in Diagram 12.1.

The rainfall of the Bahamas is not heavy, the annual total being between 1 000 and 1 500 millimetres in most places. Some 80 per cent falls in heavy showers, usually between May and October. Because rain soaks quickly into the ground, the people are dependent on wells for most of their water supply. Water shortage is often a handicap to agriculture. For instance, farmers have to wait for the rains to set in before they can plant their crops, and so they can

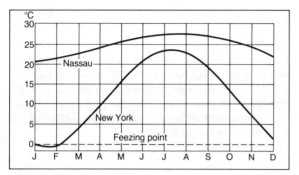

Diagram 12.1 Average monthly temperatures of Nassau and New York.

reap only one harvest a year. Much of the water supply in Nassau has to be obtained by desalinating sea water and by carrying fresh water in barges from Andros.

Differences in climate between the islands have not yet been recorded but as they stretch through 7° of latitude and vary in size from mere rocks to more than the size of Trinidad, they must exist. For instance, the average annual rainfall for Inagua may be as low as 600 millimetres. Again, Andros is known to be a major source of thunderstorms which sometimes spread eastwards to affect New Providence.

Map 12.2 The Bahamas and the Turks and Caicos Islands.

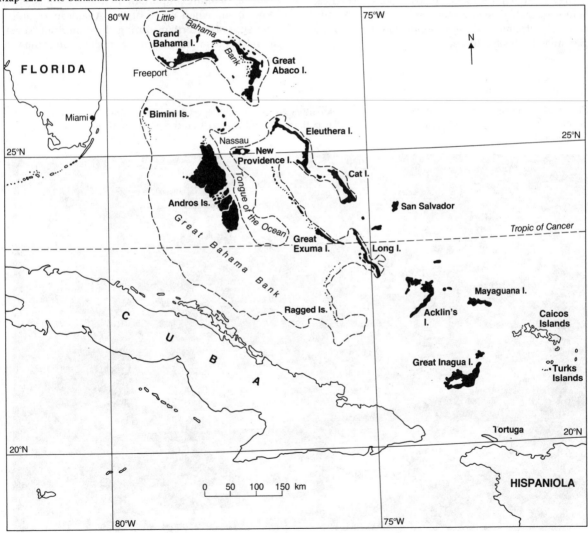

Position

Though they have never had valuable natural resources of their own to provide an income, the Bahamas have been able to share in the prosperity of other countries. This has been possible because of their position. In the seventeenth century they controlled the sailing ship routes leading out of the Caribbean and were the lair of many buccaneers and pirates. Since then their proximity to North America has been more important. They prospered from the slave trade, from the contraband traffic to the continent during the American Civil War, and from smuggling liquor into the United States during the years of prohibition in the 1920s. Today, American tourists provide the largest source of income. In 1988 tourists outnumbered the resident population of the Bahamas by twelve to one.

Occupations

Forestry

Some of the islands, notably Andros (6 000 square kilometres), Grand Bahama (1 370 square kilometres) and Abaco (1 680 square kilometres) are extensively forested with pine trees. The sale of pulpwood was the major source of income on Andros until production ceased in the mid 1970s.

Agriculture

Only for one short period of their history was plantation agriculture important in the Bahamas. This came about when some of the American colonists who supported Britain during the American Revolution left the mainland with their slaves after the war

Cruise ships in Nassau harbour. Because thousands of visitors go ashore here every year, the shops shown in this picture concentrate on the sale of tourist goods. Similar patterns of land use exist on the waterfronts of several other Caribbean towns.

in 1783 to settle in the Bahamas, notably on Harbour Island, Long Island and Abaco. There they established cotton plantations which flourished at first but quickly declined as the soil lost its fertility and insect pests appeared. Production ceased after the emancipation of the slaves in 1834.

Those Bahamian soils best suited to cultivation take up little more than 1 per cent of the total area. They exist in pockets between low ridges where they are sheltered from the salt-laden sea air. Even here they are often thin and are easily exhausted. Moreover they drain very quickly. Most of the small farmers who carry on most of the agriculture today have taken few measures to maintain the soil fertility or conserve the moisture in it. Bush burning dries up the soil, leaves it exposed to strong, drying winds, and reduces its humus content, thus lessening its power to retain moisture.

Yields, naturally, are often low. Nevertheless, small farmers grow food crops for their own needs and supply hotels with a variety of tropical fruits and tropical and temperate vegetables. Altogether, the foodstuffs produced in the Bahamas meet about 15 per cent of the needs. In an attempt to raise this figure the government has, with American assistance, set up an agricultural research and training project in the northern part of Andros. Its aim is to expand the area devoted to Bahamian family farms, improve their yields, and increase rural employment.

In recent years a number of large mechanised farms have been established on Andros, Grand Bahama and Abaco. Each farm concentrates on a single crop such as tomatoes or onions for export to the USA or for the local tourist market. Most have failed after a short time but because so much American money is available for investment in the Bahamas, others have taken their place. As a result, agricultural exports differ from one year to the next.

Eleuthera (414 square kilometres) is the most important island for commercial agriculture. Output includes oranges, grapefruit, pineapples, tomatoes, onions, pork, beef cattle, milk, and eggs. Exuma (290 square kilometres) and Long Island (600 square kilometres) produce onions, and Abaco and Andros produce onions, tomatoes and cucumbers.

Fishing

The shallow waters of the Great Bahama and Little Bahama Banks are rich fishing grounds. Fishing is a major occupation in Abaco, Grand Bahama, Harbour Island and St George's Cay (1 square kilometre). Most of the catch is consumed in Nassau, but large quantities of frozen lobsters are sent to Florida. Conchs are eaten locally and the shells are sold as souvenirs to tourists. Other shells are painted and made into jewellery.

Before the war, the Bahamas, especially Andros, had a prosperous trade in sponges, but during the 1940s the beds were so severely affected by disease that they had to be closed to fishing for some years. Since their reopening the export has been smaller than it used to be.

For conservation purposes some parts of the sea have been declared underwater protection areas, and some parts of some islands have been declared wildlife reserves and bird sanctuaries.

Tourism

The mainstay of the economy of the Bahamas is tourism, particularly from the USA. In the late 1980s American tourists accounted for 85 per cent of the hotel guests. The attractiveness of the climate is one reason for this. The Atlantic Ocean on one side and the 80 kilometre-wide Gulf Stream (at a temperature of over 21°C) on the other, ensure that the islands have a winter warmth unknown on the American continent. As winter is also the dry season it is naturally the most popular time for visitors. However, others are attracted there in summer when hotel rates are cheaper. September and October are the months with the lowest number of stop-over visitors.

A second reason for the success of tourism is that there is excellent sea-bathing from white sand beaches, not only on the two most developed islands – New Providence and Grand Bahama – but also on the others which together are called the Family Islands.

A third reason is that the islands are easily and quickly accessible by air, by cruise ships, by yachts and by motor boats from the mainland. Flights from New York to the international airports at Nassau and Freeport take 2½ hours; those from Miami to Nassau only 45 minutes.

The Bahamas have made much of their advantages. By any standards the resort areas centred on Nassau in New Providence and Freeport-Lucaya in Grand Bahama are big ones. Many large luxury hotels have been built there, and tourist attractions include shopping centres, sports clubs, championship golf courses and casinos. Though developments elsewhere are on a much smaller scale, the provision of about 50 airstrips and the construction of marinas for yachts and motor-boats has encouraged the spread of tourism to several of the Family Islands. The photograph on page 8 in chapter one shows one example, that of Bimini, famous as a centre for big game fishing.

Tourism grew with great rapidity in the 1960s; the number of visitors doubling from 1960 to 1965 and doubling again from 1965 to 1970. In the 1970s tourism not only levelled off but declined during the business recession which took place in America following the rise in the world price of petroleum. Prosperity in the Bahamas is inescapably linked to prosperity in the United States. Since then growth has

been resumed. In 1984 the number of stop-over visitors totalled 1 310 000. Of these, 759 000 stayed in New Providence, 326 000 in Grand Bahama and 225 000 in the Family Islands. In addition 908 000 cruise-ship passengers and 107 000 day trippers visited the Bahamas for a few hours. Altogether they spent about US$ 750 million.

About half of the money spent by tourists in the Bahamas goes towards accommodation, drinks and meals in hotels. The rest is spent on shopping, entertainment, gambling and other things. There are therefore many businesses besides hotels that depend for their existence on tourism. They include restaurants, night clubs, casinos, laundries, taxis, and firms with boats, fishing gear and sports equipment for hire. There are also market stalls which sell souvenirs and handicrafts (including straw goods made mainly in Long Island and Nassau) and shops selling duty-free liquor, cameras, china, glassware

Part of the tourist complex at Lucaya on Grand Bahama. This hotel has the sea on one side and an artificial harbour for yachts and other pleasure boats on the other side.

and other duty-free luxury goods. Directly or indirectly tourism provides two out of every three jobs in the Bahamas.

Banking, business and manufacturing

The taxes that businesses have to pay in most parts of the world are not charged in the Bahamas. For this reason, between 300 and 400 banks have branches and offices in the Bahamas where they carry out many of their international transactions. This 'off-shore banking' as it is called is the second most important economic activity in the Bahamas. It provides direct employment for bank officials, and indirect employment for lawyers, accountants and those who sell and repair computers, typewriters, word processors, photocopiers and other kinds of office equipment. Recently, also for tax purposes, ship-owners throughout the world have registered so many ships in the Bahamas that the only two countries with a larger number of ship registrations are Liberia and Panama.

Several factors explain why local manufacturing is of little importance in the Bahamas. They have few raw materials, no cheap source of power, no cheap labour, little local capital, and a very small internal market for industrial products. However, two factors have attracted some foreign industries to the islands. One is the tax policy. The other is the ease of access to the North American continent through the many ports along the eastern seaboard. Freeport at the western tip of Grand Bahama Island has become the main centre for these industries. Over 600 square kilometres (that is an area about the size of St Lucia) have been set aside there for industrial development.

Freeport-Lucaya

The main attraction of Freeport is an agreement by which industries located there pay no taxes, including income tax and customs duties, for a 99-year period ending in 2054. Despite this security, industrial development has not been altogether successful. Oil refining, the biggest business so far set up there, is one such example. When it began it imported large quantities of crude petroleum from such countries as Saudi Arabia, Libya, Iran and Nigeria, and exported the refined products to the United States. However, like other Caribbean refineries, including those in Aruba, Curaçao, and Trinidad, it became unprofitable in the 1980s. In 1988 it served only as a place where ships could take on fuel and where petroleum products could be transshipped. Two other large industries – cement and the manufacture of steel pipes – have also been closed. Those industries that remain include one of the world's largest rum distilleries and factories manufacturing chemicals and pharmaceuticals. It would seem that because geographical factors have played so small a part in the establishment of industries at Freeport they can easily go out of business.

Adjoining the industrial area is Lucaya, one of the biggest and richest tourist centres in the Caribbean. Luxury hotels, apartments, night clubs, a 12-acre shopping centre containing goods from all parts of the world, several golf-courses and a casino have been built, and there is a busy international airport. A similar, though smaller resort, with an airport of its own, has grown up 40 kilometres away at West End.

As a result of the developments on Grand Bahama, the resident population of the island rose from 8 500 in 1963 to 33 000 in 1980.

Population

At the time of the 1980 census the total population of the Bahamas was 209 500. Sixteen islands had more than a hundred people living on them. Of these, only New Providence, Grand Bahama, Andros, Abaco and Eleuthera had 7 000 or more. New Providence (215 square kilometres) with about 135 000 (65 per cent of the total) had a population density of 630 per square kilometre. The reason for this is that Nassau, the capital and only large town in the Bahamas, is situated there. Nassau is the hub of the Bahamas. It has direct air communications with most of the largest cities in the United States and with a number of European cities as well. It has large hotels situated on white sand beaches. It has shops in which luxury goods from all over the world can be purchased duty-free. It has a harbour which can berth several cruise ships at the same time.

Just off shore is Paradise Island which protects the harbour from the prevailing North East Trade winds and has its own white sand beaches. In recent years it has been developed into a major tourist centre, having several large hotels, a casino and a large shopping area. It is connected to Nassau by bridge.

The Turks and Caicos Islands

Geographically, these two neighbouring groups of islands form part of the southern Bahamas. Their position is shown on Map 12.2. Their total area is 430 square kilometres and their population was about 9 500 in 1988. Of these about 3 500 were in the capital, Cockburn Town.

The low rainfall (635–760 millimetres a year) is a handicap to agriculture, and only very small quantities of maize, fruit and food crops are grown. The old salt trade has declined, and frozen lobsters and conchs now form over 90 per cent of the exports. Since the building of an international airport on Providenciales in the Caicos Islands, there has been a rapid growth of tourism. Another recent development has been the registration of several thousand foreign companies which have been attracted there because they have no tax to pay.

A missile tracking station is located on Grand Turk. Others exist on Grand Bahama, Eleuthera, San Salvador, and Mayaguana in the Bahamas.

Questions and assignments

1 Look at the graphs in Diagram 12.1 and answer these questions:
   a) In what months does Nassau have i) its lowest average temperature, and ii) its highest average temperature?
   b) What are the lowest and highest average monthly temperatures in Nassau? What, therefore, is the range of temperature?
   c) In what months does New York have i) its lowest average temperature, and ii) its highest average temperature?
   d) What are the lowest and highest average monthly temperatures in New York? What is the range of temperature there?
   e) Give one reason to explain why the two places have their lowest and highest temperatures at the same time of year.

   f) Give one reason to explain why the winter temperature of New York is much lower than that of Nassau.
   g) Give two reasons why Nassau has a much smaller temperature range than New York.

2 Use the table showing tourist visits to answer the questions that follow.

Tourists visiting the Bahamas, 1980–84 (figures to the nearest thousand)

	1980	1981	1982	1983	1984
Stop-over tourists	1 181	1 031	1 101	1 240	1 310
Cruise-ship passengers	578	597	720	854	908

   a) What were the total number of tourists visiting the Bahamas in each of the five years?
   b) What was the average number of tourists over the five-year period?
   c) What was the percentage of cruise-ship passengers in i) 1980, and ii) 1984?
   d) On one diagram (like Diagram 12.1) draw and label three graphs to show i) cruise-ship passengers, ii) stop-over tourists, and iii) the totals in each of the five years.
   e) Using the graphs you have drawn, briefly describe the changes that took place over the five-year period in the numbers of i) cruise-ship passengers and ii) stop-over tourists.

3 Use the information given below to answer the questions that follow.

Stop-over tourists in the Bahamas in 1980, 1982, and 1984 (figures given to the nearest thousand)

Year	New Providence	Grand Bahama	Family Islands	Total
1980	583	382	216	1 181
1982	543	352	206	1 101
1984	759	326	225	1 310

   a) How many stop-over tourists visited Grand Bahama in 1982? How many more visited New Providence in the same year? What was the growth in stop-over tourism in the Family Islands between 1982 and 1984?

b) Briefly describe what happened to tourism in all three parts of the Bahamas in the period between 1980 and 1984.

c) For each area draw and label three vertical bar graphs (like the one below) to show the number of stop-over tourists in 1980, 1982, and 1984.

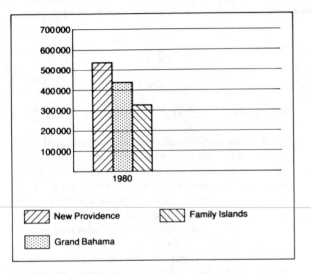

4 Use the information given below to answer the questions that follow.

Percentage share of stop-over tourists by country of residence in 1980, 1982 and 1984

Year	USA	Canada	Europe	Other
1980	75	11	10	4
1982	83	8	5	4
1984	87	6	3	4

a) Briefly describe the changes that took place in the percentages of tourists from the USA and Europe between 1980 and 1984.

b) Draw and label three horizontal bar graphs (like those in question 7 at the end of chapter eight) to show the percentages from the USA, Canada, Europe, and other parts of the world in 1980, 1982 and 1984 (one bar for each year).

c) Construct a divided circle (a pie chart) to show the percentages for 1984.

5 Use the information given below to answer the questions that follow.

Monthly percentages of tourists visiting the Bahamas

Month	Stop-over visitors	Cruise-ship passengers
January	7.5	7.2
February	9.3	7.0
March	11.6	8.0
April	10.2	8.6
May	9.0	9.3
June	8.3	9.3
July	9.3	10.3
August	8.9	9.9
September	5.5	6.1
October	6.0	7.5
November	7.6	8.5
December	8.5	8.3
Total	100.0	100.0

a) Which four months are the peak period for i) stop-over tourists, and ii) cruise-ship passengers? Which is the poorest month for i) stop-over tourists and ii) cruise-ship passengers?

b) Suggest two reasons which might explain the peak and the trough you have identified.

c) Draw a graph (like one of those in Diagram 12.1) to show the monthly percentages of stop-over tourists. Label the peak and the trough. Do the same for the cruise-ship percentages.

6 Imagine that a syndicate is planning to build a hotel on one of the Bahamas. What information would be needed before work could begin? To what extent would this information provide a geographical account of the island on which the hotel was to be located?

165

13

Cuba

Area: 114 500 square kilometres; population (1988): about 10 000 000; density of population: 87 per square kilometre.

Landforms

Cuba is by far the largest island in the Caribbean; in fact, it is almost as large as all the other West Indian islands put together. It is over 1 200 kilometres long and from 40 to 160 kilometres in width.

Almost three-quarters of the land surface is a rolling plain. The only really high mountains occur in Oriente. In the south-west of this province the narrow, precipitous ranges of the Sierra Maestra rise steeply from the sea, reaching a maximum height of about 2 000 metres in Pico de Turquino. To the east lie the Baracoa Mountains, separated from the Sierra Maestra by the Nipe plateau (see Map 13.1).

Two other parts of Cuba are mountainous. Near the south coast of Las Villas province lie the Trinidad and Sancti Spiritus Mountains which rise above 900 metres in places. In the most westerly province of Pinar del Rio there is the Cordillera de Guaniguanico which contains several separate ranges including the many isolated limestone peaks of the Organos Mountains and the long ridges and valleys of the Rosario Mountains.

There are few other places which rise above 300 metres on the island and so, in contrast to the other West Indian islands, it has been possible to construct a railway and main road along the watershed from one end of the country to the other. There are nearly 15 000 kilometres of railway in Cuba including the narrow-gauge lines used to take sugar cane to the factories.

Minerals

Most of the metallic minerals are concentrated in the mountains of Oriente. Ores of nickel, copper, manganese, chromium and iron are all present there. Of these, nickel (combined with cobalt) is by far the most important. Cuban reserves are the fourth largest in the world. The main refining and exporting centre is Moa. Nickel exports which amounted to about 40 000 tonnes a year in the late 1980s, were second only to sugar. Nearly all of them went to Russia and other communist countries for use in hardening steel. Some copper is mined in Pinar del Rio.

Petroleum has been obtained for many years from a small oilfield north of Sancti Spiritus in central Cuba. Recently another oilfield has come into production just off the coast near Havana (see Map 13.2) so output can be expected to rise. In the mid 1980s Cuba produced about one-fifth of its requirements. Most of the imports are supplied by the Soviet Union.

Climate

Cuba experiences greater extremes of temperature than any other West Indian island. There are three reasons for this. The first of them is latitude. Because Cuba almost touches the Tropic of Cancer, the midday sun is overhead only once a year – for about four weeks before and four weeks after 21st June. The hottest weather is therefore concentrated into a single season lasting from June into August. As Diagram 2.1 on page 13 shows, islands farther

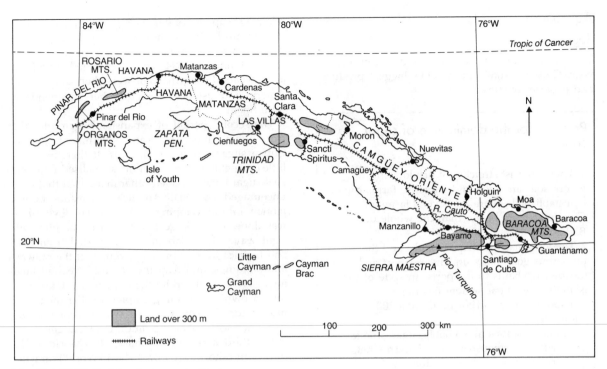

Map 13.1 CUBA: Relief and communications.

south have a longer hot season or two periods of maximum temperature a year.

The second reason is the size of Cuba. Because land· heats up and cools down more quickly than the sea, days tend to be hotter and nights cooler in Cuba than they are in any of the small islands. Thus in the hot season, day temperatures in the lowlands may reach 38°C (100°F). The third reason is the proximity of Cuba to the North American continent. In mid-winter, when northers are blowing out from the bitterly cold continental interior, temperatures on the lowlands drop to 4°C or even a little below. At such times frost can occur in the highlands.

Rainfall is typical of the northern Caribbean in that about three-quarters of the total falls in the six months from May to October. One part of Cuba – the province of Oriente – is very similar to eastern Jamaica in that the mountain summits and their northern slopes receive over 2 500 millimetres of rain a year, while the coastal strip to the south receives 1 000 millimetres and less. Elsewhere there is no such contrast. The rest of Cuba is far too narrow for rainfall to be affected by distance from the sea, and too low for any marked rain shadow to occur. In the hot months, powerful convection currents produce towering cumulus clouds from which heavy showers fall, particularly in the afternoon. In addition, easterly waves frequently pass over the island from east to west, bringing more general rain. In winter the whole pattern changes, the generally dry easterly winds being interrupted by occasional northers which move across the island from the north and north-west bringing light rain to the lowlands and heavy rain to the mountain summits.

The position, size and shape of Cuba make the island particularly prone to hurricanes. Those moving on a north-westerly track in the western Caribbean frequently pass over the island. Those moving towards Cuba from the east may either swing northwards through the Windward Passage, thus affecting the eastern tip of the island, or continue to the south of the Sierra Maestra and then swing northwards, as shown on Diagram 2.9 on page 23. The heavy rains that hurricanes bring with them cover a much wider area than the area destroyed by high winds.

Agriculture

Sugar

Though the output varies considerably from year to year, Cuba is usually the world's biggest producer and exporter of sugar.

Reasons for the dominance of sugar cane:

1 There are vast stretches of rich lowland where soils are good and immense farms can be established. There are several farms in Cuba which are bigger than the whole of Barbados.

2 The long, narrow shape of Cuba and the numerous good harbours ensure short and inexpensive hauls to the ports. In spite of the island's size, sugar seldom has to be transported overland for more than 100 kilometres.

3 Rainfall is sufficient to enable sugar cane to grow without expensive irrigation. This helps to keep down the cost of production.

4 The great period of sugar expansion came at a later date in Cuba than in the rest of the Caribbean. Virgin lands were being opened up at a time when Jamaican soils, for example, were almost exhausted. This late start also enabled Cuban planters to use production methods that had been developed at considerable expense elsewhere. For example, most factories in Cuba were able to use steam power from the outset. Furthermore, before the end of the nineteenth century all new estates were laid out with narrow-gauge railways to carry the cane quickly and cheaply to the factories. Thus larger and more efficient factories could be built in Cuba than in other Caribbean countries.

The expansion of the Cuban sugar industry took place in several distinct stages. The first began when Haiti went out of production after the slave revolt there in 1791. Cuban farmers were encouraged to grow more cane to fill the gap in European supplies at a time when the price of sugar was very high. Expansion continued throughout the nineteenth century as Cuba benefited from the rise of sugar consumption in industrial Europe and America, the relative cheapness of her slave-grown sugar[1] and the change in British economic policy from colonial protection to free trade. Production rose to over 1 million tonnes in 1894. Then it declined sharply for a few years during the civil war when Cuba – with American assistance – gained her independence from Spain.

The second period of expansion began after that war, when the American government granted Cuban sugar a preferential tariff. It therefore faced little competition even from the subsidised European beet sugar which flooded other markets at that time. Encouraged by this, American investors poured money into developing Cuban sugar. Everything was done on the largest scale and in the most efficient way. Cheap labour was imported from Haiti and Jamaica to clear the land, construct the railways and buildings, and reap the harvests. Peasant holdings were assimilated by the huge new estates, their former owners becoming employees. For them, and indeed for the country as a whole, economic dependence accompanied political independence.

The third and biggest phase of expansion came during and shortly after the 1914–18 World War when

Loading cane in Cuba. Some of the machinery was made in Russia.

[1]Slavery was not abolished in Cuba until 1886.

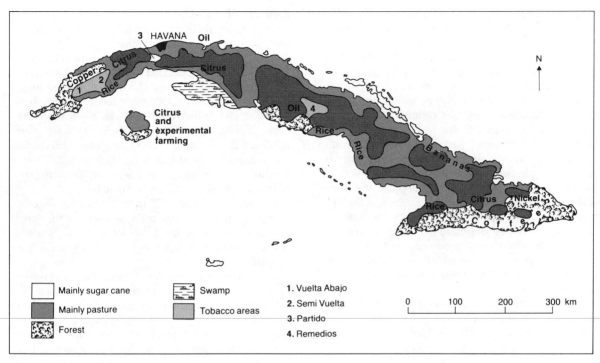

Map 13.2 CUBA: Land use.

demand for sugar was greater than ever before. This brought another flood of investment and a new wave of immigration, including many refugees from Europe. But prosperity ended a few years later, when overproduction and the world economic slump combined to send sugar prices crashing. The depression was very severe because the whole economy of Cuba had become geared to sugar and there was nothing else to take its place.

Production increased only when the United States entered the 1939–45 World War and agreed to buy all the sugar Cuba could supply. Following the pattern set thirty years before, output continued to rise after the war was over. It reached 7½ million tonnes in 1952. This was more than could be sold, and again the country was threatened with disaster. Measures were therefore taken to limit output at about 5 million tonnes a year.

The result was economic stagnation. For the four months of the crop season, 400 000 people were employed in the canefields. For the rest of the year, most of them were thrown out of work. Employment could have been found for them, and the economy

strengthened, if the sugar companies had been willing to release idle land for the cultivation of other crops. But because this would have threatened their labour supply they took no action. New industries could have been started, but because trade agreements with the United States opened Cuba to American manufactures, Cuba was unable to compete.

Almost every manufactured item in the country was imported, and three-quarters of the imports came from the USA. Throughout the 1950s, growth in the economy was restricted to tourism, and that was confined largely to Havana. The poverty of the bulk of the population, and the lack of prospects in a seemingly rich land, were the mainsprings of the revolution of 1959.

After the revolution large private farms were no longer allowed to exist. In some cases their land was cut up into smallholdings. Each was at least 66 acres in size – the 'vital minimum' for a family of five. Other large properties were converted into state farms and it is on these that 90 per cent of the sugar cane is grown.

For some years after the revolution, sugar production declined. One reason for this was that Cuba hoped to escape from the domination of cane. Another was that the increase in the number of independent farmers brought about a decrease in the number of available cane cutters. However, it was found that if Cuba was to pay its way in the world, this state of affairs could not continue. Though the trade with the United States had come to an end, petroleum, fertilisers, trucks, tractors, buses, machinery, tools, electrical equipment, metals, medicines, plastics, foodstuffs, and a host of other imported goods had to be obtained from somewhere; and all had to be paid for. Sugar was the only commodity that Cuba could produce in sufficient quantities to bridge the trade gap. The government therefore decided to raise production to higher levels than ever before. With much effort production was raised to over 8½ million tonnes in 1970. This was an all-time record.

Output in the 1980s has averaged 7½ million tonnes a year. Local needs account for ¾ million tonnes. The rest is exported. The Soviet Union and other communist countries in Eastern Europe take nearly 5 million tonnes a year at a preferential price. China takes a further ¾ million tonnes.

Since 1970 there has been a big decline in the number of sugar industry workers. This has made it difficult for Cuba to raise the output of sugar. Several measures have been taken to try to do so. One has been to extend the area under cane. Another has been to mechanise the field operations. All the cane is now planted by machines. Two-thirds of it is reaped by mechanical harvesters. In addition, many of the island's 150 sugar factories have been enlarged and modernised to make them more efficient. For a long time the lack of spare parts hindered development. Now Cuba is manufacturing its own, and is even exporting them to other sugar producing countries. It is also manufacturing the harvesters used in Cuban canefields.

The annual output of 20 million tonnes of bagasse is not wasted. Some is used as fuel for the sugar factories. Some is used in cattle feed. Some is manufactured into paper and board in several large factories.

The dominance of sugar in the Cuban economy is illustrated by the following facts: cane occupies over half of the cultivated land; sugar and its by-products make up over 80 per cent of the exports; 150 large factories are needed to process the crop. The cane-growing areas where these factories are located are shown on Map 13.2. The greatest concentration is in the two eastern provinces where over half of the island's sugar is produced.

In Cuba the problem of finding sugar workers is being met to some extent by townspeople who spend 15 days a year in the cane fields. Is there a similar labour problem in the territory where you live? How is it being met there?

Tobacco

If quantity makes Cuba famous for sugar, quality makes the country famous for tobacco. This crop occupies only 3 per cent of the cultivated land but is the second most valuable agricultural export. Cuban leaf is so fine that it is exported to many countries, where it is used for blending. Cuban 'Havanas' are the best and most expensive cigars in the world.

Cultivation is in the hands of small farmers and co-operatives because the crop needs much skill and attention while it is growing and being processed. In contrast to sugar cane, every separate leaf is important. The seedlings are planted in nurseries in August and September and transplanted to the carefully fertilised fields in October and November. Those plants to be used as the outer wrapping for cigars are shaded by cheese-cloth spread over a framework of poles. The leaves take two months to mature. After harvesting, they are hung to dry in large sheds for one to three months. Then they are packed in small bundles and fermented for another month. After that they are sorted, graded and packed into large bales for the market.

Tobacco is grown mainly in the four regions shown on Map 13.2, where the soil is specially suitable. The most famous district is the Vuelta Abajo in the province of Pinar del Rio, which produces a cigar of incomparable flavour. Blending tobacco is produced in the nearby Semi Vuelta district and around Remedios, while the Partido area south-west of Havana specialises in cigar wrappers. The bulk of the tobacco for the local cigarette industry is grown in Oriente.

As a good Havana cigar may cost several hundred times as much as an equal weight of Cuban sugar, the markets for the two products are as different as they could possibly be. As we have seen, Cuban sugar is sold in bulk, mainly to communist countries. Havana cigars go to the world's luxury markets, to expensive hotels and big cities where wealthy people are to be found.

Tobacco needs careful attention if it is to grow well.

Coffee

Coffee, like tobacco, is grown by small farmers and co-operatives. For most of the year the trees can be easily tended by the family, but from September to December, the busy harvesting season, help is obtained from gangs of migrant labourers who move from one farm to another. As coffee grows best above 300 metres, it is not found in the cane or tobacco areas. As much as 90 per cent comes from South and East Oriente, and most of the rest from the Trinidad Mountains. Cuba grows enough coffee to satisfy its needs and export a small quantity.

Other crops

Citrus fruits are grown in several parts of Cuba. One important area is the Isle of Youth. Another is the foothills of the Sierra Maestra. Exports of fresh and canned fruit, mainly to Eastern Europe, are growing rapidly.

Rice production has increased greatly in recent years. Output is more than twice that of Guyana – the leading producer in the Commonwealth Caribbean. Much of it comes from new high-yielding varieties grown on irrigated land. Bananas are produced on the northward facing slopes and the narrow coastal plain of Oriente where rain is plentiful throughout the year. Cocoa comes from the hills of Oriente. Co-operatives are being encouraged to increase their output of food crops and to plant cotton, soya beans and groundnuts in order to reduce imports of textiles and edible oils. Until this is achieved, Cuba is having to ration certain foodstuffs. Maize, which never gave good yields in Cuba, is being phased out.

Livestock

For many years after the discovery of the island, Cuba was taken up by huge cattle ranches established on the savannas. Livestock farming declined as sugar became supreme. Later it recovered, and in recent years much work has been done to improve the quality of the cattle so as to produce more beef and dairy products. There are now probably over 10 million cattle in the island. The largest single area of grassland lies in the provinces of Camaguey and, to a lesser extent, Las Villas. Butter, cheese and canned milk are made in the towns of Havana, Sancti Spiritus and Bayamo. Cuba is almost self-sufficient in animal products.

Forests

The forests which originally covered about 60 per cent of the island have been reduced, particularly in this century, to 18 per cent of the total area. Most of that which remains is in inaccessible mountain country, especially in the Sierra Maestra, which is the last remaining area of large stands of pine trees. The result of the clearing of forest that has accompanied the spread of sugar cane is that Cuba can now supply only 20 per cent of its timber requirements.

Other occupations

In recent years Cuba's industrial base has been expanding. Large oil refineries have been built to refine local and imported supplies of crude petroleum. There is a growing iron and steel industry. Cement, chemicals, agricultural fertilisers and combine harvesters are made. Sugar technology is well developed. Stoves, refrigerators, TV sets and radios are made as are many other household products.

Cuba has not hurried to enter the tourist boom which has brought social problems along with its economic benefits to the rest of the Caribbean. Even so, the number of tourists is growing. There were about 220 000 in 1988.

The people

While Cuba was a Spanish colony, its economic backwardness retarded settlement and until the end of the nineteenth century the population was relatively small. The rapid development that then took place attracted many immigrants. Half a million people entered the island between 1907 and 1919. Of these more than 60 per cent came from Spain. Because so many immigrants entered Cuba after the last slaves were brought from Africa, about 30 per cent of the population is white, a much higher proportion than in Haiti and the Commonwealth Caribbean. Puerto Rico, which was also underdeveloped in the slave days, has an even higher proportion of white people than Cuba.

For the past thirty years emigration has taken the place of immigration. Most of the people who have left Cuba have done so because of their dissatisfaction with political and economic conditions there. Nearly a million have gone to the United States, particularly to Miami where they form 40 per cent of the population. Many of them have opened their own businesses. Today, most shop signs in Miami are written in Spanish as well as in English.

The settlement pattern is considerably influenced by the sugar industry, not only because it employs so many people, but also because it enforces a marked contrast between the busy villages and towns and the empty expanses of cane fields surrounding them. Some towns have grown very large in handling the trade and catering for the needs of so many agricultural wage-earners. At least a dozen towns contain over 100 000 people. Towns and villages are fewer and smaller in the subsistence-farming areas where population is spread more evenly throughout the countryside and where there is less money to be spent. Settlement is sparse in the grasslands and sparser still in the mountains.

Towns

The capital, Havana, with over 1¾ million people, is the largest city in Cuba, and, for that matter, in the West Indies. Its importance dates back to the early colonial days when it was the centre of the Spanish convoy system in the Caribbean. Treasure fleets from Cartagena, Panama and Veracruz gathered there to refit and stock up with provisions before setting out on the final stage of their voyage to Spain. Massive fortresses, still to be seen, were constructed to protect the entrance to its harbour. Being so close to the Spanish possessions of Florida and Mexico, Havana became, as a historian wrote in 1634, 'the key to the New World, and the fortress of the West Indies'.

Since then each new development in Cuba has added to the size and importance of the city. Today the old Spanish centre is surrounded in turn by the busy commercial quarter where there are many tall, American-type buildings, and by the rapidly expanding residential suburbs.

Havana has remained the biggest port, handling some 75 per cent of the imports and 25 per cent of the exports. There are railways and main roads connecting it to all parts of the island. It is also the chief banking, shopping, industrial and university centre. Among the many industries are steel making, oil refining, the manufacture of cigars and cigarettes, drinks, canned goods, textiles, clothing, shoes, soap, matches, paint and cement.

Most of the other ports of Cuba are engaged in the manufacture and export of sugar. Matanzas, 100 kilometres to the east, has many other industries as well, notably the manufacture of rayon, shoes, ammonia and metal goods. It is Cuba's biggest oil-importing and electricity-generating town. Cardenas, not far away, manufactures sugar and alcohol and processes rice and sisal. Santiago de Cuba exports sugar, coffee and timber and refines oil. Somewhat to the east is the United States naval base at Guantanamo Bay. On the south coast Cienfuegos and Manzanillo are the largest ports. Cinefuegos is the chief centre for the export of sugar and the production of fertilisers. It has an oil refinery and will become the site of Cuba's first electricity-generating plant for nuclear fuel. Here, and elsewhere, new industries are being established as part of the government's policy of making Cuba less dependent on imports and creating new employment throughout the island.

The economy and trade

Until the revolution of 1959, Cuba was utterly dependent on American technology. It had little industry of its own. Following the revolution the supply of American manufactures was cut off. Cuba could no longer obtain even the spare parts that were needed to fix anything that broke down. Replacing imports with locally-produced goods was a difficult task. There was a shortage of capital to build and equip new factories. There was a lack of industrial raw materials. Many people holding managerial positions left the island to live in America. In addition, a great deal of time and money had to be spent on raising the level of education of children and adults, providing better housing for farm workers, extending the electricity network to rural areas, and creating and maintaining a large army to protect the island from invasion. The whole economy had to be switched from one controlled by private companies to one run by the government – an economy in which the banks, businesses, industries and many of the farms were nationalised. The whole pattern of trade had to be changed – away from America and towards the Soviet Union, China, and the communist countries of Eastern Europe. These are still the main trading partners, though Japan, Britain and other countries are becoming increasingly important to the Cuban economy.

As far as trade is concerned, things have not improved in the 1980s. Cuba's exports are still few in number and low in value. Sugar and its by-products form about 80 per cent of the total; mineral ores about 16 per cent (of which over half is nickel); and all others including tobacco about 4 per cent. If Cuba were able to sell refined sugar, the value of her exports would rise. But under the present arrangement, Russia buys unrefined sugar, processes it in factories that are used to refine beet sugar at other times of the year, and sells some of the refined product to other countries.

Because these exports are far from sufficient to pay for her imports, Cuba has built up a big foreign debt. It has to rely on economic aid from Russia believed to be worth US$ 1 million a day. Cuba has therefore still not achieved the independence she hoped for at the time of the revolution.

Nevertheless, despite many difficulties it is generally agreed that most of the working people particularly in the rural areas, are better off, better educated, better fed and healthier than they used to be. In contrast to such islands as Puerto Rico and Jamaica a determined effort has been made to equalise incomes and standards of living. Such improvements have been made possible not only by the policy of sharing wealth more widely. Cuba also has two advantages not possessed by any other West Indian island: it has a low population density, and it has plenty of good farmland available for people who wish to make use of it.

The Isle of Youth

This island, formerly called the Isle of Pines, (area: 2 600 square kilometres) lies some 50 to 60 kilometres south of the province of Pinar del Rio. Among its 60 000 inhabitants there are at any one time about 15 000 young people living in camps, improving their education and learning how to grow crops.

Questions and assignments

1 By referring to this and other chapters, copy and complete the following table about the Greater Antilles.

	Cuba	Dominican Republic	Haiti	Jamaica	Puerto Rico
Area					
Population					
Density of population					
Language					
One important mineral					
One major crop					
Capital city					
Size of capital					

2 In 1986 the main exports from Cuba were a) sugar, food and beverages 82 per cent; b) minerals 16 per cent; c) others 2 per cent. In the same year the imports were a) fuels, raw materials and metals 35 per cent; b) machinery 30 per cent; c) consumer goods 17 per cent; d) others 18 per cent. Draw two horizontal bar graphs like those in question 7 on page 148, to show these percentages.

3 In 1986 the exports from Cuba were sent to the following countries: a) USSR 70 per cent; b) other communist countries 15 per cent; c) developing countries 5 per cent; d) other countries 10 per cent. Construct a divided circle to show these percentages, and answer the following questions:
a) What do the letters USSR stand for?
b) Why is such a high percentage of the exports sent to the USSR?

4 What advantages does Cuba possess over the other West Indian islands? How has she made use of them?

5 a) At various times in history, Haiti, Puerto Rico, and Cuba have been thought of as models which Commonwealth Caribbean territories might copy. Why was this so?
b) Do you think the Cuban model would be possible, for the country in which you live? Give two reasons for your answer.

14

Hispaniola

Area: 76 480 square kilometres; population (1888): about 12 000 000

Development

On his first voyage to the West Indies in 1492 Columbus was sailing close to the north coast of Hispaniola when his biggest ship was wrecked on a reef. Some of the crew had to be left behind when Columbus returned to Spain. This, the first Spanish settlement in the West Indies, did not last long. It was destroyed by the Arawaks before Columbus revisited Hispaniola two years later. The spot was abandoned and a new settlement was built nearby. Soon afterwards the town of Santo Domingo was founded on the southern side of the island. It became for a time the base of Spanish operations in the Caribbean.

However, the island and its capital did not remain important for long. Hispaniola lacked an abundance of precious metals, and Spanish interest shifted to the Central and South American mainland where they were plentiful. The island became depopulated as the Arawaks rapidly died out and few Spaniards went to settle there. Even so, some lowland areas such as the Southern Plain and the Cibao Valley were developed into huge Spanish-owned, slave-run properties. Because of the sparse settlement, ranching rather than cultivation became the chief occupation. The more remote parts of the country fell into foreign hands. Tortuga became the chief stronghold of French buccaneers, who also settled in parts of Hispaniola itself, especially on the west coast. There they slaughtered wild cattle descended from those that had escaped from Spanish ranches,

smoked the meat and sold it to buccaneer ships. Gradually, French influence became so strong that in 1697 Spain was forced to hand over the western part of Hispaniola to France. It became the colony of St Domingue.

Under French rule buccaneering was brought to an end. Based on African slave labour St Domingue became a rich agricultural country. Indigo and tobacco were among the first crops to be exported in quantity, but sugar soon took precedence. Sugar estates were established along the north coast where little irrigation was needed, and in the Artibonite Valley and the Leogane, Cayes and Cul de Sac Plains where irrigation was essential. Coffee plantations thrived in the hills, and cotton was grown on the Arbre Plain and on those parts of the Cul de Sac Plain and Artibonite Valley which were too hot for coffee and too dry for cane.

Haiti and the Dominican Republic

At the height of its prosperity St Domingue was the richest country in the tropics. This ended in 1791 when the slaves, who made up 80 per cent of the population, rebelled and killed the French colonists or drove them out of the country. A new republic was created. It was named Haiti after the original Arawak name for the country, meaning 'land of mountains'. An English attempt to conquer the country failed when thousands of soldiers died of yellow fever. A French expedition sent by Napoleon to recapture the country also failed.

During the thirteen years of fighting many of the estates and irrigation works were destroyed and exports virtually ceased. The country was left poverty-stricken and very backward. Some other reasons explaining this state of affairs were:

1 Haiti had to pay a large sum of money to France in order to obtain recognition of its independence.

2 Much money was also spent in retaining a large army and in erecting fortifications against foreign attack. One such example is the Citadel, a colossal fortress built on a high hill near Cap Haitien. Today it is a big tourist attraction, tourism in Haiti being second to coffee as a money earner.

3 The hostility of slave-owning countries to the newly-freed nation expressed itself in an unwillingness to trade with Haiti.

4 To keep them going, estates needed skilled management backed with considerable capital reserves. The lack of a managerial class after the revolution, the backwardness of the liberated people after so many years of subjection, and the discouragement of foreign investors prevented the estates from operating. Instead they were split up into small farms, each owner producing his own crops in his own way. Sugar suffered most. Thus in 1825 virtually none was exported. Coffee exports were about half of what they had been thirty years previously.

Since 1791 Haitian history has been one of temporary dictatorships interrupted by bloody revolutions. This has handicapped agricultural and industrial enterprise.

The Dominican Republic, created in 1865, has also had a disturbed history. Both countries were occupied by American troops for a time, Haiti from 1915 to 1934 and the Dominican Republic from 1916 to 1924. Since then the differences between the two countries have grown. The Dominican Republic, with more favourable geographic conditions and with a single dictatorship between 1930 and 1961 made much more rapid economic progress than Haiti, even though much of the country's wealth was pocketed by the dictator and his relatives and friends.

Landforms

Hispaniola is the second largest Caribbean island and the most mountainous of all. It is here that the two great axes of folding which can be traced from Central America – one through Cuba and the other through Jamaica – merge in one island (see Map 1.3).

They form a series of roughly parallel east-west chains. They give Haiti its peculiar two-pronged shape.

Four main mountain ranges can be traced, one in the north, one in the south and two in between. Because they run across the international frontier, they have different names in French-speaking Haiti and in the Spanish-speaking Dominican Republic.

In the north of the Dominican Republic, behind a narrow coastal plain, is the Cordillera Septentrional which rises to over 1 200 metres. Between this and the next range – the Cordillera Central – there is a large valley which stretches from the north coast of Haiti to Samaná Bay. It is nearly 50 kilometres wide in places. In Haiti it is known as the Northern Plain; in the centre it is the Cibao, and in the east the Vega Real (see Map 14.1). It is the largest and richest agricultural valley in the West Indies, being a major producer of sisal, rice, bananas, cocoa, sugar, tobacco and smallholders' food crops (see Map 14.3). South of it lies the Cordillera Central of the Dominican Republic and its continuation, the Massif du Nord of Haiti. This is the highest range in the West Indies, containing several peaks over 2 500 metres in height. The highest of all is Pico Duarte, 3 100 metres. The narrow San Juan Valley separates the Cordillera Central from the Sierra de Neiba, which continues westwards, south of the Central Plateau of Haiti and the Artibonite River, as the Chaine de Mateaux. South of these mountains there is a rift valley, first thrown down to form a strait and then uplifted slightly in very recent times from beneath the sea. This lowland is known as the Enrequillo Plain in the Dominican Republic and as the Cul de Sac Plain in Haiti. The two salt lakes, Saumâtre and Enrequillo, which occupy depressions in the trench, are below sea level.

The 220 kilometre-long southern peninsula of Haiti contains two ranges, the Massif de la Hotte in the west, and the Massif de la Selle in the east. The latter rises to over 2 600 metres and continues a short way into the Dominican Republic.

The largest plains in the island are those in the south and south-eastern part of the Dominican Republic. Elsewhere lowlands are small and isolated from each other.

Rivers are too short and too steep to be of much use for navigation. In the dry season from December to April they dwindle and may dry up altogether, especially in limestone areas. In some places rivers have been harnessed to generate hydro-electricity.

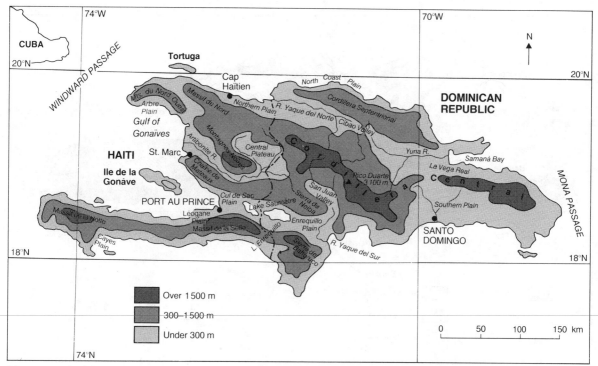

Map 14.1 HISPANIOLA: Relief.

Map 14.2 HISPANIOLA: Rainfall.

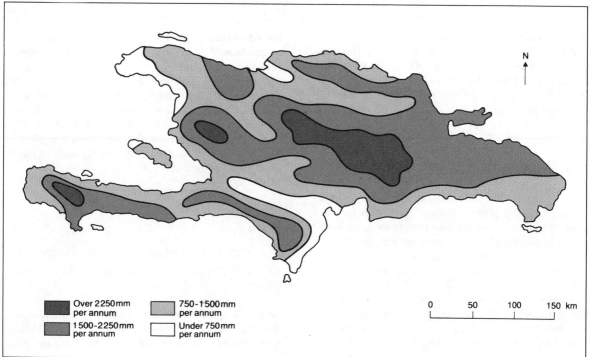

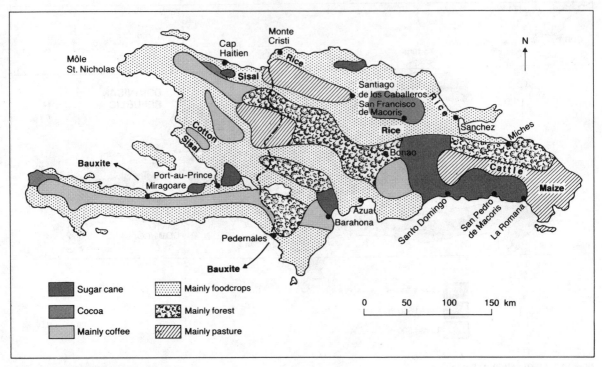

Map 14.3 HISPANIOLA: Land use.

Two examples are the gorge of the Arbitonite River which lies between the Central Plateau and the coastal lowland, and the Jimenoa Falls in the Cordillera Central. The lower courses of many streams, especially those in the Dominican Republic, provide water for irrigation.

Climate and vegetation

Because the landscape of Hispaniola is the most irregular in the West Indies, the climatic and vegetational contrasts are also the greatest. Thus the peaks of the Cordillera Central are the coolest and wettest in the West Indies, and the western lowlands are the hottest and driest. Haiti, lying on the leeward side, is drier than the Dominican Republic. The Arbre and Cul de Sac plains, for instance, get only 500 to 750 millimetres of rain a year (see Map 14.2). The heaviest rains come between May and October. Caribbean Pine forests cover the upper slopes of

the Cordillera Central and certain other ranges such as the Massif de la Selle. Lower down, lush tropical forests occur in the wetter areas and thorn forests in the drier ones. Savannas are numerous and in such places as the Cibao and the north-western part of the Central Plateau they are extensive. Cactus and thorn shrubs occur in the driest areas. A belt of this type of vegetation extends all the way from the Môle St Nicholas to Port-au-Prince. It covers much of the Ile de la Gonâve as well.

Haiti

Area: 27 750 square kilometres; population (1988); about 5 500 000; density of population about 200 per square kilometre.

So much of Haiti was divided into smallholdings at the beginning of the nineteenth century that Haitian agriculture is mainly in the hands of peasants rather than estates. Today over 80 per cent of the population are smallholders. With the land as their only resource they have had to make a living for themselves and their families. In doing so they have been the cause of the worst soil erosion in the West Indies. Over 40 per cent of the total area of the country is ruined or severely affected. The reasons for this are set out on the right.

Agriculture

The most important export crop, coffee, brings in about 30 per cent of the foreign earnings. It is grown by many peasant farmers on land between 300 and 1 500 metres in height. There are no large plantations. Although the trees are usually grown with a minimum of care and much of the crop is poorly processed, the coffee itself has a good flavour and sells well in America and in several European countries. Output is about the same today as it was at the beginning of the century; that is between 30 000 and 40 000 tonnes a year.

Sugar cane is grown on the Northern, Léogane and Cul de Sac Plains. Output has declined to the point where considerable quantities of sugar are being imported from the Dominican Republic. The largest sugar factory is located near to Port-au-Prince. It is owned by the government and operates at a loss.

Sisal plantations have been established in the areas shown on Map 14.3, particularly the one in the north. Some is exported and some is made into hats, shoes, handbags, curtains and carpets which are very popular with tourists. Sisal and straw handicrafts formed about 5 per cent of the exports in the mid-1980s.

Cocoa is grown at heights of 100 to 750 metres in some parts of the Northern Peninsula and particularly in the western part of the Southern Peninsula. Most of it is poorly processed and prices are low. Output is rather less than it was a century ago.

Essential oils are extracted from vetiver, amyris, lemongrass and other plants. They are sent to America and to France, where they are used in the making of perfumes. They form about 3 per cent of the exports.

Rice, corn, cassava and many other vegetables and fruits are grown primarily for consumption within the country. In good years some are exported,

Soil Erosion in Haiti

Three main factors have contributed to soil erosion in Haiti.

1 The population of Haiti has grown rapidly. It is now more than ten times what it was at the time of the revolution. This has had three consequences. First, it has increased the demand for agricultural land. Farming has spread higher and higher up the hillsides, destroying the forests that once existed there. Second, it has increased the demand for building materials and for fuel for cooking. The only readily available source has been wood: indeed, wood provides three-quarters of Haiti's fuel supply. Third, it has increased the demand for food crops which can be reaped two or more times a year rather than tree crops, such as coffee, which bear only once a year.

2 The replacement of forests and tree crops by food crops means that trees are no longer present on the land to break the force of the rain and soak up rainwater. Nor are their roots available to hold the soil in place. During heavy rains, water streams down the hillsides and washes away the soil. This affects not only the upper slopes but all the cultivated land below.

3 Measures for preventing soil erosion are seldom used. One reason for this is that peasant farmers have only hoes and machetes to work with. They lack heavy equipment for levelling and terracing the land. A second is that the peasant communities in the hills are isolated and largely illiterate. They therefore lack access to information on improved farming techniques. A third reason is that individual farmers acting on their own cannot prevent erosion from spreading on to their land from neighbouring property. Soil conservation has to be undertaken over a wide area if it is to be successful (see chapter eighteen.)

All this was summed up in a United Nations report written in the 1950s. It said: 'The fundamental economic problem of Haiti derives from the relentless pressure of a steadily growing, insufficiently educated population upon limited, vulnerable and – as far as agriculture is concerned – alarmingly shrinking natural resources.' The situation has, if anything, worsened since then.

Sisal being dried. What can you tell about the landscape and the climate of Haiti?

In rural Haiti a basically subsistence economy is supplanted by small earnings from agricultural products. Here coffee beans and sisal hats are being prepared for sale.

especially to the Bahamas; in bad ones, rice and corn have to be imported.

Livestock is kept on the grasslands. Some beef, hides and skins are exported.

Manufacturing

Attracted by wage rates of US$50 a month (less than a tenth paid in Puerto Rico) American companies have set up light manufacturing industries in which cheap labour is a special advantage. Examples are electrical and electronic equipment, cassettes, textiles, garments (including underwear), baseballs and toys. The fact that the export of these goods brought in about half of the export earnings in the mid 1980s does not mean that Haiti is a rich industrial country. In fact, the island's exports are small, amounting to only a third of those of Jamaica which has a much smaller area and population.

Bauxite, once an important source of income, is no longer produced. Copper, manganese and silver are known to exist, but they are not worked at present. Nor are the deposits of lignite which occur in the north-west of the Central Plateau and near Aux Cayes. The only industry based on mineral resources is the manufacture of cement.

Towns

Port-au-Prince (800 000) has grown to prominence by having the best harbour in the country and the easiest access to the most productive lowland. It is the capital, the only port with an international trade, and the biggest industrial and commercial centre. In recent years it has grown rapidly as people leave the depressed rural areas to seek a livelihood there. Some find employment in various forms of trade; others, particularly women, in light manufacturing industries. About 85 per cent of Haiti's industrial output is located in Port-au-Prince.

There are few other towns and all of them are small. Les Cayes (35 000) serves as a regional centre for the south coast. Cap Haitien (70 000) performs a similar function for the north, as does Gonaives (50 000) for the north-west. Many small settlements exist at the junction of the highlands and the lowlands where peasants sell their produce to small traders and buy household goods in exchange. As in Jamaica, most of this trade and the city marketing is handled by women.

Living conditions and migration

Haiti is the only one of the West Indies to appear in the World Bank's list of the world's twenty-eight poorest countries. In the mid-80s, the income per head was only US$350 a year. In contrast, that for Puerto Rico was about $5 000 a year. Despite large amounts of international aid supplied by the United States, other governments, and by a wide range of international organisations, the situation is not improving. Indeed, the people in the rural areas are getting poorer because their numbers are growing faster than the output from their farms.

One of the consequences of poverty is that some 60 per cent of the population is illiterate. Another is poor health brought about by malnutrition and the fact that only 40 per cent of urban and 5 per cent of rural people have access to piped water. Some 12 per cent of Haitian babies die before their first birthday compared with under 3 per cent elsewhere in the Commonwealth Caribbean islands.

The escape from poverty has been the main factor underlying emigration. For many years large numbers of cane cutters have gone on contract to the Dominican Republic to work the sugar harvest. Others have slipped across the frontier. Despite the hostility they encounter from time to time, many have not returned home. It is thought that about 300 000 Haitians are now living in the Dominican Republic.

Unlike Puerto Ricans, Haitians have not been able to travel freely to the United States. Even so, many have found their way there. In the 1970s they included boatloads of illegal immigrants who made their way to Florida. A similar movement twenty years earlier took Haitians to the Bahamas where they replaced Bahamians who were leaving low-paid jobs to work in tourism.

French-speaking countries have been another destination. There has been a considerable migration to France and also to Montreal, the largest French-speaking city in Canada. Smaller numbers have gone to Martinique, Guadeloupe and French Guiana. Altogether about a million Haitians are believed to be living abroad.

The Dominican Republic

Area: 48 730 square kilometres; population (1988): about 6 500 000; density of population: about 133 per square kilometre.

There are few similarities between Haiti and the Dominican Republic. The Dominican Republic, with nearly twice the area and about the same number of people has much less pressure on greater and more varied natural resources. The population density is nearly the lowest in the West Indies.

Another contrast is that the stable political conditions that existed during the dictatorship which lasted from the 1930s to the 1960s encouraged the investment of foreign capital for agricultural and industrial development. Though wealth was concentrated in a few hands, a stable economy was built up which, with considerable support from the United States, has since been able to grow. The main task now is to distribute the wealth more fairly among the people and raise the general standard of living.

Agriculture

Santo Domingo was the site of the first Spanish cane fields in the West Indies. But the development of a large-scale sugar industry dates from the 1870s, when civil war in Cuba curtailed the sugar output from that country and the Dominican Republic was able to capture her markets. Very large sugar estates were established mainly with American capital.

Santo Domingo at the mouth of the Ozama River. Using the picture, suggest reasons which explain the original choice of the site and the city's subsequent development.

Three cane-growing areas became particularly important and remain so today. One is round Barahona, where the Rio Yaque del Sur provides irrigation water. The second is the southern plain, where irrigation is also essential. The third is the north coast plain.

Though the Dominican Republic is the second largest sugar producer in the Caribbean (after Cuba), there has been a big decline in recent years. The main reason for this has been the difficulty of selling sugar overseas. Unlike Commonwealth Caribbean countries, the Dominican Republic has no access to the European Economic Community under the Lomé Agreement. It has therefore had to rely on selling sugar to the USA. As we have seen in chapter four, this market has declined because of competition from high fructose corn syrup. Sugar exports from the Dominican Republic have fallen from over 1 million tonnes a year in the late 1970s to under $\frac{1}{2}$ million tonnes in the late 1980s. Over the same period the value of the sugar exported has fallen from half to a quarter of the total exports. Santo Domingo, San Pedro de Macoris, Barahona and La Romana (see Map 14.3) are the main sugar shipping ports. Among the purchasing countries are Haiti and those Commonwealth Caribbean countries in which sugar production has declined or died out altogether.

The second most important crop is coffee. With government encouragement and assistance, output has risen to three times the amount produced in Haiti. The United States takes over three-quarters of the exports. Local consumption has risen with the growth of tourism.

The Dominican Republic is also a large producer of cocoa, most of which is grown on the rich soils of the Cibao round San Francisco de Macoris and exported from Sánchez. The bulk of the crop is sold in the United States. Lesser amounts are sent to the Netherlands, Germany, Puerto Rico and elsewhere. Chocolate is manufactured both for local consumption and for export.

Tobacco, grown on the Cibao round Santiago de los Caballeros, is exported to many countries including Spain, Germany, Algeria, the Netherlands and France. Some of the crop is made into cigars for sale in the USA where Cuban imports are banned. In addition, cigarettes are made for local sale. The rice output of some 500 000 tonnes a year permits a certain export. The chief growing areas are those round Monte Cristi and San Francisco de Macoris. Some of the maize produced in the country is sold to Puerto Rico. Bananas and groundnuts are also exported, and cotton is grown on the Enriquillo Plain.

In an attempt to diversify agricultural exports to the USA, such crops as tomatoes, melons, and pineapples are grown on land once under sugar cane.

There are about a million cattle in the Dominican Republic; that is, about ten times as many as in Haiti. Hides and skins are sold abroad, and some beef is sent to Puerto Rico.

Mining and Timber

Minerals are important. The most valuable is nickel, mined near Bonao (see Map 14.3). Gold and silver are mined at Pueblo Xinejo, Miches and elsewhere. Output is largest in the Caribbean. Gypsum is mined near Barahona. Iron occurs together with nickel. Deposits of cobalt, chrome, graphite, titanium, copper and platinum are known to exist. Until 1983 large quantities of bauxite were mined in the Sierra de Bahoruco and exported from Pedernales on the south coast near the Haitian frontier. Production is now very small.

About 40 per cent of the Dominican Republic is still in forest, the highest proportion in the Greater Antilles. Some timber is exported. Large reserves await future exploitation.

Industry

Though the Dominican Republic is not an industrial country, its heavy industries include oil refining based on imported crude petroleum, and cement. In addition, the number of light manufactures is growing in response to the United States Caribbean Basin Initiative (see chapter four). Several free trade zones have been set aside for them. In this connection, some firms in Puerto Rico which are exporting manufactured products to the USA have set up 'twinned' factories in the Dominican Republic where some of the work is carried out. There are three reasons for this. One is the political pressure put on Puerto Rico by the US government. Another is that Puerto Rico and the Dominican Republic share a common language. The third is that although wages in the Dominican Republic are twice those paid in Haiti, they are much less than those paid in Puerto Rico: twinning can lead to increased profits.

Tourism

The Dominican Republic resembles Jamaica in having many attractive beaches along the north coast which are within easy reach of the USA. Throughout the 1980s hotel development has been rapid, and the number of tourists has risen to about 1 million a year.

The people

In contrast with Haiti, where nearly all the people are of African descent and there are very few white or coloured inhabitants, just over 70 per cent of the people of the Dominican Republic are coloured, and 15 per cent are white.

The population is concentrated in two areas, the South-Eastern Plain, and the Cibao and Vega Real. The former area is served by the capital and chief port, Santo Domingo, and the latter by Santiago de los Caballeros. In recent years urbanisation in the Dominican Republic has been rapid. Santo Domingo has a population of about 1½ million and Santiago de los Cabelleros has over ¼ million.

Trade

In 1985, about 70 per cent of the exports went to the United States. The remainder was shared by many countries, including the Netherlands, Belgium, Puerto Rico and Japan.

Questions and assignments

1 Look at the information given about the exports from Haiti in 1980 and 1984, and answer the following questions:
   a) What was the value of the bauxite exported in i) 1980, and ii) 1984?
   b) Which product decreased most in value between 1980 and 1984?
   c) Draw bar graphs to compare each product in 1980 and 1984.
   d) Calculate coffee's percentage of the total exports in 1980 and in 1984.

Exports from Haiti in 1980 and 1984
(figures given to the nearest million US dollars)

Products	1980	1984
Coffee	90	54
Essential oils	5	6
Sugar	6	1
Cocoa	5	5
Manufactures	55	64
Bauxite	20	0
Others	35	85
Total	181	130

2 Use the information given below about the exports from the Dominican Republic in 1984 and answer the questions that follow.

Exports from the Dominican Republic in 1984
(figures given to the nearest million US dollars)

Products	1984
Sugar	300
Coffee	95
Cocoa	76
Tobacco	24
Nickel	109
Gold & silver	132
Others	129
Total	865

   a) What was the value of the combined exports of i) coffee, cocoa and tobacco, and ii) nickel, gold and silver?
   b) Calculate the percentage of the total exports formed by i) sugar, ii) coffee, cocoa and tobacco, iii) nickel, gold and silver, and iv) other products.
   c) Construct a divided circle to show these percentages.
   d) Draw a bar graph to compare the total exports of Haiti and the Dominican Republic in 1984.
   e) Give two reasons to explain the difference.

15

Puerto Rico

Area: (with dependencies): 8 897 square kilometres; population (1988): 3 300 000; density of population: 371 per square kilometre.

Landforms

Puerto Rico, the smallest and most easterly of the Greater Antilles, is roughly rectangular in shape. As can be seen from Map 15.1, there are two mountainous areas. The main backbone of the island is the Cordillera Central. It contains the highest mountain, Cerro de Punta (1 340 metres). Separated from the Cordillera Central by the valley of the Caguas River is the much smaller Sierra de Luquillo in the northeast. Here the second highest peak, El Yunque, is to be found. Together these mountainous areas take up about half the area of the island. Their core is mainly composed of volcanic and metamorphic rocks. On their northern and southern flanks is a limestone plateau which, particularly on the northern side, has been severely eroded to produce a cockpit type of karst scenery with isolated conical buttresses separated by narrow pockets of fertile lowland. Surrounding the highlands is a coastal plain, mostly made of limestone but covered in places by alluvial deposits. It is about eight kilometres wide in the north and rather less than that elsewhere.

Climate

Lying in the same latitude and having much the same shape and topography as Jamaica, Puerto Rico has much the same climate. Mean temperatures on the plains range from 24°C in January and February to just under 27°C in July, August and September. The heaviest rain falls on the mountains, especially the upper north-eastern slopes of the Sierra de Luquillo which directly face the Trade winds. The coastal plains have much less, particularly in the south, where a small area has under 1 000 millimetres a year. The rainy season lasts from May to November with September and October being the wettest in the south, and May being the wettest in the north.

Puerto Rico has occasional summer hurricanes. Over ninety have been recorded since the island was first settled in 1508.

Development

Puerto Rico was ruled by Spain for four centuries. In 1898 it was ceded to the United States. Since then, though the island has become economically tied to the mainland, it has achieved a degree of political independence. Today, Puerto Rico is a 'Free Associated State'. This means that it is self-governing in all matters save defence and foreign relations. It elects no representatives to the United States Congress and, as a result, has been able to use to its own advantage the American maxim 'no taxation without representation'. No taxes are paid to Washington, and any customs duties collected on Puerto Rican goods entering the USA are handed back to the Puerto Rican treasury.

Under the Spaniards Puerto Rico was not a great sugar producer. Some estates were established on the coastal plains, and some sugar was exported, but the industry was never as large as those in Jamaica and Hispaniola. The main reason for this was a

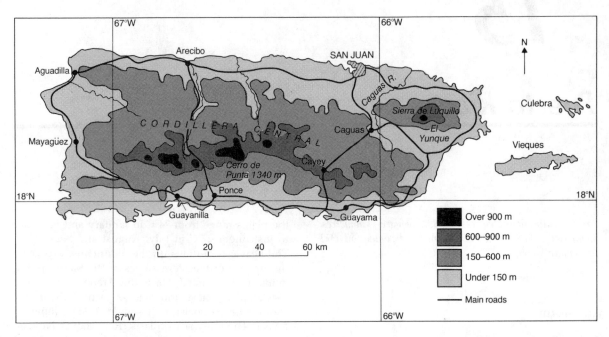

Map 15.1 PUERTO RICO: Relief.

Map 15.2 PUERTO RICO: Rainfall.

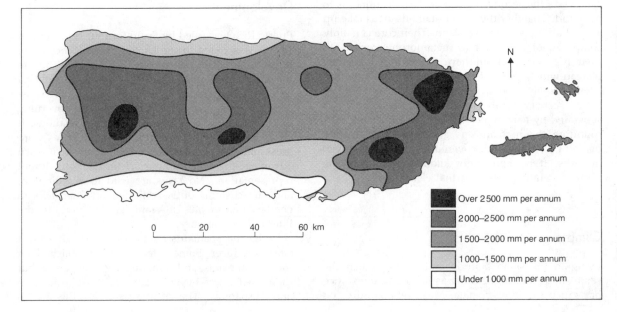

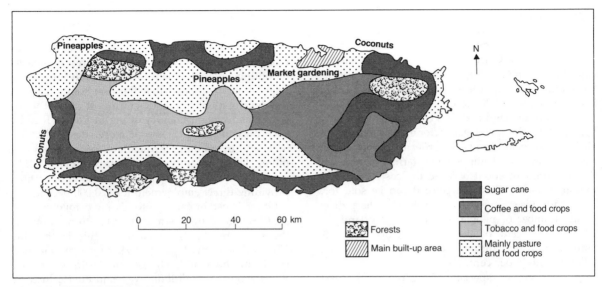

Map 15.3 PUERTO RICO: Land use.

Spanish law that said that Puerto Rico could trade only with Spain. The law remained in force for three centuries. Of course it was broken; in fact it is believed that in some years the illegal trade was larger than the legal one. Even so, development was retarded and the population was little more than a half that of Jamaica when the law was repealed in 1815. By this time, however, the slave trade had ended and as a result Puerto Rico was unable to expand the sugar lands quickly.

Cattle hides, tobacco, and ginger were the chief exports of the seventeenth century. In the next century cotton was added and in the nineteenth century the exports of sugar increased. In addition, coffee spread rapidly throughout the hills. Coffee exports were worth three times as much as sugar when the island came under American control in 1898.

More changes then took place. Assured of a large and seemingly prosperous market at home, American businessmen bought land from many of the smallholders in Puerto Rico and set up big modern sugar estates. In thirty years sugar output multiplied fifteen times. A similar expansion took place in the export of tobacco. Coffee declined, however, partly because Spain imposed tariffs on goods from her old colony, and partly because Brazilian coffee was more popular in America. Then in 1928 a world slump began. Puerto Rico suffered severely, the price of her chief commodities falling to such low levels that it was rarely profitable to sell them. To add to her distress the island was struck by hurricanes in 1928 and 1932 and suffered a serious drought in 1931. For over ten years the mass of the workers faced starvation and were only kept alive by vast relief funds from the United States.

Since the 1940s the Puerto Rican government has been acquiring land from some of the American corporations, for, by law, no private property should be more than 500 acres in size. On some of this land, government-owned 'proportional profit farms' have been set up, where labourers, in addition to being paid standard wage rates, share in the profits and use a few acres of their own to grow food crops. Others have been encouraged to borrow money from the government to buy farms for themselves. Land reform has, however, been slow. The main reason for this has been a shift in emphasis in the economy from agriculture to manufacturing. The area under crops is steadily declining, as is the number of farms.

Very little land has been left under the original forest cover, the chief remaining areas being the Sierra de Luquillo and the higher parts of the Cordillera Central.

Agriculture

Puerto Rico was at one time one of the leading sugar producers in the Caribbean. In the 1950s it had an export quota to the USA of 1 million tonnes a year. Since that time output has steadily declined. By 1975 it was down to 300 000 tonnes; by 1987 to 96 000. A large part of the land that was once under cane now lies unused. The few sugar factories that remain are all in government hands. In order to preserve jobs the government subsidises sugar farmers and bears the loss brought about because the cost of producing sugar is less than the price it can be sold for. Even with this support, there has been a sharp drop in the number of people working on the land. In 1950 36 per cent of the island's workforce was employed in agriculture. By 1980 the figure had fallen to only 5 per cent.

In some areas, especially along the north coast plain, pineapples, oranges, grapefruit and bananas are grown. Some are exported to America. Some are canned in order to reduce the risk of fetching low prices in a fluctuating market. Puerto Rico is also the largest exporter of fresh coconuts to the United States. Most are grown in a narrow belt close to the sea, mainly along the northern and western coasts of the island.

The main coffee-producing area is the rugged western mountains between heights of 300 and 1 000 metres. Though, as we have seen, coffee was once the leading export, very little is now sent abroad. Some tobacco is grown on small hill farms in the east-central part of the country. Most of the crop is exported as leaf to the United States to be manufactured there. Some is made into cigars in Cayey and Caguas.

A large proportion of the arable land is under food crops, particularly in the hills. Maize, sweet potatoes, bananas, plantains, avocado pears, yams and beans are the most widespread. In some places, as shown on Map 15.3, they are more important than cash crops.

Cattle rearing is another occupation. Those animals that are reared on the dry southern plain are used for beef production; those on the wetter northern plain for dairy products.

In general, agriculture has become an unpopular way of earning a living. As a result, by the late 1980s, Puerto Rico was producing only a quarter of its food needs. The rest had to be imported, mainly from the USA.

Manufacturing

In the 1950s the government of Puerto Rico was faced with the problems of low living standards, mounting unemployment, and a rapidly increasing population. It decided that the best solution lay in the development of manufacturing. It offered to assist firms to begin manufacturing in Puerto Rico by such measures as providing factory sites and buildings, and by granting tax holidays for ten years and more. These incentives were successful. By 1977 some 2 000 manufacturing plants were in operation, providing direct employment for 120 000 people.

Other West Indian territories have followed the lead originated by Puerto Rico but with nothing like the same result. The reason for this is that the United States, the biggest market for manufactured goods in the world, charges no tariffs on Puerto Rican exports. In addition, wages in Puerto Rico are less than those in North America. As a result some types of goods can be produced more cheaply in Puerto Rico than in America itself despite the cost of transport. If wages were to be equalised, Puerto Rico would lose its advantage and many factories would be threatened with closure.

The first industries to be set up under the new scheme were those in which cheap labour was an important factor. They included textiles, footwear and other leather and plastic goods, needlework and many different items of men's and women's clothing. Small factories were opened throughout the island to produce them. This kind of development has slowed down in recent years as wage rates have risen to the point where Puerto Rico cannot easily compete with similar products made in other countries where wages are still low.

A second and very different kind of industrial development consisted of oil refining and the manufacture of petrochemicals. These were large-scale industries located in a few major ports such as San Juan, Ponce, Guyama and Guayanilla (see Map 15.1). Each of them employed a large labour force. They relied entirely on supplies of imported crude petroleum as Puerto Rico had none of its own. Whilst the world price of petroleum was low, the industries were successful. However when the price rose in the mid-70s, profits fell and some of the industries were closed. For the time being at least, this kind of development has not continued.

Those industries to have remained most successful are those in which the tax advantages gained by manufacturing in Puerto Rico are big enough to offset rising wages. Pharmaceuticals are one example. Some of the world's major manufacturers of pharmaceuticals have set up businesses there. They export their products to the USA. The assembly of electrical and electronic equipment is another example. Because goods like these are light in weight and small in volume, they can be sent abroad by air freight.

Supporters of the Puerto Rican policy point out the following economic benefits. First, though industrial wages are considerably lower than they are in the United States, they are higher than those in the rest of the West Indies; higher even than those paid in some European countries. Second, the per-capita income rose from under US$ 300 in 1950 to nearly $5 000 in 1988. Housing is better than it was then, and so are health and education. Critics hold a different view. They point out that the wealth that has been generated has not been distributed evenly throughout society and some people remain very poor. Another point is that because many of the manufacturing companies are American owned, Americans hold the best jobs and the biggest share of the profits go to the USA. Most serious of all, the creation of new jobs is not keeping pace with the increasing size of the work force. In 1988 manufacturing employed about 20 per cent of the workforce. However, about the same percentage was out of work and living on welfare benefits mainly paid by the United States government. This has aroused some resentment in the United States. Critics there point out that although manufacturers make big profits in Puerto Rico and avoid paying taxes in the United States, they are not fulfilling their original purpose of reducing unemployment.

As a result of these and other criticisms, the government is assisting manufacturers to set up a twinning arrangement with other Caribbean countries. In this arrangement work is split in two. Part of it is undertaken in the firm's factory in Puerto Rico. The rest is carried out in a twinned factory in another Caribbean country with lower wage rates. Some manufacturers in Commonwealth Caribbean countries have entered into this arrangement.

Tourism

During the 1960s there was a big increase in tourism in Puerto Rico, and by the end of that period a million people were visiting the island each year. One reason for this was the closing of Cuba to tourists after the Castro revolution. Another was the low air fares which made Puerto Rico the best bargain for Americans taking a holiday in the Caribbean. A third was the number of American businessmen who combined a business visit and a vacation. A fourth was the provision of tax concessions to investors in tourist facilities. So many new hotels have been built that parts of Puerto Rico more closely resemble Miami Beach than any other part of the Caribbean. Some have special convention facilities, and some operate casinos. In 1987 some 1 300 000 stop-over tourists and over 700 000 cruise-ship passengers visited the island.

Population and emigration

One reason for the high rate of unemployment in Puerto Rico is the rapidity of the rise in population. Between 1960 and 1987 the number of people living in the island rose by almost a million. This figure might have doubled had it not been for emigration to the USA which Puerto Ricans can enter without restriction. About a million are now living there, 60 per cent of them in New York.

In 1988 the density of population in Puerto Rico was about 370 per square kilometre. This is higher than the United States would have if all the people in the world were living there! Despite the gigantic resources of the United States, the problem of maintaining such a population is beyond imagination. Yet in the West Indies a population density of 370 or more per square kilometre is not uncommon, and economic conditions are better than they are in many other parts of the world. This comparison with the United States indicates the scale of the problem that the West Indies have had to surmount in achieving present-day living standards.

Towns

A few years after Spaniards colonised the island, which at that time was known as San Juan Bautista, they chose the best harbour on the north coast as the most suitable place to establish their chief port. This they called Puerto Rico – the 'rich port'. In later years the names were interchanged, so that the island became known as Puerto Rico and the capital San Juan.

The older part of San Juan lies on an island which almost encloses the mouth of San Juan Bay. Several old forts, notably El Morro at the harbour entrance (see page 40) remain to show how well it was protected. It is connected by a bridge to the new part of the town. This, as can be seen from the photograph below, contains many high-rise buildings; more than in any other West Indian city. Multi-lane highways connect the city centre with well planned residential suburbs covering some 150 square kilometres of the lowlands. In all, over a million people live in and around San Juan.

The port is by far the most important in the island. Because easy, efficient transport is needed for the importation of industrial raw materials and components, and for the export of finished manufactured goods, the port has the most modern facilities in the Caribbean. They include a service by which trucks or their trailers can be driven aboard ship at one end of the journey, and driven off at the other. The time taken for the journey from San Juan to New York is 60 hours.

San Juan airport is the busiest in the Caribbean. There are direct flights to all major cities in the USA and to many other places. Between them, two American airlines had over 100 flights a day in the late 1980s. Many planes – including jumbo jets – carry nothing but cargo, and there is a constant traffic of private planes flying from Puerto Rico to the United States.

Ponce (190 000) on the south coast, is the second

With its high-rise office blocks and wide roads, this part of San Juan looks more like an American than a West Indian city.

largest port on the island. It exports sugar and rum, and has an oil refinery. Other large ports are Mayaguez (100 000), important for the canning and export of tuna fish, and Guayanilla, Guayama and Yabucoa, which import petroleum for their oil refineries.

Trade

Exports to the United States are over 80 per cent, and imports from the United States over 60 per cent of the total. As we have already seen, a great deal of the island's present prosperity is due to the availability of such a large and rich market for the exports. On the other hand it also means that Puerto Rico has to buy in return some of the world's dearest goods, so the cost of living is high.

The dependencies

The outlying small islands of Vieques, Culebra and Mona are unimportant. Most of Vieques is controlled by the US Navy which maintains a large base to control shipping entering and leaving this part of the Caribbean. The people in Culebra make a poor living by grazing and fishing. Mona is practically uninhabited.

Questions and assignments

1 Use the figures given below to answer the questions that follow.

Stop-over tourists to Puerto Rico in 1980, 1982, 1984, and 1986
(figures to the nearest thousand)

	1980	1982	1984	1986
Puerto Rico	1 627	1 564	1 866	2 042
Total for the Caribbean	6 860	6 853	7 513	8 400

   a) How many tourists visited Puerto Rico in 1982? How many visited the Caribbean in 1986?
   b) Draw bar graphs to show the number of tourists who visited the Caribbean in 1980, 1982, 1984 and 1986. Within each of these four bar graphs show the number who visited Puerto Rico.
   c) What percentage of the total number of tourists who visited the Caribbean went to Puerto Rico in 1982 and in 1986?
   d) How many tourists visited Puerto Rico in 1980 and in 1986? What was the percentage increase over the period?
   e) Give two reasons which explain the popularity of Puerto Rico for tourists from the USA.
2 Name: a) two measures taken by the Puerto Rican government to encourage industrial development; b) three of the earliest light manufacturing industries to be successful; c) two industries to have become unsuccessful; and d) three of the most successful industries in the late 1980s.

191

16

Belize

Area: (including cays): 22 960 square kilometres; population (1988) about 175 000; density of population: under 8 per square kilometre.

The Central American setting

Stretching south-eastwards from Mexico for 1 600 km is a long, tapering twisted isthmus in which lie Belize and the six Central American republics.

The republics are:

	Area (square kilometres)	Population (1988)
Guatemala	109 000	8½ million
Honduras	112 000	4½ million
El Salvador	21 000	5 million
Nicaragua	139 000	3½ million
Costa Rica	51 000	3 million
Panama	77 000	2¼ million

The mountain chain which forms the backbone of the isthmus contains many volcanic peaks, some of which rise to over 3 600 metres. A few of the volcanoes (eg Masaya Caldera in Nicaragua and Mt Irazú in Costa Rica) are active.

The mountains are a source of minerals, especially silver and gold. As Diagram 16.1 shows, the highest peaks lie above the forest line. Some of these are snow-capped; all have cold, windswept grasslands suitable only for sheep rearing. Further down, three climatic and crop belts are recognised. On the cool plateaux of the tierra fria live the majority of the people of Amerindian descent. Their subsistence economy is based on maize, potatoes, beans and livestock. Lower down, between 600 and 1 800 metres, is the tierra templada. This land of large farms, many of which are European owned, produces mainly coffee. Large quantities are grown in most of the republics. Coffee forms over half of the exports of El Salvador and Guatemala.

The hot, moist coastlands of the tierra caliente have a higher proportion of people of African descent, many of whom emigrated to Central America from the West Indies to work on the banana plantations and construction of the Panama Canal. The Central American republics supply most of the banana requirements of the United States. The plantations were originally developed on the Caribbean seaboard, but when the fruit was struck with Panama disease, the bulk of the production shifted to the Pacific coastlands. When new methods were found to combat the disease much of the cultivation returned to the eastern lowlands which are more easily accessible to the big markets of north-eastern North America. In the west, cattle farming has become important, and cotton is being grown for the Japanese market. Other lowland crops are sugar cane, cocoa, rice and sisal.

The Panama Canal has been built at the lowest and narrowest part of the isthmus. As it shortens some sea routes by thousands of kilometres it is of great economic and strategic importance, especially to the United States which currently owns the strip of land on either side of the canal. An arrangement to hand over control to Panama has been negotiated.

Settlement and development of Belize

The first Europeans to see the coast of what is now Belize were a party of Spaniards who in 1506 sailed

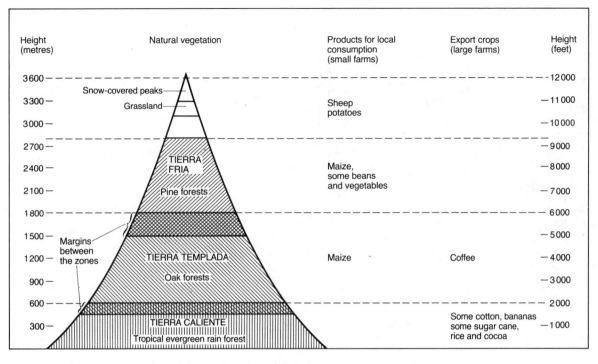

Diagram 16.1 The effect of height on land use in Central America.

along the coast of the Yucatán peninsula. They made no attempt to settle there; the swamps and forests were too unattractive for them. What they did not know was that the land had once been densely peopled by Mayan Indians with one of the world's most interesting civilisations. However, several hundred years before the arrival of the Spaniards the Mayas had left the area, leaving the forest to creep back and hide their cities and temples. The reason for this migration of perhaps three-quarters of a million people is a mystery. War, sickness, a rebellion of the peasants against their priests, a climatic change, and the ravages of soil erosion after centuries of intensive cultivation, have all been suggested to explain it.

The Central American coast, deserted by the Mayas and unsuited to the Spaniards, became instead the haunt of buccaneers who learned to navigate the channels through the reefs off-shore. They hid their ships on cays and in river mouths and attacked the Spanish treasure ships leaving Mexico, Panama and Cartagena.

In the early seventeenth century, British settlements were established in Yucatán and along the 'Mosquito' coast farther south to export logwood. This tree, from which dyes were obtained for the British woollen industry, was at that time fetching very high prices. Such a profitable trade attracted many ex-buccaneers and also settlers from Jamaica after its capture in 1655. For a short time the area became as valuable as any British colony then established in the Caribbean.

In the treaties between Spain and England the position of the British settlers in Central America was never clearly defined, and on a number of occasions Spaniards seized their ships and destroyed their homes. Gradually the logwood cutters became concentrated on the stretch of coast between the Belize and Hondo rivers. Even there they were far from safe. It was not until after they had beaten off an unusually powerful Spanish attack in 1798 that they were left in peace. During the revolutionary wars of the early nineteenth century, when the Central American republics gained their independence,

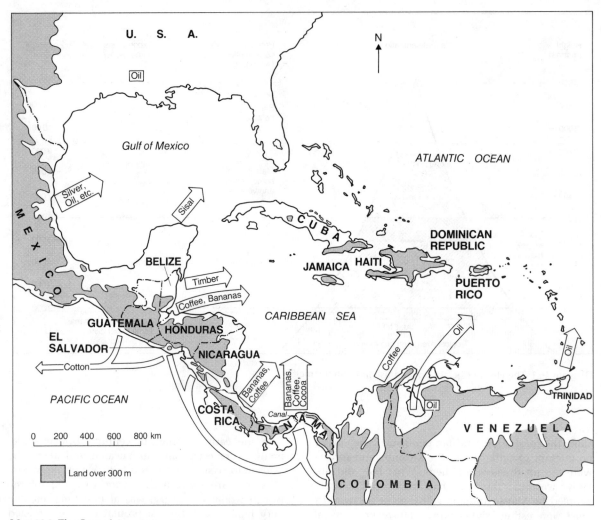

Map 16.2 The Central American setting.

Belize was the only country left untroubled and unchanged.

At the beginning of the nineteenth century, when the population numbered some 200 whites, 1 000 coloured people and free Negroes, and 3 000 slaves, a unique immigration took place. Several thousand Black Caribs, the offspring of Caribs and Negroes in St Vincent, were deported from the island after an unsuccessful rebellion against the British and taken to Belize. Many of their descendants still form a distinct agricultural and fishing community on the southern coastlands. Others are to be found in business and in the professions (particularly teaching) in all parts of the country.

As there was a steady drift of escaped slaves away from Belize to neighbouring countries, the population remained small until emancipation, after which it grew fairly rapidly. This natural increase has been supplemented by further immigration of several different groups of people. For example, about the middle of the nineteenth century Spanish refugees settled in and around Corozal in the north of the country (see Map 16.3) after fleeing from a Mayan uprising in the Yucatán. They began a sugar industry there but its success was limited and it remained small until the 1960s. Also about a century ago, small parties of Mayas began moving across the Mexican and Guatemalan frontiers into Belize. This movement has continued. Today Mayas form about 15 per cent of the population. A further 20 per cent consists of people of mixed Spanish and Mayan descent. The main language of both these groups is Spanish not English. Black and coloured people comprise 55 per cent of the total population, Black Caribs about 8 per cent. Among recent arrivals are Mennonite Christians from Europe and North America. Though small in number, they are making an increasing contribution to agricultural development.

In 1859, Guatemala agreed in a treaty with Britain that the southern frontier of Belize should be the Sarstoon and not the Sibun River. This doubled the size of the country. On its part, Britain undertook to share the cost of building a road from the capital of Guatemala to the Caribbean Sea. The road was never built. Mainly for this reason the Guatemalan government claims that Belize should belong to Guatemala. They say they will drop the claim only if certain conditions are met. The main one is access to the Caribbean Sea. If you look at Map 16.2 and Map 16.3 you will see why this is so important to Guatemala.

While Belize was a British colony it could rely on Britain for protection against invasion. Now that it has become an independent country, national defence has become a problem as it cannot afford large armed forces of its own.

Landforms

Belize, the only Commonwealth country in Central America, is long and narrow in shape. It extends for 280 kilometres from north to south. At its widest it is only about 110 kilometres from east to west. The frontier with Mexico follows the lower part of the Hondo River to its mouth. That with Guatemala runs for many miles along the mountains in the west and for a short distance along the Sarstoon River in the south. The area is about double that of Jamaica.

The Maya Mountains, an eastward extension of the much higher mountain backbone of Guatemala, take up over one-third of Belize. They rise steeply from the surrounding lowlands to a rolling plateau surface somewhat below 900 metres in height. Occasional ridges and individual summits rise several

hundred metres above that level, and in places there are deep gorges carved by swift-flowing rivers. The heart of the plateau is composed of ancient sedimentary rocks, mainly sandstone and shale, with many granite intrusions which have brought minerals, including gold and tin, to the surface. Weathering of the granite itself has produced kaolin or white china clay. As the various mineral deposits are so inaccessible, little is known about them and no mining operations have yet been attempted.

Map 16.3 BELIZE: Its position, relief and main features.

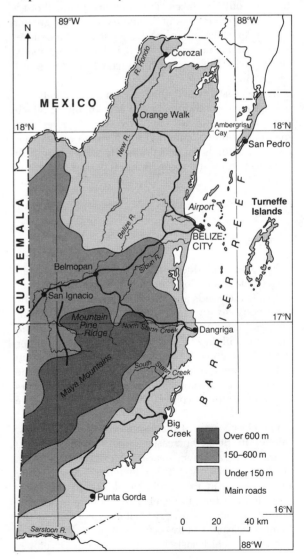

The Maya Mountains end so close to the sea that the coastal strip connecting the northern and southern lowlands is only about 15 kilometres wide. The large northern lowland is a raised limestone platform, mostly under 150 metres in height, though on the flanks of the mountains it is higher and gives rise to typical karst scenery. Along the coast marine silting has created many shallow lagoons, some of which have been entirely cut off from the sea. All the principal rivers and many of their tributaries follow old fault lines and flow for long distances in a north-easterly direction parallel with the coast. They are often bordered by swamps, and in places they broaden out into lakes. The southern plain, though more limited in extent, contains a much greater variety of sedimentary rocks, which include limestone, sandstone and shale. It is crossed by many short, swift streams which radiate from the Maya Mountains.

In the coastal waters there are numerous reefs and associated sand and mangrove cays, many of which are large enough to support coconut groves and maintain fishing communities. The main reef farther offshore extends for practically the whole length of the coast and is the second longest barrier reef in the world.

Climate

Belize, lying as it does on the eastern side of Yucatán between latitudes 16°N and 18°N, stands in the path of the Trade winds and therefore has similar climatic conditions to the rest of the Caribbean. Mean temperatures on the lowlands range from 27°C in the hottest month to 24°C in the coldest. On hot summer days the temperature may rise to 36°C while in winter, when a cold norther is blowing out from the United States, it may fall to below 10°C. The winters are thus rather colder than elsewhere in the Caribbean.

Largely because of the location of the mountains, rainfall in Belize increases rapidly from north to south. Corozal Town, near the Mexican border, has an average of only 1 250 millimetres a year, while Punta Gorda in the south has 4 500. In the rainy months from June to October the climate is hot and humid, though a short dry spell known locally as the Maugre Season usually occurs in August. The winter dry period which lasts in the north from December

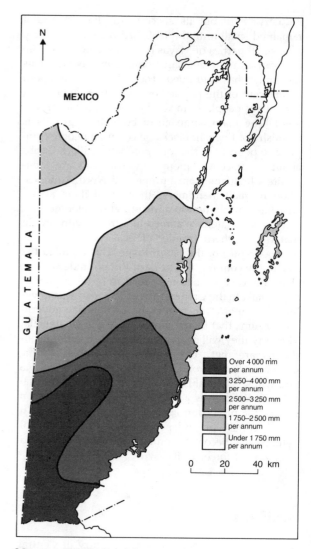

Map 16.4 BELIZE: Rainfall.

to May is long enough to suit the cultivation of sugar cane, while in the south, where it is limited to February, March and April, conditions favour tree crops such as bananas, cocoa and citrus.

Belize was long thought to lie outside the normal hurricane belt, but in recent years all parts of the country have suffered from severe storms. A thousand lives were lost when Belize City was struck in 1931 and nearly 300 when it was struck again in 1961. Punta Gorda in the South, Dangriga in the centre and Corozal in the north have also been badly damaged by hurricanes and in 1978 much of the Stann Creek citrus crop was destroyed.

Vegetation

Nearly 90 per cent of Belize is clothed with tropical forest, the character of which varies from place to place. Rain-forest takes up the greatest area. It contains a great variety of trees. They include mahogany, rosewood (found only on the southern plain), bullet-wood, the cohune and other palms, and sapodilla from which chicle is obtained. Cedar and breadnut grow on limestone soils. Pine forests occur in large stands or 'ridges', chiefly where there are poor sandy or gritty soils. In Belize the term 'ridge' has nothing to do with relief. Instead it refers to a region having a distinct type of vegetation. Much of the pine ridge country in both northern and southern plains is perfectly flat. On the other hand pine trees grow in the highlands too.

One of the most recently developed areas is the Mountain Pine Ridge lying between 300 and 900 metres on the northern flanks of the Maya Mountains. Under the pine trees grows a poor wiry grass which merges into savanna at the edge of the forest and into swamp vegetation on the lowest, most waterlogged land. Mangrove forests fringe the coast, the lower portions of the river valleys and some of the inland lagoons.

Mountain Pine Ridge country.

197

Forest products

From the time of the earliest settlement up to 1960, forest products provided Belize with its chief source of income. The logwood trade begun by the original settlers lasted until the nineteenth century. Then, as a result of the discovery of synthetic dyes with a greater range of colours, exports declined and today they are negligible. The place of logwood was taken by mahogany, first for the European and later for the American market. There was also a small export of cedar. At the beginning of this century there was a rapid rise in the export of chicle to satisfy the demands of chewing-gum consumers, mainly in America. For some years this proved very profitable, but because chewing gum is now mostly made from artificial products, the export of chicle has declined to a very small quantity. In the 1950s, timber-cutting was extended to the pine forests, but the accessible areas were soon exhausted and exports ceased.

The depletion of the pine and mahogany resources of Belize has been called a classic case of colonial exploitation. Foreign companies have taken away a valuable resource, and given little or nothing back, they have employed only cheap, unskilled labour. They have developed no local woodworking industries which could have increased the value of the exports.

Enormous quantities of timber were shipped abroad, and Belize was little better off as a result. Up to 1950, forest products formed 80% of the exports. In 1987 the figure was only 2%.

Though forestry will never regain its former importance, there are some signs of recovery. Tree cutting is being controlled. Better quality logs are being produced. New seedlings are being planted to take the place of those that have been cut.

Of the seedlings, four varieties are of particular importance. One of them is mahogany which takes about 50 years to grow to maturity. Another is cedar, which takes about 20 years. The third, teak, grows well in the southern part of the country. The fourth, gmelina, though not as beautiful a wood as the others, matures quickly (in 12 to 18 years) and is used locally in the furniture and construction industries.

Only the pine forests of Belize grow in pure stands. Elsewhere, the forests in their natural state are composed of mixed species. When seedlings are being planted care is taken to space trees of the same kind well apart so as to work with nature and not against it. For example, mahogany trees grow best when they are an acre or more apart from one another in a forest. When they are closer together, insect pests multiply and spread from tree to tree, and the risk of timber disease increases.

Of the many other tree species in Belize, only rosewood and santa maria are well known outside the country. One reason for this is that no species can be produced in sufficient volume to meet the needs of manufacturers. Another is that some are denser than water. They have to be tied to floater logs if they are to be floated down river the coast, thus adding to their cost.

Mahogany planks awaiting export.

Land holdings

Partly because land was cheap and partly because the trees suitable for cutting were scattered throughout the forests, the people controlling the timber trade acquired large properties. In the mid-

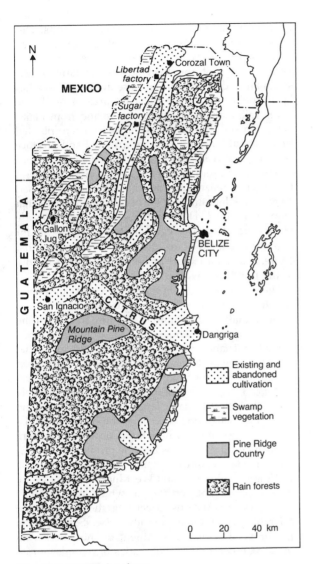

Map 16.5 BELIZE: Land use.

About 60 per cent of the total area is government land. Most of it is confined to mountainous districts. Only a small amount of it is suitable for cultivation.

Commercial farming

At various times a number of export crops have been established in Belize. In the late 1980s three were commercially successful. These were sugar, citrus and bananas.

Sugar

As we have seen, the sugar industry in the north was established about 1850. With its moderate rainfall, long dry season, flat land and good soils, the area was very suitable for cane cultivation. On the other hand this was the period of West Indian decline, when Britain abandoned her preferences on colonial sugar and when the output of beet sugar in Europe was soaring. Nevertheless, with the aid of some Chinese and Indian indentured labour, Belize was able to satisfy local needs and at times produce a small surplus for export.

In 1936 a small factory was built at Pembroke Hall (since renamed Libertad) to produce both white and brown sugar. It replaced a number of older, less efficient mills in the neighbourhood and encouraged cane farmers to increase their supplies. In order to give further encouragement, in 1959 the Commonwealth Sugar Agreement allotted Belize an export quota of 25 000 tonnes at a time when the actual exports were virtually nil. With this encouragement the area under sugar cane grew, sugar output rose and a second factory was built at Tower Hill near Orange Walk (see Maps 16.3 and 16.5).

Supported from 1975 onwards by a European Economic Community sugar quota of about 40 000 tonnes under the Lomé Agreement and by a further quota to the USA, the output of sugar continued to rise. It reached a maximum of 116 000 tonnes in 1983. The decrease that followed was due mainly to a fall in the US quota as America made more use of home-produced high fructose corn syrup and reduced the import of cane sugar. The output in 1987 was about 84 000 tonnes. By then the Libertad factory had been closed. However there were plans for a Jamaican business concern to re-open it. The intention is to manufacture ethanol from cane and export it by way

1960s it was estimated that about 2 million acres (35 per cent of the total area) were owned by fifty people. Of these, only three were nationals of Belize. No other West Indian territory had so high a proportion of absentee landowners. At least one-third of their land is suitable for agriculture, but less than $\frac{1}{2}$ per cent of it is under cultivation. In an attempt to change this situation the government is charging special taxes on land that is left unproductive. So far the results have been small.

of Jamaica to the United States so as to obtain the tax concessions on new products made available under the Caribbean Basin Initiative. Ethanol is an industrial chemical. Mixed with gasolene it can be used as a motor vehicle fuel.

Citrus

The main citrus-producing area in Belize is the Stann Creek Valley, where the alluvial lowlands support high yields of very good quality oranges and grapefruit. A secondary producing area exists farther inland. Some of the production comes from small farms, some from large ones. On the latter, most of the fruit is picked by migrant workers from Guatemala as local labour is in short supply. The area under citrus and the output of fruit are growing rapidly. Oranges form 70 per cent the supply. Two factories, both in the Stann Creek Valley, have been built to process the fruit. Together they process 85 per cent of the crop, converting it into citrus concentrates which are exported from Dangriga. Most of the concentrates go to the USA which imports them duty free under the terms of the Caribbean Basin Initiative. In 1987 they earned 18 per cent of the country's income, compared with 37 per cent from sugar and molasses.

Bananas

Before the 1939–45 World War, Belize was an important supplier of bananas to the USA. They were grown in the Stann Creek area and exported from Commerce Bight. The combined effects of Panama disease and the wartime shipping shortage brought an end to large-scale banana farming. This lasted for forty years. In the 1980s the area under bananas began to grow again. Exports were resumed, this time to Britain. Bananas formed 8 per cent of the total exports in 1987. Port facilities are being developed at Big Creek (see Map 16.3) to handle the crop.

Other crops

Cocoa was once produced in quantity in the south of the country. It then declined. However, in the 1980s new high-yielding disease-free cocoa trees have been planted on small and medium farms. This should result in an increase in output in the 1990s.

A small quantity of rice has long been grown in various parts of the lowlands particularly in the south around Punta Gorda. Recently a new area has been opened up in the Big Falls area of the Belize River valley about 30 kilometres inland from Belize City. Several thousand acres have been planted there, about half of which are irrigated and produce two crops a year. The rice is reaped with modern machines and sent to two mills – one at Big Falls and the other at Belize City – for milling. Output reached 10 million kilograms in 1981 but dropped to half that amount in 1987. Here and elsewhere attempts are being made to grow vegetables on a large scale for sale to the United States during the winter months. There is a small export of honey, produced mainly in the north and west of the country.

There can be no doubt that the present population which amounts to only 8 per square kilometre is too small to make use of more than a tiny fraction of the 5 000 square kilometres or so of potentially good agricultural land. At first sight it would seem that the best way of bringing the land into production would be to encourage the immigration of experienced farmers, perhaps from the densely populated West Indian islands. In practice this is no easy task. Belize does not have the money to assist settlers in opening up new lands or to sustain them for years until their crops become profitable. Besides, there are few countries in the world whose people welcome immigrants, and West Indian territories are no exception. The territory in which you live may have strict regulations governing the entry of immigrants, West Indian or otherwise. Some people favour such regulations; others do not. See what views you can find on both sides of the question.

Traditional Mayan agriculture

The Mayas base their agriculture on a form of shifting cultivation known as the *milpa* system. They rent a few acres from a landowner on a year-to-year basis, burn and clear the bush, and use the land to grow a variety of crops and rear a few animals. After two or three years the weed growth becomes so thick that the easiest thing to do is to prepare another clearing. They therefore need at their disposal many times the area they can cultivate in any one year. Fortunately, the abandoned land rapidly reverts to bush, and so soil erosion is not serious. Nevertheless, it is an inefficient and wasteful system and does nothing to improve the land. The staple crop of the Mayas is maize, but they also grow rice, beans, sweet potatoes, yams, cassava, tomatoes and green vegetables. Most of the produce is kept for family subsistence, but an increasing amount is sold.

In order to promote better farming, the government is assisting farmers to buy their own land. In addition, farmers' co-operatives are being encouraged, and farming machinery can be hired cheaply.

In the southern coastlands some traditional Black Carib agriculture still exists. The men undertake the heavy work of burning and clearing the land but then return to their principal occupation, fishing, while the women plant, tend, and reap the crops. Rice, cassava, maize, beans and root crops are the chief crops.

Livestock and fish

In recent years pastures and herds have been improved. This is particularly noticeable on the lowland areas around San Ignacio, and commercial livestock rearing has developed at a rapid pace. Belize is self-sufficient in beef, but exports are handicapped by a shortage of shipping. Mennonites in the Cayo and Orange Walk Districts are supplying fresh milk to Belize City and other places. The output of poultry and eggs has also increased.

Though Belize is in reach of some of the finest fishing grounds in the Caribbean, local fishermen are restricted to the coastal waters and the cays by the size of their boats. Ample supplies of fish are caught for the local market, and a big export trade in lobsters, conchs and shrimps has developed. The extent of this business is shown by the fact that in 1987 these products brought in over 9 per cent of the country's foreign earnings. This was four times the value of lumber which was at one time so important.

Tourism

Though the tourist business is small in comparison with that of Jamaica or neighbouring Mexico, it is growing. The cays are the principal attraction, and

hotels have been built on a few of them. The main tourist centre is San Pedro on Ambergris Cay (see Map 16.3). Other tourists visit prehistoric Mayan remains and go on adventure holidays in the interior.

Belize City and Belmopan

In the days of the ancient Mayan civilisation, Belize was a self-sufficient country. The people produced what they consumed, and consumed what they produced. There was no overseas trade, and therefore no need for any ports. But when Belize became a colony it was developed as an exporter of forest products and an importer of almost everything else. A major port had to be established, and Belize City was chosen as its site. No ports could be built further north because the sea was too shallow to take any but the smallest boats. To the south, deep-water harbours existed, but their hinterlands were too restricted by the Maya Mountains to support a large volume of trade. The situation of Belize City is therefore the best that could have been found. However, it suffers from several disadvantages. One is that ocean-going ships have to cross the reef at a point over 20 kilometres south, and, on reaching the town, must stand a kilometre and more off-shore and be loaded and unloaded by barges. This creates many problems, and is perhaps the biggest handicap to the development of the sugar industry. Another disadvantage is that the town itself is built on low-lying reclaimed land only a foot or two above the sea. Drainage is therefore difficult, and pure water has to be piped several miles into the town. In addition, it is open to flooding during hurricanes, as happened in 1961 when the sea was driven almost a kilometre inland. A further disadvantage is that Belize City is surrounded by a useless, insect-infested, crab-ridden swamp, across which roads have had to be built at great expense.

In spite of these drawbacks, people moved back to Belize City after the 1961 hurricane. At the time of the 1980 census the population numbered 40 000, that is, about a quarter of the total for the whole country. The town has continued to dominate the trade, banking and business of Belize. But it is no longer the capital. A new capital, Belmopan, has been established close to the geographical centre of the country at the most important inland road junction. However, it has not proved a popular place to live. In 1980 its population was less than 4 000.

Belize City and Belmopan have developed some light industries. Of these by far the most important is the manufacture of jeans and other clothing in small factories built with American, Korean and Hong Kong capital. In 1987 garments formed the country's second biggest export. Other light industries are cigarettes, soap and edible oils, sawn timber, furniture, matches, beer, flour milling, footwear, mattresses, car batteries, and some aluminium products.

Reasons for Belize City being the chief port are shown on map 16.6. Sketch maps like this are easy to draw and present geographical information more clearly than a written account. When you are drawing one, the important things to remember are to concentrate on only one topic, to select a few points about it, and to present them so that they can be understood at a glance. A sketch map can therefore be thought of as a cartoon, not a portrait. As in a cartoon, captions are used. These should be carefully worded so as to stress the topic you are illustrating. So if you wanted to illustrate the disadvantages of the site of Belize City, you could use the same outline as that in Map 16.6, but the captions would have to be differently worded.

Belize City from the air. Compare the width of the river shown here with that of the Demerara shown on page 218. What other differences can you see?

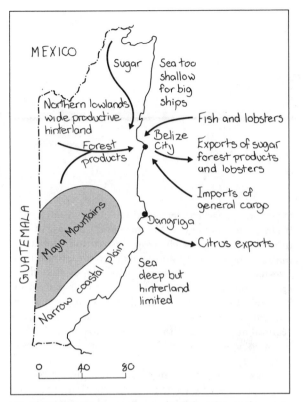

Map 16.6 Sketch map to show why Belize City is the chief port of Belize.

Communications and trade

Until recently there were so few roads in Belize that the bulk of the traffic had to be carried by river. The Belize River, navigable by shallow-draught vessels to San Ignacio, was always the chief waterway, a fact which contributed to the site and growth of Belize City.

In order to connect the chief towns, to develop existing forest and agricultural areas and to open up new ones, major and feeder roads are being constructed. However, even today Belize has only one kilometre of motorable road for every 30 square kilometres of territory. It is true that this compares favourably with Guyana, which has 1 kilometre of road to every 200 square kilometres, but it is much worse off than developed countries. For instance, in Barbados there are 2 kilometres of road to every 1 square kilometre of land.

Considering the size of the country, the overseas trade of Belize is small. Even so, it is larger than that of any of the Commonwealth Eastern Caribbean states, several of which have about the same population.

Because of its position. Belize handles some of the imports and exports for that part of Mexico near its frontier. It is ideally placed to do the same for Guatemala, but because of the disturbed political relations between the two countries this trade is very small. Re-exports in 1987 were worth about one-fifth of the export of the goods produced in Belize itself.

Questions and assignments

1 Trace an outline map of Belize, and mark and label the following: a) three neighbouring countries; b) an area of mountains; c) three rivers; d) an area where sugar cane is grown; e) an area where citrus fruits are grown; f) an area where rice is grown; g) a popular tourist area; h) a town from which sugar is exported; i) a town where citrus products are exported.

2 Name: a) three varieties of forest trees that grow in Belize and one use of each of them; b) two similarities and two differences between milpa farming in Belize and peasant farming in the West Indian islands; c) two problems arising out of the low population density of Belize; d) one advantage and one disadvantage of Belmopan as the capital.

3 The percentage of each of the main exports from Belize in 1987 was: sugar and molasses 37 per cent; citrus products 18 per cent; fish products 9 per cent; bananas 8 per cent; lumber 2 per cent; and garments 18 per cent.

   a) What was the total percentage of these exports?

   b) What, therefore, was the percentage of other exports?

   c) Draw a horizontal bar graph to show these percentages.

   d) Construct a divided circle to show these percentages.

4 Compare Belize with Jamaica by writing one sentence about each of the following: a) area, b) population, c) population density, d) sugar production, e) banana production.

5 Name three important changes that have taken place in Belize since 1950. Give three reasons to explain one of those changes.

17

Guyana

Area (estimated): 215 000 square kilometres; population (1988): about 800 000; density of population: under 4 per square kilometre

The South American setting

That part of South America which lies north of the Equator is occupied almost entirely by the republics of Colombia and Venezuela, and by Guyana, French Guiana and Suriname. Colombia has an area of 1 140 000 square kilometres and a population of 30 million, and Venezuela has an area of 912 000 square kilometres and a population of 18 million.

The Andes, which fork into a number of separate ranges known as cordilleras, are the source of several precious minerals, in particular emeralds, platinum, gold and silver. Between their summits, which are capped with snow above 4 500 metres, and the hot coastal plains there are several zones of cultivation. They resemble those of Central America (see page 193). But because the Andes are higher, the mountain grasslands, known as the paramos in South America, are more extensive. And because the Andes are closer to the Equator, each of the zones extends upwards to a higher altitude. Thus the tierra caliente rises to about 900 metres, and the tierra fria to about 3 000 metres.

On the coastlands, the valleys and the lower slopes, bananas, sugar cane, rice, and cocoa are the chief crops. Some rubber, balata, balsa wood and other forest products are also produced. Coffee, grown on the middle slopes, forms 50 per cent of the total exports of Colombia and is the chief agricultural export of Venezuela. Here, and higher up, there are dense clusters of population in sheltered basins, such as Bogota, Valencia and Caracas. In addition to coffee, such crops as cotton, tobacco, maize, wheat, barley and vegetables are grown and livestock is reared. Further up the slopes, the chief crop is potatoes. Finally, on the wide expanses of poor wind-swept grasslands above the upper limit of cultivation, sheep and other animals are kept. Natural approaches into the mountains are provided by such valleys as the Magdalena and Cauca (see Map 17.1).

Venezuela is one of the world's leading oil exporting countries. The principal fields lie along the eastern and western shores of Lake Maracaibo and to some extent under the eastern part of the lake itself. Another smaller field, together with a pitch lake, occurs at Guanoco near the Gulf of Paria and there is a third lake north of Ciudad Bolivar. Oil and its products add up to 95 per cent of the exports of Venezuela. Colombia is a less important producer, the largest fields lying on the Venezuelan frontier near Lake Maracaibo and in the Magdalena Valley. Iron ore and coal exist in both countries and some steel is manufactured. Venezuela mines bauxite and has its own aluminium industry.

Large expanses of savanna occur in the interior of both Venezuela and Colombia. They are sparsely settled and little developed, the chief occupation being cattle ranching.

Most of the people of Guyana, Suriname and French Guiana live on a very narrow strip of land near the coast where they cultivate sugar, rice and a variety of other crops. Gold and diamonds are produced in small quantities in the interior. Guyana and Suriname produce large quantities of bauxite. French Guiana is the place where European space rockets are launched.

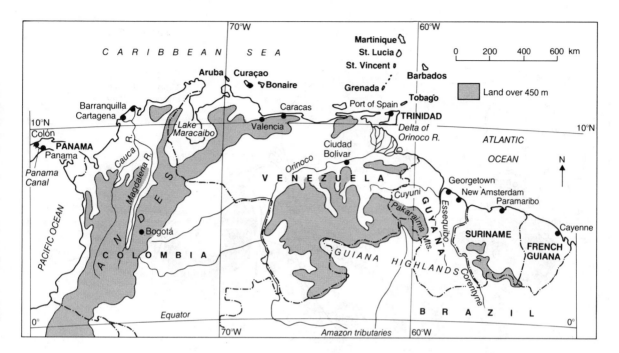

Map 17.1 The South American setting.

Development of Guyana

Considering its distance from Europe and the difficulty of penetrating its forests, the north-east shoulder of South America became known to Europeans at a surprisingly early date. The first to arrive were parties of fortune hunters. At various times in the sixteenth century they explored the rivers in search of a city they believed the Incas had built to hide themselves and their gold from the Spaniards. The next to arrive were the Dutch who began to settle in the area in 1616. This they were able to do because the area lay on the borderline between the possessions allocated to Spain and those allocated to Portugal by the Treaty of Tordesillas, and both those nations hesitated to colonise it.

Instead of seeking precious minerals the Dutch established plantations along the banks of such rivers as the Essequibo, Demerara, Berbice, Corentyne, Coppename and Suriname. The ruins of one of their forts – Kykoveral – built at the junction of the Cuyuni, Mazaruni and Essequibo Rivers, is still to be seen. It is not far from Bartica (see Map 17.2).

An export trade in tobacco, sugar cane, cocoa, coffee and cotton was developed. But the riverside settlements did not last long. The soil, poor to begin with, gradually became exhausted. By the 1720s the estates were being abandoned. The forest crept back over them and there is scarcely a trace of them today.

The settlers had only one place to turn. Penetration farther upstream was barred, for, as you can see from Map 17.2, nearly every river has a waterfall or rapid not many kilometres from its mouth. No ship could cross these barriers. The settlers were therefore forced to move down to the coastlands and develop them. This was a gigantic task. The land was so low and so flat that great areas were covered by the sea at high tide. To reclaim it two things had to be done. First, a wall had to be built to keep out the sea. Second, canals had to be dug to drain the swamps left behind. To speed up development the Dutch allowed in other people, particularly French and British settlers. Using slave labour the settlers gradually created new plantations. With these improvements the area became an attractive prize and it changed ownership several times. In the end, three of the Dutch colonies – Essequibo, Demerara

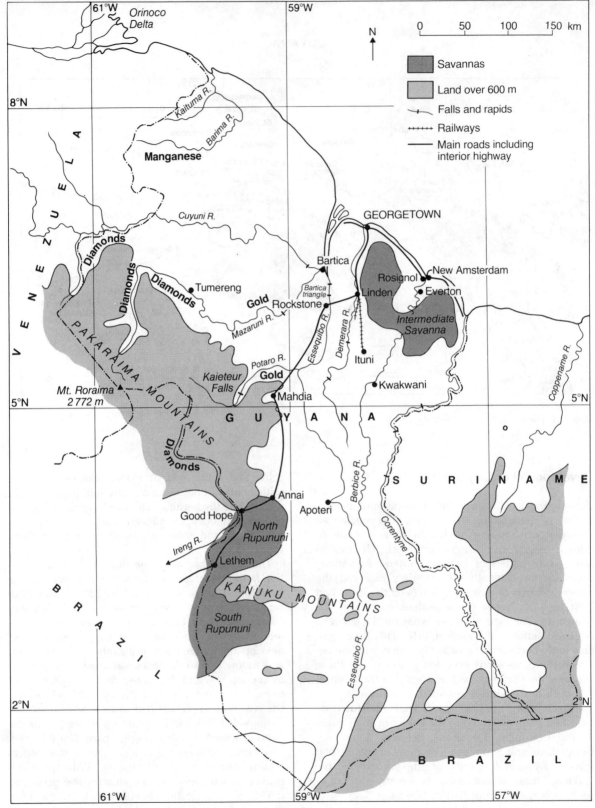

Map 17.2 Guyana and her neighbours.

and Berbice – were ceded to Britain.

The work of draining and improving the coastlands continued. Sugar cane was planted on all the new estates and sugar became by far the most valuable export. This development was still going on when the slaves were freed. Many of them left the estates to fend for themselves. To preserve the sugar industry other sources of population had to be found. There was a new wave of immigration, largely from India. Today, people of Indian descent form a little over half the population. Many are still engaged in the sugar industry. Many others cultivate rice, the second most important crop in the country.

Landforms

Guyana can be divided into four physical regions: the alluvial coastlands, the sand and clay lowlands, the Pakaraima Mountains, and the southern uplands.

The alluvial coastlands

Along the coast there is a narrow strip of lowland at most 30 to 50 kilometres wide. It is made of thick sediments, mainly clay deposited by the rivers entering the sea. Wells drilled into it provide a valuable source of pure water. In contrast with the other regions it contains no mineral wealth, though drillings have been made off-shore in the hope of finding oil.

Many areas in the West Indies suffer from the erosion caused by swift-flowing streams, but this is the only one where the threat comes from the sea. In places the sea has encroached by as much as 4 kilometres in the past 200 years.

The sand and clay lowlands

Inland from the alluvial belt is a region of undulating land. It lies between 15 and 120 metres above sea level and is about 160 kilometres wide. Originally part of the interior plateau, it was worn down to a lowland ages ago. Then, it is believed, the action of heavy tropical rain weathered the crystalline rocks along its edge. The result was the formation of a layer of bauxite, sometimes over 10 metres thick.

The next thing that happened was that the land submerged beneath the sea. During that period deposits of clay and white sand were laid on top of the bauxite. This white sand, composed mainly of silica, protected the bauxite from further erosion when the land emerged from the sea.

Bauxite is the ore from which aluminium is obtained. Alloys of this metal are used in the aircraft, packaging, food-processing and electrical industries as well as for making many other things such as the pots and pans of the kitchen. Most of the world's bauxite is made into aluminium. Some kinds of high-quality bauxite can also be used to make electrical insulators and the fire-resistant bricks needed for lining the insides of furnaces. Guyanese bauxite has this quality. It therefore has the advantage of being in demand for several purposes.

At least 500 million tonnes of this high-grade bauxite (ie bauxite containing 60 per cent alumina) are known to exist in readily accessible parts of the lowlands. Still larger quantities of low-grade ore exist further south and in the Pakaraima Mountains. Mining is concentrated in three areas – one around Linden on the Demerara River, one at Ituni a little over 60 kilometres south, and one at Kwakwani on the Berbice River (see Maps 17.2 and 17.5).

Nationalisation

Up to 1971 the chief exporter of bauxite was a giant Canadian company which, by owning bauxite deposits, alumina factories, hydro-electric plants, and aluminium factories in various parts of the world, controlled all stages of the production of aluminium. Then the Guyanese government took the bold step of nationalising the company's operations in Guyana. One reason for this was the government's dissatisfaction over the slow pace of development. Thus, though bauxite had been mined in Guyana for over fifty years, the country's output had been outstripped by that of Jamaica, where production had started much later. In addition, while Jamaica had been exporting alumina since 1953; its production in Guyana had been delayed until 1961, and it had never been developed on the same scale. As for the metal itself, there was little likelihood of its being made in Guyana for although the country possessed the potential hydro-electric resources needed to smelt aluminium, the company already owned all the hydro-electric stations it needed in Canada. It therefore seemed that Guyana would continue to be no more than a moderately large producer of bauxite, a small producer of alumina, and a non producer of aluminium. With bauxite valued at $18 a tonne, alumina at $150 a tonne, and aluminium at $1 000 a tonne, the government felt that Guyana was receiving too small a share of the benefits.

Taking over the ownership of bauxite and alumina production in Guyana was the first large-scale act of nationalisation in the West Indies outside Cuba. Since then the nationalisation of other foreign-owned companies has continued in Guyana and spread to other Commonwealth Caribbean countries. Nationalisation, or other forms of government participation in business, has therefore become an important political issue. If you carry out an enquiry, you will find that different people have different views on the subject. For example, some people believe that a country's most important resources should be controlled by the government and not by foreign companies whose first concern is profit-making and not national development. Other people say that a government and its civil service are less capable of running a commercial enterprise than a company is. Governments are not competitive businesses; companies are, and they must be run efficiently if they are to remain in being. Still others are opposed to foreign control of West Indian resources, but even more opposed to nationalisation which inevitably increases a government's power.

The bauxite mined in Guyana is a pinkish, fairly hard, clay-like rock. Before it can be reached, the forest has to be burned or chopped down and bucket wheel excavators or powerful hoses must strip or wash away the overburden of white sand. Below the layer of sand is a layer of clay, sometimes 15 metres thick, and this has to be removed by draglines and bulldozers. The mineral is therefore more expensive to mine than Jamaican bauxite which lies on the surface. On the other hand it is of better quality. In the Linden area it is blasted loose with dynamite, taken to stockpiles, and loaded on to railway trucks which are hauled by diesel locomotives to the town. There

most of the ore is crushed, washed, dried in huge oil-fired kilns, and loaded on to ships for export. Because heavily-laden vessels are unable to cross the sand-bars at the mouth of the Demerara River, this bauxite is taken in special bulk-carriers, half-empty ships, and small vessels to Trinidad. There it is stored and transferred to large ships for the remainder of its journey to major industrial countries where it is made first into alumina and then into aluminium. Exporting the ore mined at Kwakwani is no less difficult. Barges carry it down the Berbice River to Everton, some 16 kilometres from the sea, where it is dried and stored for shallow-draught freighters to take overseas. Exports from Everton are much smaller than those from Linden.

As we have seen, some Guyanese bauxite is used for special industrial purposes and is not made into aluminium. At Linden this bauxite is heated to a very high temperature in special furnaces so as to purify it before it is exported. The product is called 'calcined bauxite'. Until the late 1970s over 80 per cent of the world's supply of calcined bauxite was made in Guyana. Since then output has declined, partly because of competition from Chinese exports and partly because other products are taking the place of calcined bauxite.

In addition to calcined bauxite and metal-grade bauxite, Guyana exports 'chemical-grade' bauxite which is used to make aluminium chemicals for industrial purposes.

Another product from Linden used to be alumina made in the same way as in Jamaica (see chapter five). Like the rest of the bauxite industry, alumina consumed large quantities of oil fuel, all of which had to be imported. When oil prices rose in the 1970s, Guyana found it hard to compete with bauxite and alumina produced in other parts of the world. Alumina production ceased in 1982. As for bauxite, the output in 1988 was 1 300 000 tonnes, much less than in the 1970s when output averaged well over 3 million tonnes a year.

The Pakaraima Mountains

In the west and north-west, 300 and more kilometres from the sea, there is a mountainous region which takes up about one-seventh of the country. It is a huge plateau about 600 metres high, surmounted in places by steep-sided flat-topped ranges which rise considerably higher. The highest point, of all, Mount

Mining bauxite in Guyana. Compare this picture with the one on page 62. Why are the mining methods so different?

The Kaietur Falls at the edge of the plateau.

Roraima, on the frontier with Brazil and Venezuela, reaches 2 772 metres. These ranges are the source of many rivers which are renowed for their waterfalls when they reach the edge of the plateau. The best known are the Kaieteur Falls on the Potaro River, a tributary of the Essequibo. It has a sheer drop of 226 metres, nearly five times that of Niagara. The region was virtually inaccessible until the coming of air transport and even today few people live there. Most of them are Amerindians.

Waterfalls of such size are obvious potential sources of hydro-electricity; the reason they have not been developed is that they lie so far inland. They are also extremely difficult to reach, and are a long way from the centres where the electricity is needed. In the 1970s there was a scheme to build a large dam across the upper Mazaruni River in the Pakaraima Mountains so as to generate hydro-electricity there. The costs of doing so were more than the country could afford and the scheme was abandoned.

The plateau is composed mainly of ancient sandstone, with igneous and metamorphic rocks in places. It contains gold and diamonds. Rivers have carried down both these minerals and deposited them on their beds, where they are sought for by small groups of prospectors known locally as 'porknockers'.

Most of the diamonds come from the Upper Mazaruni River where Tumereng is the chief collecting centre. Gold is more widespread, but the Potaro River is one of the richest sources. At present gold and diamonds form only a small fraction of the total exports, but in periods of depression in the sugar industry the number of porknockers has risen and output has increased.

There are many other minerals in the mountains. One of them, manganese, was mined and exported for a time in the 1960s. Others known to exist are mica (use in electrical industries), tungsten, copper, nickel, platinum and columbite-tantalite (used in making jet engines).

The southern uplands

The southern part of Guyana is little known. It is believed to consist largely of ancient metamorphic rocks and granite. Near the rivers the land is low and there are large swamps. Elsewhere there are some low plateaus, including the Kanuku Mountains, which reach a height of 1 200 metres in places. Guyana's right to the ownership of the south-eastern corner of the country is disputed by Suriname.

Climate

The climate of Guyana is classified as Equatorial; that of the Caribbean islands as Tropical Marine. In fact, on the coastlands when, as often happens, a sea breeze blows by day, the two climates are indistinguishable. The main difference is in the amount of rainfall. When showers fall they tend to be heavier and longer than those in the islands, and when the area is under the influence of the Intertropical Convergence Zone, prolonged rain may fall. The average annual rainfall of the coastlands is about 2 300 millimetres. Its distribution, month by month, is shown in Diagram 17.3. Further inland, rainfall increases to 3 500 millimetres a year in the Pakaraima Mountains and decreases to about 1 500 millimetres in the rain-shadowed lowlands to the south. In this, the least rainy area, the forest which covers most of the rest of Guyana is replaced by savanna. Monthly rainfall distribution in the savanna area is shown in Diagram 17.4.

The interior

From the point of view of settlement, there are only two important regions in Guyana – the densely peopled coastal strip and the sparsely settled interior. A large proportion of the inhabitants of the

Diagram 17.3 Average monthly rainfall of the Rupununi savanna

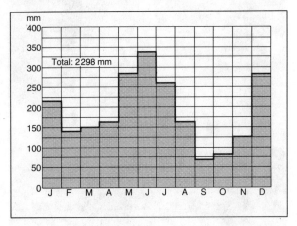

Diagram 17.4 Average monthly rainfall of the coastal belt of Guyana.

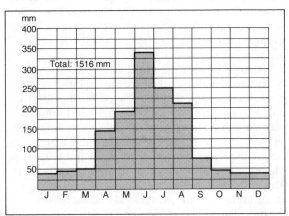

Greenheart logs being transported by truck. What can you tell about the trees?

timber cutting has to take place close to the banks of navigable rivers. This restricts operations to some 35 000 square kilometres. At present the bulk of the logging and saw-milling takes place in the area known as the Bartica triangle, bounded by the Essequibo and Mazaruni Rivers (see Map 17.2).

The forests contain hundreds of species of trees, but only a few are in demand. The most important is greenheart, found only in Guyana. It is used all over the world for marine construction as it does not rot in water and resists the attack of sea creatures which can destroy even steel. Amongst other trees cut are crabwood, used locally to make furniture; purple heart, used to make floors; mora, used for railway sleepers; and wallaba, used for firewood and charcoal. Many other excellent varieties of wood exist and are gradually being exploited as their qualities are recognised. Some of the softer timbers are being chemically treated so as to make them termite resistant. Some re-forestation, using Caribbean pine and other trees, is being undertaken.

In two parts of the interior the forests give way to large expanses of grassland.

1 The Rupununi Savannas take up over 13 000 square kilometres of land in the south-west close to the Brazilian border. They are divided into two sections, a northern and a southern, by the thickly forested Kanuku Mountains. The rainfall of these savannas is lower than elsewhere, being less than 1 500 millimetres a year in most places. Moreover, as shown in Diagram 17.4, there is a dry season from October to April.

Four factors have hindered development. First, during the rainy season, large stretches of the savannas are flooded. Second, except in the river valleys, the soil is generally infertile. Third, because of the poor soil and the long drought, the quality of the grass is poor. As a result, though the savannas support about 55 000 cattle, each animal needs over 30 acres of grazing even in the best areas. (On the best West Indian pastures a cow can be kept on less than 1 acre.) Fourth, the remoteness of the district makes marketing a problem. This has been solved by slaughtering the cattle at Lethem and sending the carcasses by plane to Georgetown.

Several thousand Amerindians live in the Rupununi Savannas. As they are expert horse riders, many of them earn a living as cattle-men on the large ranches in the region. Others rear small herds of their own. Still others cultivate tobacco, cassava,

interior are Amerindians. Some of them still live a tribal life, speaking their own dialects and preserving their own customs. They produce enough cassava, sugar, plantains and vegetables for their own needs. They obtain fish from the rivers, and meat from the animals they keep and from wild animals they may hunt in the forests.

In the early days of colonisation the Amerindians suffered severely from slave raids and from European diseases. Now only a fraction of their former numbers, they have been allotted reservations where they can live protected from further exploitation. One of them is as large as Jamaica.

Many Amerindians have left the reservations and are employed in mining, cattle ranching and cutting timber in the forests.

Different types of forest cover some 180 000 square kilometres of Guyana, that is, over 80 per cent of the total area of the country. The most important type is the rain-forest which occurs in the wetter lowland areas. Because of the difficulty of transporting logs,

211

Cattle on the Rupununi savanna. The animals are of a hardy, quick-maturing breed capable of resisting heat, drought and flies. Their long legs enable them to cover large areas of grazing land.

cotton, maize, beans and vegetables, on the fertile land at the base of the Kanuku Mountains. They burn and prepare the fields in the dry season and plant their crops when the first heavy rains arrive.
2 The Intermediate Savannas lie east of the Demerara River and extend to within a short distance of the coast. Here the grass is of poorer quality than that of the Rupununi and fewer cattle are reared. However, numbers are increasing, both on the savannas themselves and between the savannas and the sea. There is also a CARICOM project in which Trinidad, Guyana and St Kitts have combined to grow maize, soya beans and black-eye peas on part of the Intermediate Savannas.

Other savannas occur on plateau summits in the Pakaraima Mountains, but they are not used in any way.

The coastal fringe

Ever since the first successful cultivation of the coastlands began, virtually all further settlement has grown up there and the interior has remained almost unaltered. However, even on the coastlands progress has been limited, for after two centuries of effort less than one-tenth of their area has been drained and cultivated. Settlement is still almost entirely confined to that section about 160 kilometres long and 3 to 12 kilometres wide between the Essequibo and Corentyne Rivers (see Map 17.5). Even here development efforts have often proved fruitless, and large areas of land which were once brought under cultivation have since been abandoned.

It is therefore a mistake to think of Guyana with less than four people per square kilometre as an obvious home for large numbers of emigrants from the overcrowded Commonwealth Caribbean islands. On the cultivated land, which amounts to $1\frac{1}{2}$ per cent of the total area of the nation, the population density is about as high as that of Barbados. This is more than agriculture can support, and the usual features of overpopulation – poverty, bad housing and insufficient employment – are all present.

Unfortunately, it is not easy to open up new land in Guyana in spite of the enormous area available. It seems certain that the vast forests and savannas can never support dense settlement. Though new land is being opened up on the coastal strip and a

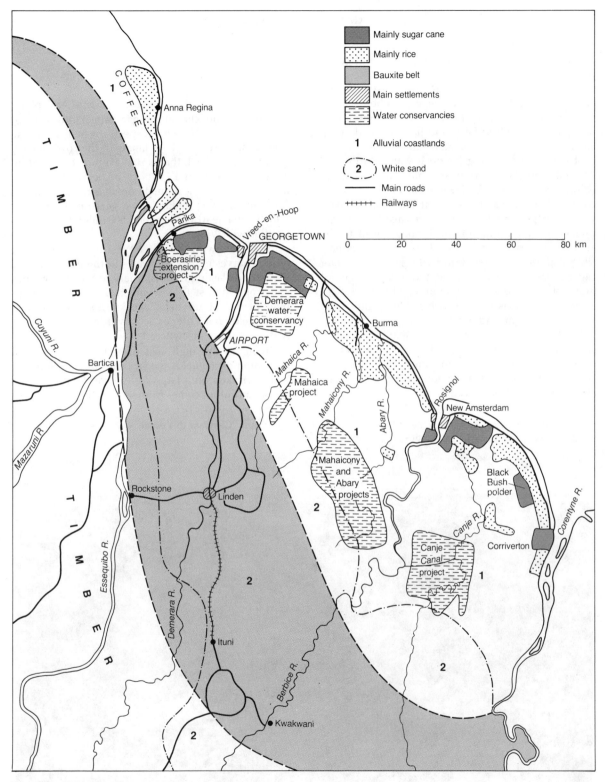

Map 17.5 GUYANA: The main productive areas.

few parts of the interior, this is a slow and costly process.

The difficulty of developing the coastlands has arisen because they lie, almost everywhere, a few feet below high-tide mark. As we have seen, a wall has had to be built to keep out the sea. In addition, all residential and cultivated areas have to be protected from flooding by fresh water during the frequent periods of very heavy rain. This protection is afforded by an elaborate system of dams which collect any flood water in large, shallow inland reservoirs or 'conservancies' as they are called. These are drained by thousands of canals. Some lead to the lower stretches of the rivers where drainage is possible at all times. Others lead to the sea where water can be drained away only at low tide so that for much of the time it has to be pumped out. In these circumstances it is not surprising that so little land has been brought under cultivation.

The chief crops grown are sugar cane, rice, coconuts and provisions. In addition, some 200 000 cattle are kept, mainly in ones and twos on smallholdings, and there are large numbers of pigs, sheep, goats and poultry.

Crops

Sugar

Partly because of the nature of the land and partly because of the climate, sugar cane cultivation in Guyana differs in some respects from that in the West Indian islands. The climate of the coastlands is typically Equatorial; that is, the average temperature is never more than 1°C above or below 27°C, and, more important, the annual rainfall is heavy, ranging from about 2 000 millimetres a year on the frontier with Suriname to a little over 2 500 millimetres on the frontier with Venezuela.

In contrast with the other West Indian countries, cane is harvested twice a year – in the two relatively dry periods lasting from February to the end of April and from August to November. This gives a cropping period of up to 30 weeks, and the workers therefore do not suffer as acutely from an out-of-crop season as those elsewhere.

Owing to the high cost of reclaiming land and maintaining canefields, sugar cane cultivation has to be undertaken on a large scale. Over 90 per cent of the sugar output comes from ten estates – all govern-

Sugar estates in Guyana are large. One of them has 7 000 acres under cane. Compare this estate with those shown on pages 90 and 108 and list the similarities and differences.

Canals, cane fields and punts on an estate in Guyana.

Some irrigation canals run parallel to these while others branch off at right angles, so that each field is bounded by one drainage canal and three irrigation canals as shown on Diagram 17.6. On some estates waterways exceed 500 kilometres in length. As they are expensive to maintain, every possible use is made of them. For instance, irrigation canals are brought into use to flood the cane fields for a few days whenever the rainfall is inadequate. They are also used for transport during the harvest. The reaped canes are carried from the fields and stacked in steel barges. Trains of five or six of these, each carrying 5 to 6 tonnes of cane, are drawn to the factory by mules, oxen and tractors. Where the punts on the irrigation canals have to cross over the drainage canals they do so by means of greenheart bridges.

Guyana has usually been able to meet its European Economic Community sugar quota (currently 159 000 tonnes) and its local needs (35 000 tonnes). However, the price of sugar on the world market in recent years has been too low to encourage additional production. Output has fallen from an average of over 300 000 tonnes in the 1970s to 260 000 tonnes in the late 1980s. In 1988 it was 171 000 tonnes.

ment owned since the mid-1970s. The remainder comes from self-employed cane farmers and a few small co-operatives on the fringes of the estates.

The estates are situated along the sea coast and a little way up the Berbice, Demerara and Corentyne Rivers as shown in map 17.5. The nature of the land has influenced their layout. They have a narrow frontage on the sea and a much greater length stretching inland. The soil, for perhaps one kilometre behind the sea-dam, is not suitable for sugar cane, but sometimes provides pasture or is used to grow rice. The main road and most of the agricultural settlements are also close to the sea. Then, extending perhaps as much as 11 kilometres inland are the estate's cane fields. Each estate is terminated by the back-dam which separates it from the swamp of the shallow waters of the conservancy behind.

Drainage canals stretch from the back-dam where they obtain water to the sea-dam where they drain.

Diagram 17.6 Land use near the coast.

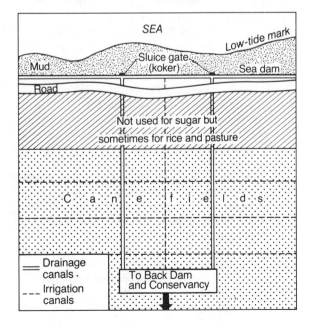

215

Rice

Owing to the constantly high temperature and the two wet seasons it is possible to grow two rice crops a year on the coastlands of Guyana. Because the mid-year rains last longer and are more dependable, three-quarters of the crop is planted in April and May and reaped between September and November. The remainder is planted towards the end of the year and is reaped in March and April.

Most of the output is produced by Indian families on smallholdings 2–15 acres in size. Where, as is often the case, these farms have been established on abandoned cane lands, water control is a difficult problem. Originally these lands were provided with drainage and irrigation canals. But to be of any use these canals must be properly maintained all the way from the back dam to the sea. This was possible while the land was under one management, but it is difficult to do now that it has been split into many separate holdings. Thus, in spite of recent developments, about 40 per cent of the rice is grown on land lacking proper drainage and irrigation and there are considerable losses in very wet or very dry years.

To increase rice and vegetable production and improve living conditions for farmers, several government-planned land reclamation schemes have been developed. The first was the Mahaicony-Abary Rice Development Scheme which was started in the 1939–45 World War when British rice supplies were cut off by the Japanese invasion of south-east Asia. Thousands of acres of land near the mouths of the Mahaicony and Abary Rivers were reclaimed and in a few years it became, and still remains, one of the largest areas of mechanised rice production in the Commonwealth. Other more recent schemes are the Boerasirie Extension Project, the Canje Project, the Tapacuma Project and the Black Bush Polder on the Corentyne coast. Several of these are being extended. The conservancies already built or planned to serve these projects are shown on Map 17.5.

Other developments have been the building of a large rice mill at Burma which handles about one-third of the crop, the improvement of many of the smaller mills, and the introduction of high-yielding rice which matures more quickly than traditional varieties. In addition, small farmers are able to borrow government-owned tractors, ploughs and combine harvesters when they need them.

Despite these developments, the output of rice has fallen in recent years. After reaching a peak of about 215 000 tonnes in 1977, it fell to an average of about

Sugar cane being fed into the mill.

150 000 tonnes by the late 1980s. About two-thirds of the output is exported. Most of it is sold in bulk to CARICOM countries at a preferential price above the world market price. Packaged white and parboiled rice is also exported, some going to countries outside the Caribbean region.

Coconuts and oil palms

Most of the coconut plantations have been established on long, narrow sand reefs which stand a metre or more above the level of the surrounding land. These reefs, which run parallel to the coast, are thought to be old sea beaches. Mainly because labour is hard to obtain output is declining. Guyana is not self-sufficient in coconut oil and other coconut products. To increase the supply of edible oil, the area under oil palm is being enlarged.

Other crops

Coffee grows well on the better drained soils. Some is exported, but most is sold locally, partly in the form of instant coffee. Citrus fruits take up a larger area, but output is barely sufficient to meet local demand. Cocoa is grown and exported in small quantities. All kinds of fruit, green vegetables and root crops are grown. Much of the output comes from smallholdings on the strip of land near the coast, but some is produced by new settlements being developed with government assistance in the interior.

In keeping with the national policy of becoming more self-sufficient, agricultural imports are being replaced with local products. One example is the blending of cassava flour with wheat flour in making bread. Another is the salting and smoking of locally caught fish to replace imports of salt cod and smoked mackerel. The rivers and coastal waters are well stocked with fish.

Tourism

In recent years the prices paid for the major products exported from the West Indies have been low, and the prices of goods imported from industrial nations have been high. This situation has created a serious balance of payments problem throughout the region. However, by developing tourism most Caribbean countries have been able to make a substantial reduction in the gap between their exports and their imports. Some have even been able to bridge the gap.

Guyana has not shared in the economic benefits of tourism. One reason for this is that it is the most distant country from North America and Western Europe, the two main sources of tourists to the Caribbean. Another is that Guyana has fewer dry sunny days than all but the most mountainous West Indian islands. A third reason is that Guyana lacks the white-sand beaches, clear blue sea, and off-shore coral reefs that are the main Caribbean tourist attractions. Guyana therefore cannot expect to rival the islands for mass-market tourism. Whatever developments take place are likely to depend on the beauty of the inland waterfalls and on the opportunities provided for adventure holidays.

The people

With the rise of the coastal sugar plantations in the late seventeenth century, labour was needed and slaves were imported in such large numbers that by 1837 there were 85 000 in the country. Since then the number of people of African descent has grown, partly because of immigration from Africa and from some West Indian islands, but mainly by natural increase.

The first Indians landed in 1838. By 1917, when the indenture system was stopped, nearly a quarter of a million had arrived. This was over half the total who came to the Caribbean. Though many chose to return home when their contracts expired, the majority remained in Guyana as field workers on the estates or as rice cultivators on their own holdings. Since then their numbers have increased more rapidly than that of other racial group and they form over half of the entire population.

Plural societies

People who support the theory of plural society (see page 95) point out that the distinction between the African and the Indian elements of the Guyanese population is even more marked than in Trinidad. For one thing there are notable differences in the distribution of population. Thus Indians form a high proportion of the agricultural population and a small proportion (15 per cent) of the townspeople. In addition there are, along the coast, some villages that are peopled almost entirely by Indians and others that are peopled mainly by Africans. Another consideration is the way that the Indians maintain their religious and other customs, and retain a close connection with India and Pakistan. Still another is the fact that in politics the Indians and the Africans tend to vote on racial lines.

Those who are opposed to the theory of the plural society point out how successfully the language barrier has been overcome, how Indians are entering the professions, the civil service, the police and the army, and how education is helping to build a united community. In 1970 Guyana was declared to be a Co-operative Republic, and one of the aims of developing co-operatives in all forms of community life is that of overcoming racial differences.

Other races are present in small numbers only. The groups at the time of the 1980 census were as follows: Indian descent 389 800; African descent 231 300; Mixed 83 700; Amerindians 39 900; Chinese 1 800; White 800. Those not classified totalled 1 100. It is believed that in the period between the 1970 and 1980 censuses about 130 000 more people emigrated from Guyana than entered the country from other parts of the world.

Towns

Georgetown, with its suburbs, contains about 200 000 people, that is about one-quarter of the population of Guyana. It first grew up as a small Dutch fort protecting the settlements along the Demerara River and became a small township when the riverside estates were abandoned in favour of the coastlands and sugar became the dominant export. A capital city and a port were needed, and as Georgetown was selected to fulfil both these functions it soon became by far the most important settlement. The residential sections developed when many of the estate-owners built themselves large houses on the outskirts of the town with the money they received from the British government at the time of the emancipation of their slaves. At the same time many of the freed slaves also left the plantations to settle in the city, and the proportion of people of African descent in Georgetown has been high ever since.

Most of the buildings in Georgetown are made of timber obtained from the interior forests. Today, however, many of the large buildings are being made of concrete. Development has always been hampered because Georgetown lies on flat land about 1 metre below the level of the sea. Drainage has been the most difficult problem and the vast majority of the dwellings in Georgetown and elsewhere along the coast are raised on wood, brick or concrete piles to protect them from the damp. Many open, muddy drainage canals, or 'trenches' as they

Looking across the Demerara River from Georgetown. What can you tell about communications?

are called, lead through the city to the river, but even these may flood during periods of very heavy rain. In the city centre, some canals have been covered over, and trees and grass have been planted on them to provide shaded walks in the midst of busy streets.

Georgetown, which handles practically all the country's trade except the export of bauxite and some of the sugar, has two fronts, one on the sea and the other on the Demerara River. All the wharves, or 'stellings' as they are called, have been built on the river bank, for only along the river is there deep, sheltered water right up to the shore. However, even the river suffers a disadvantage in that the sand-bar at its mouth has a clearance of only 5 metres at high tide, which prevents large vessels from docking at Georgetown.

Georgetown is the administrative centre and by far the most important shopping and banking town in Guyana. It has several light industries, such as textiles, food processing, brewing, saw-milling, ship-building and repairing, printing and woodwork. A number of modern light industries have been sited on an industrial estate on the southern side of the town. In addition, Georgetown is the centre of the fishing industry. Shrimps in particular are plentiful in the shallow water above the continental shelf which stretches many miles off shore. Large quantities are exported to Japan and the USA.

Until 1978 the only method of crossing the Demerara River was by ferry from Georgetown to Vreed-en-Hoop (shown on the photograph on page 218). Now, however, a road bridge connects the two banks about 5 kilometres inland from the river mouth.

Other settlements on the coast vary in size from small villages to townships containing several thousand people. The inhabitants are mainly concerned with fishing and with growing food crops and rice, though they often seek employment on the sugar estates at harvest time. New Amsterdam (20 000) the third largest town in Guyana, occupies much the same position on the Berbice River as Georgetown does on the Demerara. It was founded at about the same time, but it has never rivalled Georgetown in importance as it lies on a shallower river which can take only small coastal vessels. It acts as the chief marketing and shopping centre for those people living on the eastern section of the coastlands between the Berbice and Corentyne Rivers. It is connected by ferry to Rosignol on the western side of the Berbice River. This in turn is linked with Georgetown by road.

There are only two settlements of any size in the interior. One is the mining and industrial centre of Linden (27 000). The other is Bartica (3 500), focus of almost all overland communication with the interior. It is a collecting centre for timber and gold, connected to Georgetown by a regular riverboat service.

Communications

As one would expect, the pattern of communications in the largely undeveloped interior is completely different from that in the densely settled section of the coastlands.

In the interior a few kilometres of narrow-gauge railway have been laid to carry bauxite to Linden. In addition, roads run from Bartica into the logging, diamond and gold-mining areas nearby. Attempts have been made to build a highway to connect Georgetown, Linden and Bartica with Lethem on the Brazilian border so as to expand trade links with Brazil. However, it has yet to be completed.

Apart from these developments, all heavy traffic is river-borne. Unfortunately, because of rapids, river traffic is not without difficulty. It is the distance upstream of the first rapid that limits the extent of the important logging areas, just as in bygone days it limited the Dutch estates. This distance varies from about 65 to 160 kilometres, only a fraction of the length of the rivers themselves. Punts towed by tugs carry timber, and motor-boats are used for passenger transport. Small steamers can reach Bartica on the Essequibo to load timber, and Linden on the Demerara for bauxite. Aeroplanes provide the only other link with the interior. In a couple of hours they fly to remote places which could take weeks to reach by other means. A few planes are equipped to alight on the rivers but the regular air service uses airstrips which have been prepared in the interior.

On the coastal strip roads replace rivers as means of communication. Indeed the major rivers, all over a kilometre wide near their mouths, are barriers to transport, cutting up the coastlands into four distinct segments. Only one, the Demerara, has been bridged. Elsewhere the only communication from bank to bank is by ferry. The main roads run close to the sea and connect the towns along the coast. In addition, a road runs inland from Georgetown to Linden by way of the main airport (see Map 17.5).

Questions and assignments

1 Trace an outline map of Guyana, and mark and label the following: a) three neighbouring countries; b) an area of mountains; c) three rivers; d) an area where sugar cane is grown; e) an area where rice is grown; f) an interior cattle-rearing area; g) a lumbering town; h) a town from which bauxite is exported.

2 Name: a) three varieties of forest trees that grow in Guyana, and one use of each of them; b) two similarities and two differences between rice farming in Guyana and peasant farming in the West Indian islands; three kinds of bauxite mined in Guyana, and one use of each of them; two differences between the sugar estates in Guyana and those in the West Indian islands, and give one reason to explain each of these differences.

3 Using Diagrams 17.3 and 17.4:
  a) Write down the average monthly rainfall figures for i) the coastal belt, and ii) the Rupununi Savanna, in a table like Table 2.4.
  b) Using the method given on page 19 say in each case which months are wet, moist and dry.
  c) How many dry months are there on the coastal belt, and how many in the Rupununi?
  d) Briefly compare the rainfall of the two areas.

4 a) Using the following census figures (which have here been rounded off to the nearest thousand) draw a graph to show the rise of population in Guyana.

Population of Guyana 1881–1980 ('000)

Year	Population	Year	Population
1881	252 000	1960	560 000
1911	296 000	1970	702 000
1931	311 000	1980	759 000
1946	376 000		

  b) In what years do you think the population reached $\frac{1}{2}$ million and $\frac{3}{4}$ million?
  c) Extend your graph and find what you think the population will be in 1995.

  d) In what year do you think the population will reach 1 million?
  e) By how much did the population increase in the twenty years between 1911 and 1931? What was the percentage increase?
  f) By how much did the population increase in the twenty years between 1960 and 1980? What was the percentage increase?
  g) Give one reason to explain why the percentage increase between 1911 and 1931 was bigger than that between 1960 and 1980.

5 Using the information given below, answer the questions that follow.

Composition of the population of Guyana in 1960 and 1980 (figures given to the nearest thousand)

Census categories	Numbers 1960	1980	Percentages 1960	1980
Negro/Black	184 000	231 000	33	31
East Indian	268 000	390 000	48	51
Amerindian	25 000	40 000	4	5
Mixed	67 000	84 000	12	11
Other	16 000	14 000	3	2
Total	560 000	759 000	100	100

  a) By how much did the Negro/Black population increase between 1960 and 1980? What was the percentage increase?
  b) By how much did the East Indian population increase between 1960 and 1980? What was the percentage increase?
  c) Draw two horizontal bar graphs (like those in question 7 on page 148) to show the percentages of the five population categories in 1960 and 1980.

6 Compare Guyana with Belize by writing one sentence about each of the following: a) area, b) population, c) density of population, d) composition of the population, e) major crops, f) fishing.

7 Give three reasons to explain why so high a proportion of the population of Guyana lives in such a small proportion of the country.

18

Comparisons Overseas

This chapter extends the study of geography beyond the Caribbean so that comparisons can be made with certain other parts of the world. It deals with the following:

1 The two most important soil types found in temperate regions, namely podsols and chernozems.
2 Soil erosion of different kinds that have occurred in two parts of the USA, and some soil conservation methods employed there.
3 The coniferous forests of the Canadian Shield which have given rise to one of the most productive lumbering industries in the world.
4 Large-scale commercial fishing in North America.
5 Three farming studies: the prairies of Canada; commercial beef and dairy farming in the USA; and peasant farming in Nigeria.
6 Tourism in Switzerland, an inland country with a cool temperate climate.
7 Industrial development in Britain, the United States and Japan on a scale unknown in the West Indies.
8 The growth of New York, one of the world's major cities.

Soils in temperate regions

The effects of temperature, rainfall and vegetation on soil formation are described in chapter three. They are well illustrated in two soil types found outside the West Indies. Podsols are one of these soil types, chernozems the other. Both words are of Russian origin. Podsol means grey soil, chernozem means black earth.

Podsols form in the coniferous forest regions of northern Canada, Europe and Asia. In these areas the winters are long and cold, and the summers short and cool. Because temperatures are low for much of the year, biological activity in the soil is slow. This is one reason why humus takes a long time to form. Another reason is that the tough, needle-like leaves of coniferous trees do not easily decompose. Instead they form a highly acidic layer of raw humus on the surface of the ground.

Water from the snow which melts in spring and from the rain which falls in summer acts on the soil in two ways.
1 The water picks up some of the acids as it soaks through the humus. These leach any soluble minerals including iron and aluminium compounds in the top layer of the soil and carry them down to the B horizon. This explains why the A horizon of a podsol is grey in colour and why the B horizon is reddish-brown.
2 The water eluviates any small particles of clay in the top layer, washing them down through the A horizon. They collect some 20 to 50 centimetres below the surface where they form a dark-coloured layer called an iron pan (or hard pan). If podsols are to be cultivated they need deep ploughing to break up the iron pan. Otherwise the top soil tends to get waterlogged and hinder the growth of crops.

A soil profile of a podsol is shown in Diagram 18.1.

Chernozems form in temperate grassland regions. The two biggest areas in the world are both in the northern hemisphere. One begins close to the Gulf of Mexico and extends northwards through the Great Plains of the central states of the USA to the Prairie Provinces of Canada. The other extends eastwards from Rumania through the grasslands of

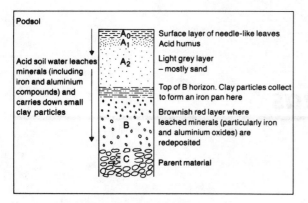

Diagram 18.1 Soil profile of a podsol.

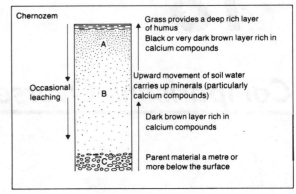

Diagram 18.2 Soil profile of a chernozem.

Russia (the steppes) and through Mongolia into northern China. In the southern hemisphere the soils underlying the grasslands of Argentina and Paraguay (the pampas) are also chernozems.

The annual rainfall in these areas is low, and the summers are long and warm. Some summer days are very hot indeed. These conditions favour the growth of grass rather than trees which require more moisture.

Grass grows quickly in spring and summer. Growth ceases in winter and many of the leaves and roots die to produce a rich humus. Where roots die, holes are left in the soil so that it crumbles easily. As we shall see, this crumbling can lead to soil erosion if the land is over-grazed or carelessly cultivated. Water soaks through the soil easily, and biological activity takes places not only near the surface but also for some distance underground. Chernozems may be a metre and more deep.

Some leaching occurs in spring when the snow melts, and also in summer if there are any very heavy rain showers. For the rest of the growing season the surface of the land loses more moisture from evaporation than it receives from rain. To replace the moisture lost by evaporation, water is drawn upwards through the soil carrying soluble minerals, particularly calcium compounds, which enrich the soil. Chernozems are the richest soils in the world.

Because of the constant movement of soil water containing humus and minerals, the A and B horizons of a chernozem are hard to distinguish. Both horizons are deep and both are dark brown in colour. Towards the surface, where there is most

humus, the colour of the soil is very dark and may even be black. Diagram 18.2 shows a profile of a chernozem.

Soil erosion in North America

We have seen in chapter three that soil erosion is a natural process. It goes on all the time, everywhere. We have also seen that soil erosion accelerates if the vegetation cover is removed. It can even get out of control. Two well-known examples in the USA show what problems can arise when that happens.

The first example is the Tennessee River system shown in Map 18.3. As you can see, the Tennessee and its tributaries begin by flowing westwards out of the Appalachian Mountains. Then the Tennessee River itself curves northwards to join the Ohio and Mississippi Rivers. It is the Mississippi that carries the water from all these streams to the Gulf of Mexico.

The problem of soil erosion in the Tennessee Valley area began in the late eighteenth century when people from Europe started to settle there and to clear the forests that covered the land. Many of the settlers had no previous experience of farming. None of them knew much, if anything, about how to grow maize (corn) or tobacco or cotton. Yet these were the crops they planted. They made the mistake of planting the same crops year after year. This took the goodness out of the soil and left it exposed to rainwater erosion. Whenever rain fell heavily, which it often did, some of the topsoil was washed downhill.

Gullies began to be carved in the hillsides. As time passed, the gullies grew and the pace of erosion increased. By the beginning of the present century so much soil had been swept into the rivers that they became choked and could no longer be used for navigation (see Diagram 18.5). After prolonged rain the rivers rose above their banks and flooded surrounding areas causing loss of life and enormous damage. The danger of flooding was not limited to the Tennessee River system. It extended all down the Mississippi to the sea.

Throughout the Tennessee Valley area crop yields fell. Some families abandoned their farms and went to live elsewhere. Those who remained were badly fed, badly housed, and very poor. By themselves they could do nothing to restore their land. The problem was too big for them to deal with. It was even more than could be handled by the seven states which suffered the effects of the erosion. Only the United States Federal Government was in a position to take effective action. In 1933 it set up the Tennessee Valley Authority (TVA) to put things right. The area controlled by the Authority was ten times the size of Jamaica.

Nine large dams were built along the Tennessee River, and over 20 more on its tributaries. These controlled the flow of river water, holding it back in times of flood and releasing it when the danger of flood was over. In addition, the dams were used to generate hydro-electric power so as to provide low-cost electricity for households and for the new industries that grew up in the area. River bottoms were dredged so that river transport could begin again. Gullies were filled, trees planted, and other soil conservation measures were implemented (see Table 18.4). Steep slopes were sown with grass and clover and used for cattle grazing. What, shortly before, had been a rural slum became a prosperous part of America.

TVA has been so successful in raising living standards in the area it serves that its methods have been copied in several other parts of the world. However, nothing similar has since taken place in the USA itself because of opposition to the idea of increasing the power of the Federal Government.

At about the same time that the TVA was set up to control soil erosion in Tennessee and its neighbouring states, another kind of soil erosion was

Map 18.3 The Tennessee Valley area of the USA.

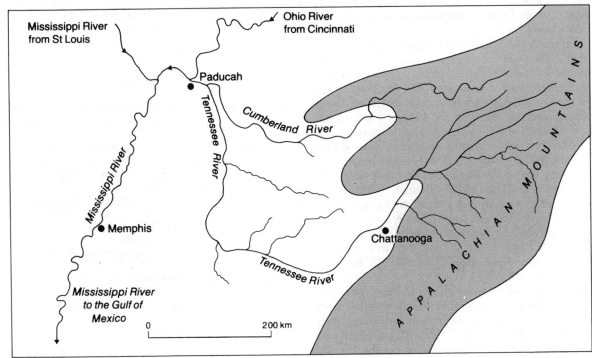

'Dust Bowl' country in the Great Plains of the United States. How can the direction of the furrows in a ploughed field affect soil erosion in areas where rainfall is low?

causing havoc some 1 500 kilometres further west. This was the famous 'dust bowl' which affected parts of the states of Kansas, Oklahoma and Texas. Inexperienced farming was again the reason for the disaster. Over large parts of the Great Plains, which for centuries had been lightly grazed by migrating herds of bison, farmers set up ranches where they raised far more cattle than the grass could support. Elsewhere, with the aid of tractors and combine harvesters, other farmers turned vast areas of grassland into wheatfields.

For many years all seemed to go well. Profits were high. The rich chernozem soils seemed inexhaustible. The bare patches of land that appeared on over-grazed land were ignored. The fact that the soil in the wheatfields crumbled more and more easily went unnoticed. Then in the 1930s a series of hot dry summers struck the region and the mistakes the farmers had made became apparent. Wind storms picked up the powdery soil and carried it away. At times the sky above cities as far distant as New York and Philadelphia was black with dust. By 1935 it was estimated that nearly a quarter of the top soil of the Great Plains had been stripped away and been lost for ever. Many farmers were ruined. They and their families left their farms and migrated to other parts of the country, particularly to California, to try to begin a new life.

The measures taken to restore the land were different from those adopted by the TVA. Apart from taking over abandoned farms and conserving their soil, the US government did little to control the way the land was used. Instead, it set up the US Soil Conservation Service to advise, assist and educate farmers in improving their methods. In some areas the land has been returned to grass and not been cultivated since. In others a crop is grown every second year. Where wheat is grown it is often rotated with other crops, particularly sorghum (an animal feed). Rows of trees have been planted across the prevailing winds in order to act as windbreaks. The land is carefully ploughed so as to prevent rain from running down the furrows or the wind blowing along them and carrying away the soil. New kinds of plough kill weeds in the soil without breaking up the surface too much. As a result of this, farming in The Great Plains is now much more prosperous and far less risky than it was fifty years ago.

Dust storms in the United States are now rare. Nevertheless do they sometimes occur. For example, in 1977 a storm which struck a grazing area in the San Joaquin Valley of California carried away some 25 million tonnes of top soil in only twenty-four hours.

Table 18.4 Some Soil Conservation Methods

Gullies	Build dams across gullies to hold back flood water Use wire mesh or trailing plants on gulley sides to hold soil in place
Steep hillsides	Build terraces along hillsides to slow down run-off
Gentle hillsides	Plough around hillsides and not up and down them (contour ploughing)
Dry areas	Improve soil moisture (eg by irrigation and by cultivating in ways that prevent soils from becoming powdery) Plant rows of trees or grass strips in large fields across the direction of the prevailing winds to act as windbreaks Grow crops every second year
General	Avoid using fires to clear land for cultivation Replant trees or grass on denuded land to bind the soil Rotate crops from year to year Prevent over-grazing

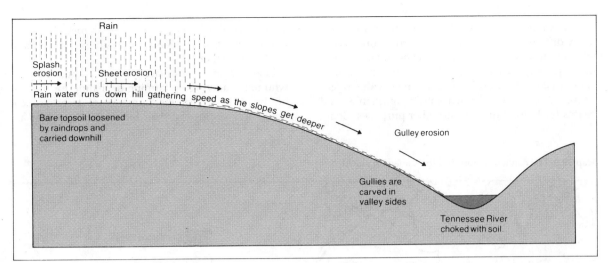

Diagram 18.5 Section through a hillside showing the soil erosion process.

Sawing up newly felled coniferous trees in Canada. What similarities and differences can you see between the trees shown in this picture and those in the photographs on pages 30 and 197?

The forests of the Canadian Shield

The Canadian (or Laurentian) Shield occupies some 2½ million square kilometres of northern Canada (see Map 18.6). It is an area of ancient (Precambrian) rock which has been uplifted and worn down several times in its 500 million-year history. Its surface features owe much to the immense ice sheets which moved across it during the last Ice Age. When the ice melted it left behind a rounded rocky landscape with thin soils and many lakes and rivers.

Winters on the Shield are cold. For several months rivers and lakes are frozen and the land is covered with snow. Summers are warm but short. Few kinds of vegetation survive in these conditions. Coniferous trees can do so for the following reasons:

1 Their tough needle-like leaves are not killed by freezing winter temperatures.

2 Their leaves remain on the branches all winter (which is why the trees are called 'evergreen'). They are therefore able to take advantage of the first warm days of spring.

3 Their leaves shed snow easily, so branches are not broken off by the weight of accumulated snow.

4 Their trunks and branches are supple and do not easily snap in high winds.

5 Their roots are adapted to absorb nutrients from thin, acid podsolic soils.

Vast forests of coniferous trees cover the Canadian

225

Shield. Unlike Caribbean forests in which there are many different kinds of trees, coniferous forests contain very few species. Spruce is the main variety, but fir, pine and larch are important in places. All four varieties are very useful. Being tall trees with straight trunks, they can be sawn into long planks and beams for house-building and other purposes. Being softwoods, they are easily cut and shaped. Most important of all, their wood can easily be pulped and made into paper.

Most logging takes place in winter, often by men who make a living by farming or fishing for the rest of the year. Enormous numbers of trees are cut down and stripped of their branches. Some logs are

Map 18.6 The coniferous forest of the Canadian shield.

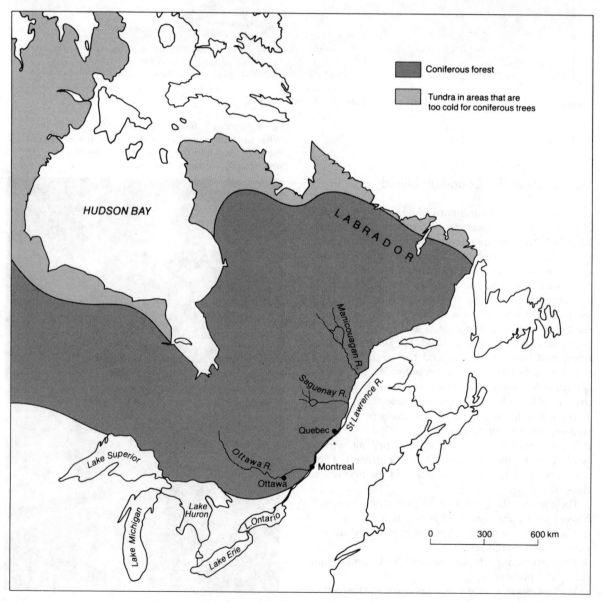

sawn up immediately. Others are hauled to river banks where they are stacked until the spring floods arrive and the logs can be floated downstream to big sawmills and pulpmills.

The forests of the Canadian Shield produce about 40 per cent of Canada's output of timber, pulp and paper. The region is particularly important for the export of newsprint to the United States. Power for the timber, pulp and paper industries is obtained from hydro-electricity generated on the Ottawa, Saguenay, Manicouagan and other rivers.

Because so many of the trees in the more accessible areas have been cut down, logging is gradually moving northwards across the Canadian Shield. Fortunately, the forests are so large, and the replanting programme so extensive, that the supply of lumber is unlikely to run out. A much greater danger is that the forests could be killed by acid rain caused by air pollution in the USA. The pollution comes from two sources. Vehicle exhaust fumes are one of them. Gases emitted by power stations are the other. Throughout this part of North America electricity is in great demand not only for industrial purposes but also for winter heating and summer air conditioning. Much of the electricity is generated in power stations that run on coal or oil. Both of these fuels produce gases containing oxides of sulphur, nitrogen and carbon. If these gases are not prevented from entering the atmosphere they combine with rain drops and make them acid. Recently it has been found that acid rain can do much damage to the environment. It can kill fish in lakes. It kills coniferous trees by slowing down the growth of new leaves so much that the trees are not able to survive.

Large-scale commercial fishing in North America

The Atlantic and Pacific coasts of North America support two of the world's biggest fishing industries. The two areas are very different from each other.

Off the coast of Newfoundland, the Maritime provinces and the New England states (see Map 18.11) there is a continental shelf which is nowhere more than 180 metres deep and often as much as 150 kilometres wide. Because the sea above the shelf is rich in nutrients it supports vast numbers of fish. The three most important varieties are cod, which may reach two metres in length; haddock, which

resembles cod but is smaller in size; and herring, which is smaller still and is found in huge shoals. Because the sea is shallow, fishing boats can easily catch the fish at all levels from the surface down to the sea bed.

Commercial fishing has been undertaken on the Atlantic continental shelf for over 300 years. It was from here that the West Indies imported dried salt cod (the cheapest available source of protein) from slave times onwards. Nowadays only a small proportion of the catch is dried and salted. Most is filleted (ie the bones are removed), cut into portions, frozen, and packed in cartons for export in refrigerated containers.

Modern boats have electronic equipment which can locate shoals of fish in the water, and nets which allow few fish to escape. There is a danger that so many fish will be caught that the supply will be exhausted. The biggest danger comes from factory ships based in West Europe, Russia and Japan. They can remain at sea for months while they catch enormous quantities of fish. To protect its fisheries Canada has passed laws which control the amount of fish that foreign boats may catch within 320 kilometres of its coastline.

The Pacific coast from Oregon northwards through British Columbia to Alaska is the source of another type of fish. This is salmon, of which there are several varieties. They breed in the upper reaches of the clear, unpolluted streams that rise in the mountains of the Western Cordillera and flow swiftly down to the sea. The new-born fish live in this fresh water for a year. Then they swim downstream to the Pacific Ocean where they remain for another two or three years. At the end of that time by a miracle of nature that we do not understand they find their way back to the same rivers in which they were born. With great effort they make their way upstream against the powerful rush of water until they reach a place where they can lay their eggs. The adult fish then die.

Fishing takes place when the salmon return from the ocean to breed. Because the dates they enter the rivers are the same each year, the fishermen are prepared for their arrival. Fleets of fishing boats wait off-shore and in the river mouths; some with lines, others with nets. In addition, large numbers of anglers stand on the river banks catching the salmon with rods and lines.

Canadian salmon are in such demand in other countries that most of the catch is exported. The commonest way of preserving the fish is to can them. For this purpose large canneries have been built on the Fraser and Skeena rivers in British Columbia (see Map 18.11) and at other places along the Pacific coast. Though the salmon fishing season is short, the catch is so large that the canneries are unable to keep pace with the supply. Many fish have to be frozen until the canneries are ready to process them.

As on the Atlantic coast there is a danger of over-fishing, and the size of the catch has to be controlled by law. In addition, to preserve the supply, hatcheries have been constructed where the salmon breed so that the eggs and new-born fish are protected until they are ready to swim to the ocean.

Table 18.7 Commercial fishing: comparisons between the Caribbean and Canada

The Caribbean	Canada
Varieties such as kingfish, snapper, dolphin and flying fish.	Varieties such as cod, haddock, herring and salmon.
Few fish caught in rivers.	Salmon caught in rivers.
Most of the Caribbean is too deep for commercial fishing.	Atlantic coast has a large, shallow continental shelf.
Caribbean not rich in nutrients.	Canadian coastal waters rich in nutrients.
Small quantities of fish caught, mainly in small boats.	Large quantities of fish caught, mainly in relatively large boats.
No exports apart from lobsters (crayfish) and shrimps.	Large exports of fish to many countries.

Farming in the Canadian Prairies

The prairies occupy part of the Canadian provinces of Manitoba, Saskatchewan and Alberta. They lie at the northern end of the belt of natural grassland that stretches southwards through the interior of the United States to the Gulf of Mexico. To the north and east of the prairies lie the forests of the Canadian Shield. To the west lie the snow-capped ranges of the Rocky Mountains (see Maps 18.8 and 18.9).

The prairies are well known as being one of the most productive wheat growing areas in the world. The natural factors that account for this are set out in the box.

Natural factors favouring wheat growing in the Prairies

1 *Temperature*

The cold prairie winters are no handicap to wheat farming as the wheat is not in the ground then. It is sown in spring when temperatures rise enough for the snow to melt and provide moisture for the soil. It grows quickly enough in the long, hot summer days to be ready for harvesting before the frosts of the next winter arrive. Wheat can be grown wherever there is a growing period of a hundred days or more and where there are no severe frosts for at least eighty days.

2 *Rainfall*

It is not strictly correct to use the word 'rainfall' for the prairies or any other part of the world which has snow for part of the year. The term 'precipitation' is usually used instead, as it covers both rainfall and snowfall.

About 80 per cent of the annual precipitation of the prairies falls as rain between May and September. These are the months when the wheat is growing. The remaining 20 per cent falls as winter snow. The total precipitation averages between 300 millimetres a year in the west and 500 millimetres in the east. In parts of the west irrigation has to be used, but elsewhere the precipitation is sufficient for wheat which does not require a great deal of moisture.

3 *Flat land*

The prairies are part of the very large interior lowland of North America known as the Great Plains. Though they are higher in the west than in the east, the slope is so gentle that in most places the prairies appear to be absolutely flat. The flatness of the land is the main reason why farmers have been able to mechanise their farms. The most important machine is the combine harvester, so called because it not only cuts the wheat stalks but also separates out the

---

Combine harvesters cutting wheat on the prairies. What conditions favour mechanised farming?

grain as it moves over the ground. Trucks take the grain from the combine harvesters to large storage sheds called elevators, each of which can hold up to 2 000 tonnes. At the elevators the grain is loaded onto railway trains and taken to flour mills or to ports on the Atlantic and Pacific Ocean and on Hudson Bay for export to overseas markets (see Map 18.9).

4 Soils

The parent material of prairie soils consists of glacial deposits left behind after the last Ice Age. Climatic and biological action over thousands of years has weathered the parent material into a chernozem (see page 222). This rich, deep soil is very suitable for the cultivation of wheat and other temperate crops.

Wheat farming spread rapidly westwards across the prairies following the construction of two coast-to-coast railways in the 1880s. Land was cheap enough for each settler to be able to buy quarter of a square mile or half of a square mile in the east, and a square mile (1.6 square kilometres) in the west. The wheat grown on these large farms costs less than that grown by farmers in Europe. As a result, Europe has a ready market for Canadian wheat. A big export trade developed which has continued to this day. Canada is the world's biggest wheat-exporting country.

Though the prairies are famous for wheat, other crops have always been grown there. Monoculture is as risky a business in the prairies as it is anywhere in the world. Oats and barley are becoming increasingly important, and many farmers use part of their land to grow oilseed and other nitrogen-rich fodder for dairy and beef cattle. An added source of wealth

229

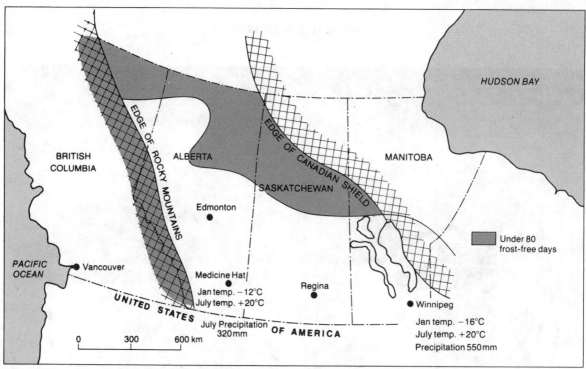

Map 18.8 The geographical setting of the Prairies.

Map 18.9 Prairie farming.

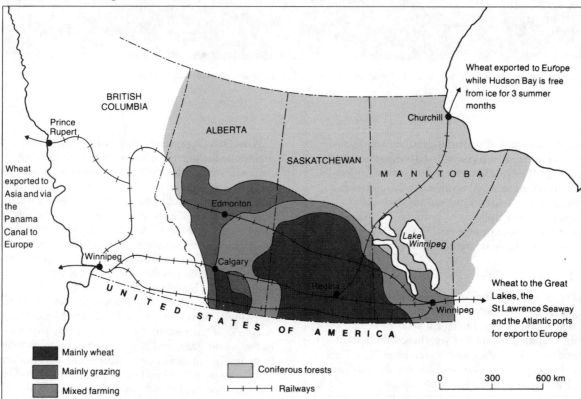

Table 18.10 Commercial farming: comparisons between sugar cane in the Caribbean and wheat in Canada

Caribbean sugar cane farming	Canadian wheat farming
Sugar cane grown in several parts of the West Indies.	Wheat grown in one very large area in Canada.
Large farms seldom run by an individual.	Large farms usually run by the individual who owns the land.
Long growing season – about a year.	Short growing season – about a hundred days.
Large labour force: few field operations mechanised.	Small labour force: all field operations mechanised.
Extra labour employed for harvesting.	Extra labour employed for harvesting.
Most of the output exported.	Most of the output exported.
Most exports sold at prices guaranteed by international agreements.	Export prices guaranteed by the Canadian government.

is crude petroleum and natural gas obtained in large quantities, particularly in Alberta.

The largest prairie town is Winnipeg with a population of over 600 000. As can be seen from Map 18.8 it is situated where the gap between Lake Winnipeg and the United States frontier narrows to only 100 kilometres. It is therefore the focus of the railways and roads that run eastwards from the prairies. Two other towns, Edmonton and Calgary, have populations of over 500 000. Like Winnipeg they are centres for flour milling, meat packing, and the manufacture of butter and cheese.

Commercial pastoral farming in the USA

The two main products obtained from cattle are beef and milk. Because Americans consume more of these products than any other people in the world, the raising of beef cattle and dairy cattle are big businesses in the USA. The businesses differ from each other in several ways.

1 Dairy cows need richer pasture than beef cattle. Dairy cows therefore tend to be kept in moist areas where grass grows best. Beef cattle can be raised where the climate is drier and the grass is less rich.

2 Dairy cows have to be milked twice a day. They need more attention than beef cattle which can be left to themselves for weeks or months at a time.

3 Milk has to be sold while it is fresh. For this reason farmers who sell milk need easy access by road to nearby towns and cities where most of their customers live. Beef can be frozen or chilled and does not have to be consumed so quickly. Beef cattle

can therefore be raised hundreds or even thousands of miles away from towns.

4 Because land prices near towns are high, dairy farms are expensive to buy, and most dairy farms are therefore small. Their area can usually be measured in tens or hundreds of acres. Land prices in remote areas are much lower, and beef cattle farms, called ranches, may be many thousands of acres in size.

Beef cattle

The semi-arid Great Plains region is the world's best known beef cattle raising area. It stretches for over 2 000 kilometres along the eastern side of the Rocky Mountains from Texas in the south to Canada in the north (see Map 18.11). Cattle rearing takes place in two stages. First the calves are allowed to graze over wide tracts of land. Then after about a year they are rounded up and taken to much smaller farms. There they are fed for a few months on highly nutritious animal feeds such as maize (corn) and soya beans to which steroids and other growth-producing pharmaceuticals are often added. During that time the cattle double their weight. They are then taken by rail to Omaha, Kansas City, Chicago, St Louis and other towns in the interior of the USA where they are slaughtered.

Though no part of the carcass is wasted, critics point out that raising beef cattle in this way is a wasteful way of producing food. The land could be put to more efficient use if crops were grown for human consumption and not for animals. However, things are unlikely to change while steaks, hamburgers and other meat products remain such popular items in the American diet.

Dairy cows

To remain in business in a highly competitive society, American dairy farmers have to produce a high volume of milk. For this reason they keep as many cows as their farms can support. The main problem is to feed the cows in winter when the grass is not growing. To do this the farmers cut as much grass as possible in summer. They mix it with other nutritious animal feed so as to make silage which is stored in large metal bins called silos.

To keep the workforce to a minimum, dairy farming is highly mechanised. At milking time the cows go to large sheds where they are milked by electrically-operated pumps. Every care is taken to ensure that the milk is kept clean. Each day's supply is collected in specially designed trucks and taken to factories where it is heated to a temperature at which any dangerous bacteria are destroyed. This process is called 'pasteurisation' after Louis Pasteur who invented it. To meet the requirements of different customers, some of the milk is homogenised so that the cream does not form a separate layer on the surface, and some is skimmed so as to remove some or all of the cream.

In addition to fresh milk, the USA is the world's largest producer of many other dairy products. These include cream; evaporated milk, which contains much less water than fresh milk; condensed milk, which is even more highly concentrated; powdered milk from which all the water has been removed; butter; cheese; and yoghurt.

Peasant farming in Nigeria

The first thing to note about Nigeria is its size. Its area is over 923 000 square kilometres. This is considerably more than all the Caribbean lands put together. If you imagine a rectangle of land with corners at the Dominican Republic, the Gulf of Maracaibo, Trinidad and Sombrero (see Map 1.2) you will have a rough idea of the size of Nigeria.

The second thing to note is the latitude of Nigeria. Its most southerly point – the delta that the River Niger has built up on entering the Gulf of Guinea – is about 4°N. The northern frontier of the country extends as far as 14°N, well within the tropics. The

Map 18.11 The main cattle-raising areas in the USA.

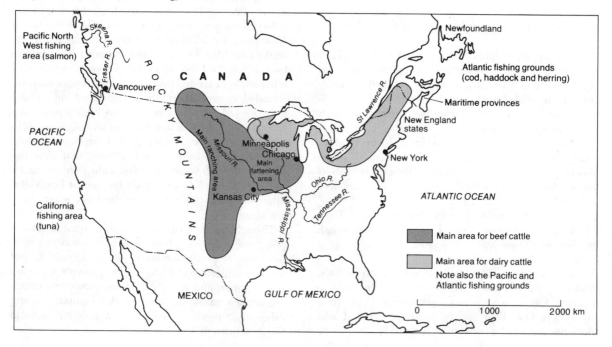

climate is therefore tropical. However, no country of such size can have the same climatic conditions everywhere. Thus the range of temperature between the hottest and coolest months is smaller at Port Harcourt on the Niger delta than at Kano in the north. In addition, the highlands have lower temperatures than the lowlands, most noticeably at night. This is particularly true of the high plateau around the town of Jos (see Map 18.12), where it is cool enough for wheat and some other temperate crops to be grown.

Rainfall contrasts are considerable. The southern coastlands have over 2 500 millimetres of rain a year. This is enough to support tropical rain forest (now mostly cleared) and such commercial trees as cocoa, oil palm, kola and rubber. Maize and rice are the main cereal crops; yams, cocoyams and cassava the main root crops. Further north, in the middle zone of the country where the rainfall is less (1 000 millimetres to 2 500 millimetres a year) the natural vegetation consists of tall savanna grass and scattered trees. Maize, yams and cassava are grown, as are okras, peppers, plantains, cowpeas, pigeon peas and various kinds of leafy vegetables. Further north still the rainfall is below 1 000 millimetres a year, the rainy season is short and droughts occur frequently. The natural vegetation consists of poor savanna grass and thorn scrub. Millet and sorghum (guinea corn) are the main cereals; groundnuts and, in places, cotton are the main cash crops. Nomadic herdsmen move from one grazing area to another with their herds of African cattle. Relatively few animals are raised in the middle zone of the country owing to a deadly cattle disease carried by tsetse flies which thrive in the moister conditions there.

The third thing to note about Nigeria is that it has two very different types of economy. One is the commercial and industrial sector. It is based on the income obtained from petroleum and petroleum products which form 95 per cent of the exports. This income supports a modern western way of life, with extremes of wealth and poverty in the main towns, some of which are large. Thus Lagos has a population of over 6 million, and Ibadan 2½ million. The other type of economy is based on agriculture. It exists throughout the rural areas and supports 70 per cent of the country's population of about 100 million. In contrast to the towns, the rural way of life is essentially traditional.

One of the most important traditions concerns the ownership of land. It developed hundreds of years ago when each village community had to produce all the food it needed and cash crops were unknown. It is based on the belief that land does not belong to the present generation alone. It belongs also to all those people who farmed it in the past and to those yet unborn who will farm it in the future. Land therefore belongs to the whole village community and not to individual community members. For this reason families may not own the land they farm. They may neither sell it nor hand it on to their children. Instead each piece of land to be cultivated is loaned for a few years to those who wish to farm it. The task of allocating the land is undertaken by the chief of the community or by a respected elder appointed for the purpose.

A farmer's first task is to clear the land he has been allocated. This is usually done by burning any bush that has grown on it and digging the soil with hand tools, the most common of which are hoes and machetes. In this task the farmer may be helped by members of his immediate family, by other relatives, and by friends and neighbours. This African custom of friendly co-operation is also carried on by smallholders in many parts of the West Indies.

Nigerian peasant produce being prepared for marketing. What similarities and differences are there between this scene and one in the West Indies?

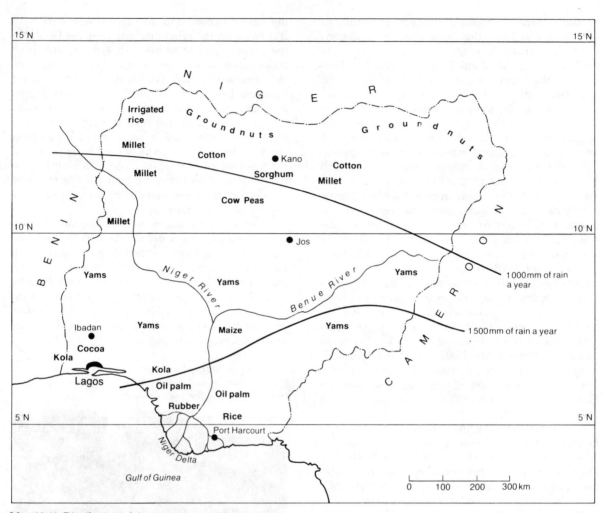

Map 18.12 Distribution of the main crops in Nigeria.

Next the farmer sows those seeds and plants those crops that grow best in his district. His main concern is to provide food for his family, but he may also grow a cash crop such as cocoa in the wet south, groundnuts in the dry north, or vegetables and fruits near to large towns. In addition he may grow a crop such as cowpeas to make silage if he keeps a few cattle. Most farmers rotate their crops from year to year. This makes the best use of the soil and gives variety to the diet. After three or four years yields decline to the point where it is best to stop using the land and allow it to lie fallow until it is needed again. In communities where plenty of land is available a piece of land may remain unused for as much as fif-

teen years. Where land is scarce the fallow period may last no more than a year or two. Whatever the period may be, when the land is to be used again it is loaned to another farmer and the process of cultivating it is repeated.

The customs relating to land ownership vary somewhat from place to place. For example, in some parts of the north a farmer may have one piece of land close to the village where he lives which he cultivates year after year, and another piece further away where he follows the bush fallow system described above. Basically however, one factor is the same everywhere. This is that the amount of land a farmer can make use of is limited to the amount he can clear, plant, weed and reap using only hand labour. This rarely exceeds five acres.

The main advantages of the traditional way of farming are that it provides food for the community and ensures that land is available for everyone who wants to farm it. On the other hand there are several disadvantages. First, where individuals may not own land there is no incentive for them to spend money improving it. Second, for the same reason, people are unable to acquire sufficient land to mechanise their farming methods. Third, because land is real-located every few years, members of the same family cannot be sure that the pieces of land they are loaned will be beside each other. They are often widely separated.

The traditional system works best in remote rural districts where plenty of land is available. It works less well where the supply of land is so limited that the soil has to be cultivated year after year without a break. A recent problem is that many young people are looking for work in the modern sector of the economy rather than on the land. As a result farmers are increasingly having to hire labour at peak periods, and this is expensive. Some critics of the traditional system of farming say that it is out of date and not productive enough. However, many of the modern commercial farms that have been set up, often with government aid, have not been successful and have lost a lot of money. Farming in the tropics is never easy, and it may well be the case that small farmers have fewer failures than large-scale enterprises.

Tourism in Switzerland

The main tourist attractions in the Caribbean are the hot sunny days, the warm nights, the beautiful beaches and the clear blue sea. Much the same is true of the European and African coasts of the Mediterranean Sea, another of the world's most popular areas for holidaymakers. Switzerland has none of these attractions. How, then, has it become world famous for tourism? Three factors are of particular importance.

1   The landscape of Switzerland, with its mountains, valleys, lakes, pastures and pine forests, has attracted summer visitors from other parts of Europe for over a hundred years. Among them there have always been some for whom the main attraction has

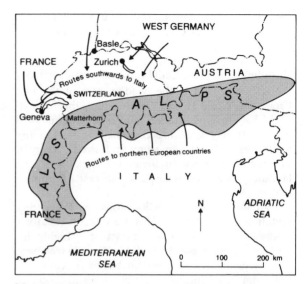

Map 18.13 The geographical setting of Switzerland.

been the challenge of climbing the Matterhorn and other mountain peaks.

2   The highest mountains in Europe – the Alps – run through the southern part of Switzerland (see map 18.13). Each winter over twelve million tourists visit the Swiss Alps to enjoy the exhilarating sport of skiing on their snow-covered slopes. The Swiss have built Alpine hotels to accommodate them, and cable railways and ski lifts to take them to the best places for skiing.

3   Western Europe has a population of about 300 million people, many of whom have several weeks' paid vacation each year and earn enough money to go abroad for their holidays. Lying at the heart of Western Europe, Switzerland is easily accessible to these holidaymakers. They can make the journey from their homes to the Alps by rail, car or coach in a few hours. Alternatively they can fly to one of the three international airports at Zurich, Geneva and Basle. In addition, people travelling overland between such countries as Germany, France, Belgium, the Netherlands, Britain and Scandinavia in the north of Europe and Italy in the south have to make the journey by way of Switzerland. A number of railways and roads have been built through Alpine passes, using tunnels in places. The Simplon railway tunnel, a few kilometres east of the Matterhorn, is the longest in the world.

Switzerland has taken full advantage of its central position. It remained neutral in the two world wars that shattered most of the rest of Europe. Because of its neutrality it has become one of the world's leading countries for banking and financial services and for international conferences. Many countries, including some in the Caribbean, maintain an embassy there. Switzerland is the headquarters of the Red Cross, the World Health Organization, the International Labour Organization, and other international bodies. It has grown accustomed to welcoming foreign visitors and to meeting their needs. Many of the staff who work in Swiss hotels, offices, restaurants and shops speak several European languages.

Tourism is not without its problems. Preventing pollution is one of them. This is a difficult task for a land-locked country in the midst of a highly industrialised continent. Indeed, like Canada (see page 227) Switzerland has been unable to prevent acid rain from damaging its coniferous forests. A second problem is that tourism offers better paid and more attractive employment than Alpine farming. When farms close for lack of labour their grassland is no longer kept short by grazing animals. Long grass does not hold the winter snow in place as well as short grass with the result that dangerous avalanches can occur. A third problem is that modern mass tourism has been accompanied by a

Alpine scenery in Switzerland. In what ways does this landscape resemble that shown in the photograph on page 7? What are the differences?

rapid expansion of the area under buildings and roads. These are unable to absorb the water created when the snow melts in spring. It therefore pours directly into the rivers and can bring about destructive flooding.

Heavy industry in Britain, the USA and Japan

The factors necessary for the development of industry are given on pages 94–5. If a place does not possess them it is unlikely to become an important industrial centre. No part of the West Indies possesses more than a few of the factors. This explains why the West Indies are not major industrial countries.

In certain parts of the world conditions are more favourable to industry. The first country to take advantage of them was Britain.

The rapid rise of industry in Britain (a growth known as the 'industrial revolution') took place in the middle of the eighteenth century. It began because of the invention of a number of machines which could make cloth cheaply and on a large scale. Factories were built to house the machines. The money to build them was supplied by private capital. Some of it came from the profits made by the owners of slave-run West Indian sugar estates.

The earliest factories in Britain were built beside hillside streams where swiftly flowing water could be used to run the machines. Then, with the development of the steam engine in the 1780s, steam power replaced water power. Steam engines needed a source of cheap fuel. This was obtained from coal, enormous quantities of which were available in several parts of Britain. Big factories were built on these coalfields. Labour, including child labour, was employed to work in the coal mines and in the factories. Families moved from all over the country to find jobs there. Towns were built to house them. Different towns tended to specialize in different industries. Some made cloth out of cotton, others out of wool. Some used Britain's plentiful supplies of iron ore to make iron. Others used the iron to make bridges, ships, steam engines, textile machinery, locomotives, railway lines and may other heavy engineering products. Each British coalfield supported several of these manufacturing towns. Each became what is called an 'industrial region'.

Owing to its early start in industrial growth, its experience of overseas trade, and its colonial possessions, Britain was able to capture a world-wide market for its industrial products. However, competitors soon arose. One of them was the USA.

Industry in the USA developed through the determination of the American settlers to cease to be dependent on British manufactured goods. Factories producing textiles, weapons and a range of other light manufactures were set up on the eastern coastlands of the country where the bulk of the people lived at that time. Then in the early nineteenth century heavy industry, based on the manufacture of iron and steel, became established on the western side of the Appalachian Mountains. The first industrial centre there was Pittsburgh. Its main advantage was its location on the Appalachian coalfield, one of the world's most productive. Also, to begin with, there were local supplies of iron ore. As these dwindled their place was taken by high-grade iron ore found in enormous quantities in the Mesabi Range and other sites close to Lake Superior. The Great Lakes themselves provided an inexpensive water transport system for much of the journey. Where difficulties existed they were overcome by building the Soo and Welland canals. In addition, the lakes were linked by the Erie Canal and the Mohawk and Hudson rivers to New York and other east coast ports (see Map 18.14). Further links were provided by the building of a dense network of railways.

The traffic was not all one way. Instead, the waterways and railways by which iron ore was carried from Lake Superior to Pittsburgh were also used to carry coal in the opposite direction. As a result, a number of towns manufacturing iron and steel and heavy engineering products grew up on the shores of the Great Lakes. Among the largest are Chicago and Gary on Lake Michigan, and Cleveland and Buffalo on Lake Erie. Another large town, Detroit, is the main automobile manufacturing town in the USA. Close by are other towns where components for automobiles are made. For the past fifty years the industrial region between Chicago and Pittsburgh has been the most important in the world.

Recently the supply of Lake Superior iron ore has begun to run down. To keep the industries going, iron ore is being brought into the region from elsewhere. One source of supply is Labrador in eastern Canada. Some of it is carried in ocean-going ships up the St Lawrence Seaway, and some enters the USA through ports on the east coast. Another source of supply is Venezuela.

The main rival to the USA as the world's leading industrial nation is Japan. Until the mid-nineteenth century the Japanese government would not permit any kind of foreign development, including industry, to take root in the country. Then the policy changed and Japanese industry began to grow. Conditions were not altogether favourable. Japan possessed very little coal or iron ore, the two essential raw materials for heavy industry. It also lacked colonial possessions to provide an overseas market for its manufactures.

Offsetting these disadvantages were a number of favourable factors. One was that at the time industrial development began Japan's population numbered thirty million. The country therefore possessed both a large workforce and a home market for its industrial goods. A second was that its mountains were the source of swift-flowing streams which could be used for water power. A third was that being an island nation Japan had a long coastline with many harbours that could be developed into ports. Above all, the country was determined to become a great industrial power. To protect its home market it prevented foreign manufactures from being imported. To obtain the raw materials it needed it conquered Manchuria on the eastern side of mainland Asia and then occupied most of China.

Much of Japan's growing industrial strength was used to manufacture military equipment for its armed forces. By the time Japan entered the 1939–45 War, its army, navy and air force were powerful enough to challenge those of the USA and Britain. Japanese troops occupied most of the Pacific islands and south-east Asia.

When the war was brought to an end by the nuclear attack on the Japanese cities of Hiroshima and Nagasaki, Japan set about rebuilding its industrial economy for peaceful purposes. Major difficulties had to be overcome. In particular, having lost its overseas conquests Japan had to obtain 80 per cent of its coal and almost all of its iron ore, bauxite and crude petroleum from other parts of the world. However, favourable factors still outweighed unfavourable ones. Japan was still determined to succeed. Its streams were able to generate sufficient hydro-electricity to provide three-quarters of the country's power requirements. Its population had grown to 100 million, providing Japan with a larger home market than any single European country. Within the population there were millions of men and women who were willing to work longer hours

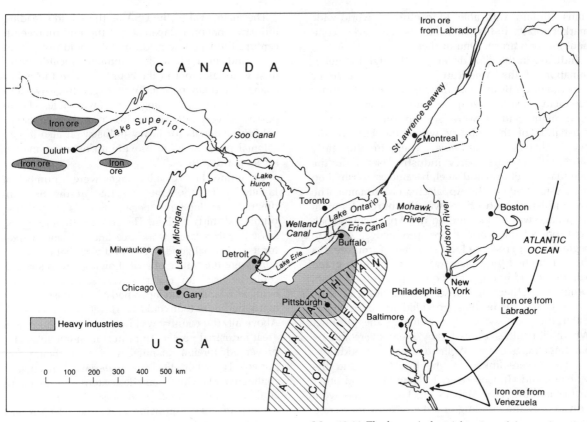

Map 18.14 The heavy industrial region of the north-eastern USA.

Map 18.15 Japan and its major industrial areas.

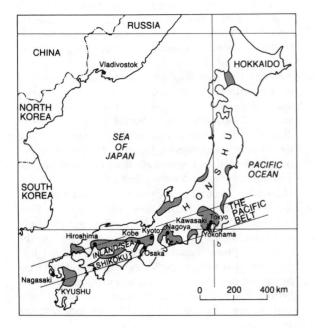

for lower wages than the workers in the USA and Europe. For a time Japan became the world's largest ship-building nation. It remains among the leading producers of iron, steel, zinc, aluminium and other industrial metals. Industrial growth has been phenomenal. In 1950 Japan had only a small automobile industry. Now in the 1980s it produces more cars, trucks and motorbikes than any other country in the world; more, in fact, than the USA and Britain put together. Other products which have enormous world-wide sales are wrist-watches; cameras and films; radios and stereos; television sets; audio and video-recorders; electronic calculators; computers; telecommunications equipment; silk,

Cars being assembled in a Japanese factory.

cotton and synthetic textiles; and office machines including photocopiers and word processors. As a result, Japan has the world's largest trade surplus. It also has the world's largest stock market where private investors can buy and sell shares in Japanese companies. Living standards have risen, and wages and working conditions are no longer poorer than those in Europe and America.

Nearly two-thirds of Japan's imports consist of raw materials brought in by sea. Most of these materials are bulky. Transporting them inland would be needlessly expensive. For this reason Japan's heavy industries and oil refineries have grown up in and around the ports where the raw materials are unloaded.

The most important industrial area is the 'Pacific Belt'. It stretches from Tokyo, the capital of Japan, south-westwards to Osaka and along the shores of the Inland Sea between the islands of Honshu,

Shikoku and Kyushu (see Map 18.15). Rectangular in shape, it is almost 1 000 kilometres long by 200 kilometres wide. Its area is about twice that of Jamaica. It contains 70 per cent of the nation's population which by the mid 1980s totalled 120 million. It accounts for 70 per cent of the nation's industrial production.

Within the Pacific Belt are several industrial centres. The biggest of them includes the cities of Tokyo, Yokohama and Kawasaki and has a population of over 14 million. Several large oil refineries are located here, as are shipyards and factories making aircraft, engineering products, scientific apparatus, textiles and chemicals. Next in size is the area containing the cities of Kyoto, Osaka and Kobe where many heavy industries are located. Light industries are more widely distributed. Many are set in the countryside where the environment is much more attractive than it is in the cities.

New York – one of the world's largest cities

In considering the growth of New York to its present size of between nine and ten million people, it is important to remember two things. One is that the population of the USA is made up almost entirely of immigrants. The other is that many millions of those immigrants came from Europe. They left such countries as Ireland, Germany, Italy, Russia and Poland to escape poverty, religious persecution, political oppression and war, and took ships to the New World in search of a better life. To handle the shipping, ports grew up wherever natural harbours existed along the Atlantic coast. Some of them, including Boston, Philadelphia and Baltimore, as well as New York, are shown on Map 18.16.

One reason why New York became the most important of these ports is the quality of its harbour. The mouth of the Hudson River is wide, sheltered and deep. It has never had to be dredged even to allow entry to the world's largest ships. In addition, there are over 1 000 kilometres of waterfront where ships can load and unload their cargoes.

A second reason is the easy access of New York to the interior of the continent. As Map 18.16 shows, the Appalachian Mountains form a natural barrier to inland communications. New York, however, stands at the end of a gap stretching northwards and westwards along the valleys of the Hudson and Mohawk Rivers. The opening of the Erie Canal in 1825 allowed canal barges to carry heavy cargoes between New York and the Great Lakes. From then on no other Atlantic port has rivalled New York in importance. Even when railways replaced canals as the main carriers of heavy goods, New York suffered no disadvantage. The Hudson-Mohawk gap became a major routeway for multitrack railways from New York to the Great Lakes and beyond.

Though New York remains the busiest port in North America, it has changed in several ways in

The central business district of Manhattan.

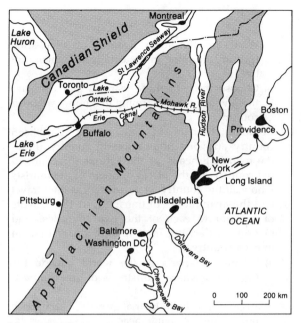

Map 18.16 The setting of New York.

Map 18.17 The site of New York City.

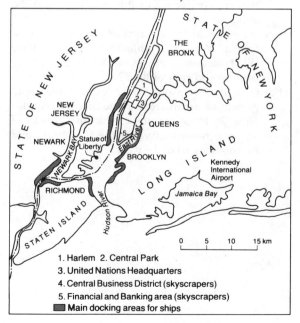

1. Harlem 2. Central Park
3. United Nations Headquarters
4. Central Business District (skyscrapers)
5. Financial and Banking area (skyscrapers)
▨ Main docking areas for ships

recent years. First, since the construction of the St Lawrence Seaway in 1959 New York has lost some of its trade as goods can be shipped abroad from ports on the Great Lakes, except for a few months in winter when the Seaway is frozen. Second, there is much less passenger traffic by ship across the Atlantic than there used to be. Its place has been taken by air transport. Kennedy International Airport is one of the busiest airports in the world. Third, many of the old warehouses beside the Hudson River have fallen into disuse because they are not suitable for handling modern containerised cargoes. They have been replaced by new loading and unloading facilities on Newark Bay.

The heart of New York is Manhattan, an island less than twenty kilometres long and seldom more than three kilometres wide. The number of people living in this small area is about the same as that of Jamaica. Land prices are so high that large buildings have to be built vertically to great heights. In two parts of Manhattan there are dense clusters of skyscrapers. One of them is the financial and banking centre at the southern tip of the island. The other is the Central Business District just south of Central Park (see Map 18.17). It is here that some of the world's most famous luxury shops, showrooms, hotels, restaurants, theatres, and other places of entertainment are located. Nearby, on the shore of the East River, is the United Nations headquarters. To the north of Central Park is Harlem where many black New Yorkers live. Heavy industry is absent, but there are a number of light industries in Manhattan. The most important of these is the manufacture of textiles and clothing, particularly women's garments.

Many of the four million people who work in Manhattan live in other New York suburbs. Their journeys to work and back are difficult and can be time-consuming. Multi-lane highways exist, but traffic often comes to a standstill at peak periods, particularly near the bridges and tunnels that connect Manhattan eastwards to Long Island and westwards to New Jersey and Staten Island. To avoid delay, many people travel by subway rather than by road. Transportation is not the only problem. Two other major difficulties are the provision of drinking water and the disposal of waste. New York is such an overcrowded and expensive place to live that more people are moving out than are moving in. The population is therefore slowly declining.

241

Questions and assignments

1 a) Draw and label soil profiles for i) a podsol, ii) a chernozem, iii) a latosol.
  b) What are the main factors that give rise to each of these soil types? Locate one part of the world where each may be found.

2 a) What is meant by the term 'soil conservation'?
  b) Compare one area of soil conservation in the West Indies with one in another part of the world under the following heads: a) why conservation has been necessary, b) the measures taken, and c) the results. Illustrate your answer with sketch maps and diagrams.

3 a) With the aid of sketch maps locate one major forest area in i) the Caribbean, and ii) North America. What natural conditions have given rise to these forests?
  b) Compare the two areas under the following heads: i) types of trees, ii) the commercial uses of the lumber, iii) forest conservation.

4 Compare commercial fishing off the coasts of Canada with that undertaken in any one named Caribbean country under the following heads: a) the types of fish that are caught, b) the size of the fishing industry, c) methods of processing the fish, d) the need for fish conservation.

5 Compare one area of commercial arable farming in the Caribbean with one in another part of the world under the following heads: a) location, b) climatic conditions, c) main crop grown, d) farming methods, e) products made from the crop, and f) markets for the products.

6 a) With the aid of sketch maps locate one important cattle raising area in the Caribbean and one in a non-Caribbean country.
  b) Name two similarities and two differences between the two areas, and give two reasons why cattle raising is important in the areas you have named.

7 a) What are the main features of small-scale (peasant) farming in the country in which you live?
  b) Choose three of these features and compare them with peasant farming in a non-Caribbean country.

8 Compare tourism in one named Caribbean country and one non-Caribbean country under the following heads: a) the natural attractions of the country, b) the places of origin of the tourists who visit the country, c) the distances they travel and the main modes of transport, d) the benefits of tourism to each of the two countries, and e) problems arising from the growth of tourism in each country.

9 a) Locate two parts of the world outside the Caribbean where industry is of great importance.
  b) Account for the industrial growth of each place under the following heads: i) raw materials, ii) sources of power, iii) labour supply, iv) markets, and v) other factors.
  c) Use the same headings to account for the growth of industry in any one named area in the West Indies.

10 a) What is meant by the term 'pollution'?
  b) What are the main factors causing the pollution of i) rivers, ii) the sea, and iii) the atmosphere?
  c) Why should these forms of pollution be controlled? Why is it difficult to control them? What measures are being taken by various countries to control them?

11 a) Give three reasons which explain the rapid growth of urban areas in the modern world.
  b) How do these reasons explain the growth of any one named city in i) the Caribbean, and ii) another part of the world.

Glossary

Magazines, newspapers and radio bulletins frequently refer to a number of regional and world-wide political and economic organisations. Those of most significance to the Caribbean are listed below. Some are dealt with in more detail in the main part of this book (see the Index).

Association of African, Caribbean and Pacific States (ACP). A group of nearly 70 countries which, under the terms of the Lomé Convention, have free access to the European Economic Community (EEC) for their main agricultural exports. All the Commonwealth Caribbean States are ACP members.

Caribbean Basin Initiative (CBI). A plan introduced by the United States Government in the 1980s to assist Caribbean countries to increase their exports to the USA, in particular to encourage them to set up new industries exporting light manufactured goods.

Caribbean Community and Common Market (CARICOM). Those Caribbean countries (at present Antigua and Barbuda, The Bahamas, Barbados, Belize, Dominica, Grenada, Guyana, Jamaica, Montserrat, St Kitts-Nevis, St Lucia, St Vincent and the Grenadines, and Trinidad and Tobago) which have agreed to co-ordinate their foreign and economic policies, raise the level of trade within the Community, plan the growth of new industries and protect them from overseas competition, strengthen agriculture and regional transport services, and work closely together to improve health, education, and other social services. CARICOM's headquarters are in Georgetown, Guyana.

Caribbean Development Bank (CDB). A bank with its headquarters in Barbados which analyses economic trends in the region and assists development by providing funds for selected projects.

Commonwealth. An association of nearly fifty countries from all parts of the world which, on freeing themselves from colonial rule, have voluntarily decided to remain in close touch with one another and to work together to foster economic, social and cultural development, Canada and Australia are the largest in area; India, Bangladesh, Pakistan, Nigeria and Britain have the largest populations.

Commonwealth Caribbean. Two categories of Caribbean countries:
1 those which were once British colonies but on becoming independent made their own decision to join the Commonwealth; and
2 those which are still British dependencies and have a Commonwealth connection through Britain.

European Economic Community (EEC). A growing number of European states (at present Belgium, Britain (i.e. the United Kingdom), Denmark, France, the Federal Republic of Germany (i.e. West Germany), Greece, Ireland, Italy, Luxemburg, the Netherlands, Portugal and Spain, which have agreed to remove trade barriers between one another (i.e. to set up a 'Common Market'). By 1992, people, goods and services will be able to move freely within the Community.

Food and Agricultural Organisation (FAO). A United Nations agency set up to improve the production and distribution of food from farms, forests and fisheries, raise living conditions in rural areas, and endeavour to eliminate hunger in the world. Its headquarters are in Rome.

General Agreement on Tariffs and Trade (GATT). An agreement between the world's major trading nations to consult one another about trade problems, to reduce tariff barriers, and to facilitate the expansion of world trade.

Lomé Convention. An agreement first made in the early 1970s between the EEC and ACP countries and subsequently renewed and enlarged on several occasions. Its main aim is to provide stable prices for ACP products (including sugar), but it also provides support to developing countries after hurricanes and other natural disasters. (See also *Stabex*.)

Organisation of African Unity (OAU). An organisation set up in 1963 to promote African solidarity, eliminate colonialism in Africa, co-ordinate defence policies, and co-operate in political economic and social matters.

Organisation of American States (OAS). A regional organisation of the United Nations which aims to achieve peace and justice, promote American solidarity, strengthen collaboration among member states and defend their independence. In the late 1980s the following countries were members: Antigua and Barbuda, Argentina, The Bahamas, Barbados, Bolivia, Brazil, Chile, Colombia, Costa Rica, Cuba, Dominica, the Dominican Republic, Ecuador, El Salvador, Grenada, Guatemala, Haiti, Honduras, Jamaica, Mexico, Nicaragua, Panama, Paraguay, Peru, St Kitts-Nevis, St Lucia, St Vincent and the Grenadines, Suriname, Trinidad and Tobago, the USA, Uruguay, and Venezuela. The headquarters are in Washington DC.

Organisation of Eastern Caribbean States (OECS). A group of seven countries in the chain of islands in the Lesser Antilles (Antigua and Barbuda, Dominica, Grenada, Montserrat, St Kitts and Nevis, St Lucia, and St Vincent and the Grenadines) which are linking themselves closer together to promote their common interests. They share the same currency.

Organisation for Economic Co-operation and Development (OECD). A group of the world's richest countries (including the USA, Australia, the EEC members, Switzerland and Japan) set up primarily to improve their own economic and social conditions but also to provide assistance to developing countries.

Organisation of Petroleum Exporting Countries (OPEC). An organisation set up in 1960 to try to regulate petroleum output from the world's major petroleum exporting countries, and thereby to stabilise the price of petroleum on the world market. Sometimes it has been successful in doing so; sometimes not.

Stabex. An arrangement made by the EEC to stabilise the export earnings of some fifty commodities produced by ACP countries (including coffee, bananas, tea, cocoa, groundnuts and cotton). It resembles an insurance policy in that it provides support in bad years.

United Nations (UN). An association of about 160 nations (nearly all that exist in the world) which have pledged themselves to work together to promote world peace and security and to co-operate in establishing political, economic and social conditions in which these aims can be achieved.

United Nations Educational, Scientific and Cultural Organisation (UNESCO). A United Nations agency which promotes educational, scientific and cultural collaboration throughout the world. Its headquarters are in Paris.

United Nations Children's Fund (UNICEF). A United Nations agency which works to improve the quality of life of children and mothers in developing countries by such means as immunising children against common diseases and helping communities to obtain pure water and undertake health projects.

United Nations Development Programme (UNDP). As the world's largest agency for technical assistance, UNDP provides most of the funds for projects carried out in developing countries by the United Nations and its agencies.

World Bank. A bank set up by the United Nations to make funds available to developing countries so as enable them to undertake large-scale development projects and obtain technical assistance. The headquarters are in Washington.

World Health Organisation (WHO). A United Nations agency which helps countries to eradicate diseases and improve the health of their populations. Its present target, 'Health for all by the year 2000', aims at 'the attainment by all citizens of the world of a level of health that will permit them to lead a socially and economically productive life.' Its headquarters are in Geneva.

Index